The
South
Atlantic
Quarterly
Spring 2007
Volume 106
Number 2

Visit Duke University Press Journals at www.dukepress.edu/journals.

Subscriptions. Direct all orders to Duke University Press, Journals Fulfillment, 905 W. Main St., Suite 18B, Durham, NC 27701. Annual subscription rates: print-plus-electronic institutions, $166; print-only institutions, $150; e-only institutions, $148; individuals, $35; students, $21. For information on subscriptions to the e-Duke Scholarly Collection through HighWire Press, see www.dukeupress.edu/edukecollection. Print subscriptions: add $12 postage and 6% GST for Canada; add $16 postage outside the U.S. and Canada. Back volumes (institutions): $150. Single issues: institutions, $38; individuals, $14. For more information, contact Duke University Press Journals at 888-651-0122 (toll-free in the U.S. and Canada) or 919-688-5134; subscriptions@dukeupress.edu.

Permissions. Photocopies for course or research use that are supplied to the end user at no cost may be made without explicit permission or fee. Photocopies that are provided to the end user for a fee may not be made without payment of permission fees to Duke University Press. Address requests for permission to republish copyrighted material to Permissions Coordinator, permissions@dukeupress.edu.

Advertisements. Direct inquiries about advertising to Journals Advertising Coordinator, journals_advertising@dukeupress.edu.

Distribution. The journal is distributed by Ubiquity Distributors, 607 DeGraw St., Brooklyn, NY 11217; phone: 718-875-5491; fax: 718-875-8047.

The *South Atlantic Quarterly* is indexed in *Academic Abstracts FullTEXT Elite, Academic Abstracts FullTEXT Ultra, Academic Research Library, Academic Search Elite, Academic Search Premier, America: History and Life, American Humanities Index, Art Index Retrospective, 1929–1984, Arts and Humanities Citation Index, Corporate ResourceNet, Current Abstracts, Current Contents/Arts and Humanities, Discovery, Expanded Academic ASAP, Historical Abstracts, Humanities Abstracts, Humanities and Social Sciences Index Retrospective, 1907–1984, Humanities Full Text, Humanities Index, Humanities Index Retrospective, 1907–1984, Humanities International Index, International Bibliography of Periodical Literature, Literary Reference Center, MasterFILE Elite, MasterFILE Premier, MasterFILE Select, MLA Bibliography, News and Magazines, OmniFile Full Text V, OmniFile Full Text, Mega Edition, Research Library, Social Sciences Index Retrospective, 1907–1984,* and *Student Resource Center College with Expanded Academic ASAP.*

The *South Atlantic Quarterly* is published, at $166 for (print-plus-electronic) institutions and $35 for individuals, by Duke University Press, 905 W. Main St., Suite 18B, Durham, NC 27701. Periodicals postage paid at Durham, NC, and additional mailing offices. Postmaster: Send address changes to *South Atlantic Quarterly,* Box 90660, Duke University Press, Durham, NC 27708-0660.

© 2007 by Duke University Press

ISSN 0038-2876

The
South
Atlantic
Quarterly
Spring 2007
Volume 106
Number 2

Late Derrida

SPECIAL ISSUE EDITOR: IAN BALFOUR

Introduction   205
IAN BALFOUR

Performativity as Performance / Performativity
as Speech Act: Derrida's Special Theory of
Performativity   219
J. HILLIS MILLER

Scruples, or, Faith in Derrida   237
REI TERADA

As If the Time Were Now:
Deconstructing Agamben   265
DAVID E. JOHNSON

Bereft: Derrida's Memory and the Spirit
of Friendship   291
DAVID L. CLARK

Suspended from the Other's Heartbeat   325
ELISABETH WEBER

Rage against the Divine   345
DAVID LLOYD

Derrida, Europe, Today   373
MARC REDFIELD

"Distressful Gift": Talking to the Dead   393
MARY JACOBUS

Notes on Contributors   419

Ian Balfour

Introduction

> Instead of time, there will be lateness.
> —David Berman (from "The Wild Kindness," by The
> Silver Jews)

This volume seeks to commemorate and to interrogate, to read with varying measures of gratitude and critique, the late or later work of Jacques Derrida. And to read these texts now that Derrida is "late." Does it make any difference for the reading of texts by Derrida that now their author is dead? Was not the author always already divorced from his texts, "writing" being famously identified since Plato, not least via Derrida's own analysis, with death and absence and thus able to—indeed forced to—function in the absence of their author, since he would always be, after a fashion, dead in relation to them and they dead in relation to him? This could well be. Yet especially for those indebted to Derrida's writing, his teaching, and his lectures, there is perhaps something new in this new absence of Derrida, especially his no longer being able to respond, to write, to speak. Derrida was tireless in responding to his—and not just his—porous community, publicly and, to an extraordinary degree, privately. Now we are left to write, think,

South Atlantic Quarterly 106:2, Spring 2007
DOI 10.1215/00382876-2006-021   © 2007 Duke University Press

and talk among ourselves. The tasks of reading, thinking, writing, and acting remain, and remain daunting, and all the more so in the absence of Derrida and the production of any new texts by him.

The essays gathered here address primarily the later work of Derrida, roughly of the last fifteen to twenty years, on the theory that this body of work—this part of his body of work—is less well known and much less well assimilated in critical discourse these days. Perhaps this can be chalked up partly to the fact that Derrida wrote so much (and granted so many interviews) that it is difficult even for devoted readers to keep up with his voluminous output. Surely some of us are still struggling with and over the writings of the 1960s and 1970s. Many of the texts are so rich as to demand and repay repeated readings, such that it is all the more difficult to get and keep "up to date" with Derrida, unless one is doing little else. It's hard not to get the impression that in his later years Derrida was writing all the more under the shadow of a looming death, whose date was scarcely knowable, even, apparently, at the very end. This contributed, it seems, to a new sense of urgency, an urgency combined with the patience and vigilance that only once in a blue moon would fail the author. These texts, then, are fast and slow at the same time.

Before and especially after his death Derrida was taken to task, by people disposed to condemn his putative skepticism, his relativism, or even just his questioning of our ability to know certain things with certainty, for improvised reflections such as the following from an interview given in the weeks immediately following what it is hard not to call "9/11," a moment when it was difficult to talk of anything else or of anything without somehow invoking that event:

> We do not in fact know what we are saying or naming in this way: September 11, *le septembre 11*, September 11. The brevity of this appellation (September 11, 9/11) stems not only from an economic or rhetorical necessity. The telegram of this metonymy—a name, a number—points out the unqualifiable by recognizing that we do not recognize or even cognize, that we do not yet know how to qualify, that we do not know what we are talking about.

In this interview, given October 22, 2001, and lightly revised afterward, Derrida goes on to complicate the status of the invocation of "9/11," as "we" now most commonly say—but it is hardly a universal appellation—all in the service of trying to figure out just what we were and are dealing with in relation to this "event," not at all simply throwing up his intellectual and political hands, as if to suggest some generalized condition of our not being able to know or not being able to act responsibly in the face of this or any other event, as if—to say it otherwise—the supposed Derridean discourse of undecidability somehow entails that we cannot or should not make decisions. The extraordinary ways the simple tag "9/11" has been invoked in the last years by the Bush administration and its occasional odd ally in the "war on terror" sometimes waged on nonterrorists, invoked also to justify nothing less than a war not on terror, is more than enough to demonstrate that "we" did indeed not know what exactly "9/11" meant or could mean in the early weeks after the event.[1] If Derrida pauses, or suspends his judgment on, say, determining what as momentous an event as "9/11" means, daring to suggest we might not yet (at least "then," so very close to event itself) know what we are talking about, he is accused of irresponsibility, whereas the opposite is far truer: his thinking, writing, and speaking is characterized, rather, by a hyperresponsibility, a responsibility to the complexities of the moment, of history, and the history to come, and to the discourses in which we think and judge, all the while committed to resisting some of the suspect and exhausted modes of thinking we have inherited.[2]

Surely some of the late and later texts are more improvised and sketchier than the early, characteristic essays, many of which seemed like compacted books ("White Mythology," for example) and which usually featured a more traditional academic rhetoric of proof (numerous footnotes, references to secondary literature, etc.). The inexorable prospect of inexorable death gives the later texts a charge and a differently personal investment not usually legible in the earlier ones, however much Derrida always "knew" that death could come at any moment, however much he "knew" that the future, as he had already enunciated in *Of Grammatology*, could be anticipated only in the form of "absolute danger," as one extravagant formulation would have it. "Every third thought shall be my grave," Shakespeare's Prospero remarks in the face of his approaching death: it is a hauntingly elliptical phrase whose primary sense seems to be that every third thought will be *about* the grave and yet, on the face of it, the third thought would *be* the grave, a thought *of* the grave in more ways than one.[3] If Derrida is to be believed, the thought of death was even more omnipresent for him despite and even because of intense moments of happiness. In much the same way that Thomas De Quincey found the contemplation of death "most affecting" in summer, when the weather was fine and when "the exuberant and riotous prodigality of life naturally forces the mind more powerfully upon the antagonist thought of death, and the wintry sterility of the grave," Derrida confesses that the thought of death is especially pressing in moments of happiness, prompting an anticipatory melancholia in the face of what would be the loss of the moment. As he says in the last moments of his very last interview: "I am never as haunted by the necessity of dying as in happiness and pleasure [*jouissance*]" (*Apprendre*, 55). Fortunately for the rest of us, this prospect of death was, for Derrida, often extraordinarily energizing, prompting him to think and write all the more, and in all the more engaged a way. Mourning was not only an immense topic for Derrida, as explored tellingly in these pages by Mary Jacobus and David Clark; it was also—including, as it were, an impossible mourning in advance for himself—a driving force of his thinking.

This striking conjunction of the vital and the mortal is audible in Derrida's last public interview, which appeared in *Le Monde* on August 19, 2004. His interlocutor recalls an enigmatic formulation from *Spectres of Marx* that suggests, in a convoluted, theatrical passage, that Derrida might not know how to live. Derrida now responds:

> As for the turn of phrase that you cite ("finally knowing how to live"), it came to me once the book was done. First of all it plays, albeit seriously, with the common meaning of the phrase: to learn to live is to mature, also to educate. To tell someone "I'll teach you how to live" means—sometimes with an undertone of menace—"I'm going to shape you, I'm going to put you right." Also the equivocation of this play means even more to me: this sigh is also an opening to another, more difficult line of questioning: to live: can that be learned? Taught? Can one learn, by method or training, by experience or experiment, to accept –better yet, to affirm—life? This worry over heritage and death resonates throughout the whole book. It is also the torment of parents and their children. When will you become responsible? When will you be accountable for your own life and name?
>
> So to answer your question without further delay: no, I never learned to live. Really, not at all! Learning to live ought to mean learning to die—to acknowledge, to accept, an absolute mortality (without positive outcome, or resurrection, or redemption—neither for oneself nor anyone else). That has been the old philosophical injunction since Plato: to philosophize is to learn how to die. I believe in this truth without giving myself over to it. Less and less, in fact. I have not learned

to accept death. We are all survivors on deferral (and regarding deferral, from the geopolitical viewpoint in *Specters of Marx*, the emphasis is especially—in a world that is more in-egalitarian than ever—on the billions of living things—human and otherwise—who are denied not only basic "human rights," which go back two hundred years and are continually being amplified, but are denied even the right to a life worthy of being lived). But I remain ineducable when it comes to knowing-how-to-die, or, if you prefer, how-to-live [*savoir-vivre*]. I have yet to learn [*appris*] or acquire anything regarding this subject. (*Apprendre*, 23–25)

From the outside, it seem counterintuitive that Derrida would, so late in life, never have learned how to live, he who would have appear to have led an extraordinarily vital life (to invoke a quasi-tautology), a variegated life as writer, husband, father, thinker, teacher, and more, to say nothing of what would appear to be his having been able to do what he wanted to do, with the exception of becoming a professional soccer (though he might have named it "football") player. As distressing as this might be for the subject experiencing this noneducation, resulting in a decided restlessness, it is a restlessness that translated into a ceaseless activity of thinking and writing, a ceaseless *affirmation*, despite massive misreadings of Derrida to the contrary.

Later in the same interview, Derrida notes that this "learning to live" is always "narcissistic" (*Apprendre*, 30), and certainly Derrida's own person—or persona—surfaces directly more often in his late texts, becomes explicit and even a theme, and not only in overtly autobiographical texts such as the moving "Circumfession" from the late 1980s, in which Derrida weaves in and out from his own life and thought to that of his fellow North African, St. Augustine, sometimes being able to shift even in midsentence from his French words to Augustine's Latin ones, or from his own mother to the fabled "Santa Monica." A text such as *Monolingualism of the Other* might also be exemplary in this regard, beginning with the peculiar, if not singular, circumstance of Derrida's own relation to language and languages, growing up in Algeria speaking a French he never felt was his own, and yet claiming it to be his only language, even if, by most standards, he could be said to know several other languages. But the "one" rarely remains just one, and the "I" not simply an "I," at least not in language, whose very medium and mechanisms work against sheer singularity being able to remain intact. Derrida, far beyond any narcissism, is interested in these conjunctions and dynamics for intellectual and philosophical reasons and for the ways in which the singular, including his own person or persona, resists philosophy.

The notion of "late Derrida" could imply that his career can be divided up neatly into phases or periods. Commentators have long made much of this or that "turn" in Derrida's itinerary or trajectory. There is no doubt that certain preoccupations or concerns now and then acquire a new prominence, as in, say, a cluster of texts about justice in the 1980s and early 1990s, or another cluster regarding religion in the 1990s and the first years of the new millennium (the latter is deftly analyzed by Rei Terada in this volume), or the concept and manifestations of the performative (as expertly treated below by Hillis Miller). Were these important changes? Yes and no. No, insofar as to an extraordinary degree so many of the major preoccupations were treated or at least announced in the trio of epoch-making books that appeared in a kind of philosophical "May '67": *Of Grammatology, Writing and Difference,* and *Voice and Phenomena,* even if sections of those texts had been published a little before and did not all appear in May. Do we recall sufficiently that ethnocentrism, for example, is taken up from the very first page of *Of Grammatology?* The shifts in Derrida, if they are indeed shifts, are such to the extent that Derrida is truly alive and attentive to the demands of the problematics and texts facing him in any given conjuncture. There are, to be sure, certain gestures and concerns that overarch his long career, even habits of thought—despite Derrida's insistence that deconstruction, if there is such a thing, is not a "method"—but Derrida had a great sense of the occasion and would like to respond, if ever he could, to the unpredictable demands of occasions, even if just to answer a request, out of the blue, to write or talk on this or that topic. And the occasions were sometimes were pressing political ones, a constant preoccupation of Derrida's: thus he would respond with pointed interventions to the plight of the *sans-papiers* in France, or the pending execution of a political prisoner—or in a more expansive way to the "state" of Europe, so to speak, addressing the prospects of the European Union, analyzed in the light of the complicated genealogy of that continent as a name, an idea, and a set of histories. In his writings on Europe, for example—the subject of Marc Redfield's searching essay in this volume—one could not quite have predicted the shape or the content of his reflections on the basis of his earlier work. Few if any of the late essays can be easily slotted into the framework of what came to be understood as classic deconstructive "method," as, say, in the demonstration that what seems to be a stable binary opposition of certain terms turns out, on inspection, to be a problematic and unstable co-implication of those very terms. The late essays are far more heterogeneous than that, and one would be hard pressed to "systematize" them, were that even deemed a desirable goal.

There are, to be sure, sometimes some pronounced differences of rhetoric and emphasis from the early texts to the late. In the early work, for example, there was a decided suspicion of the category of experience as mobilized in major and minor thinkers, such as Edmund Husserl. Then in a good many of the late works there are frequent invocations of just that term ("the experience of undecidability, the experience of . . .") where the term in question now no longer appears in quotation marks. Yet there is perhaps less of a difference than appears at first glance because so often the particular object of Derrida's critique—as "experience," in some cases—is not the term or concept as such but how that term is embedded and how it functions in a certain text or corpus of an author. To take another example: we know that Derrida is often roundly accused of being antirational—though almost nothing could be farther from the truth—perhaps because he now and then subjects certain articulations of reason to probing analyses that leave texts trembling. Yet it is hardly reason as such that is dismantled by Derrida but something on the order, for example, of the discourse of reason in Plato, where reason is more or less systematically aligned with the king and the sun, hardly necessary or unproblematic associations. And to call attention to what resists reason, in any number of its guises, is hardly to be antirational. Rather, it is precisely rational in attending to the limits of reason, a time-honored gesture of Enlightenment philosophy from Locke to Kant. It is evident that Derrida was often concerned with deflating the pretensions of a discourse of the sovereign subject, of the subject as sovereign, including the narrowest and the broadest senses, as astutely tracked in the pages below by David Johnson, which focus not by accident on the motif of "touching," traditionally conceived as not at all the most philosophical of the senses. In this way Derrida was suspicious of the pretensions of reason but, once again, always only a *certain*—and hence not universal—reason. Yet the minor matter of charting Derrida's changes and shifts can be left to historians of ideas: that task seems to pale in comparison with figuring out what Derrida has to teach us in the texts that remain to be read and the vast network of topics engaged there.

The singularity of the occasion or the conjuncture is not unrelated to what is usually Derrida's typical object of scrutiny: a text. Derrida's thinking, until the end, tended to take the form of a *reading*. It is not self-evident that this is the form thinking should take: it is certainly not the only viable or justifiable mode. Derrida, however, was trained in a tradition that engaged the history of philosophy via its *texts*, not in the first instance by more abstract reflection on this or that "problem" in philosophy, as is commonly the protocol in analytical philosophy, even if that mode of philosophy has crucially to do with the definitions of words and concepts as they come down to us. It is an unfortunate irony that what is perhaps Derrida's most often read and most widely anthologized essay, "Structure, Sign, and Play in the Discourse of the Human Sciences," is one of his least typical works, given its programmatic character, its brevity (!), and the absence of a particular anchor in a given text or set of texts. The chosen mode of reading has its possibilities and pitfalls: in his close attention to how thinking gets articulated, Derrida is always able to show surprising and problematic things that are liable to escape our attention if we confine ourselves to received ideas, vast topics abstractly conceived, or lazy habits of thought. Derrida will sometimes focus, notoriously, on a seemingly out-of-the-way feature of a text, a footnote, a figure of speech, a difficulty in translating this or that word from another language, only then to reveal larger complexities that should not escape any rigorous confrontation with the text. In this, Derrida was often, in effect, teaching philosophy and philosophers certain lessons that some modes of institutionalized philosophy were not at all anxious to learn: for example, that there may be some conceptual and practical problems attendant to the fact that most philosophy is articulated in a given, nonuniversal language (Greek, Japanese, German . . .) and that there are weighty problems of translation from one given language to the next, even within traditions that appear relatively homogeneous (the Greek and the Roman, for example). Derrida disturbs philosophy's dream of a universal language—and thus unproblematically translatable language—even before he gets to similarly thorny matters of figurative language and what we might call the genres of philosophy (the dialogues of Plato, say, where the invisible author is on record as being against theater and mimesis, or the strangely autobiographical mode of Descartes's *Discourse on Method*). Even philosophers as acutely attentive to matters of language as Ludwig Wittgenstein and J. L. Austin—and this will be all the more the case in their followers—seem little disposed to scrutinize the rhetorical character of language, including its figural texture, which cannot simply be wished away.

By such attention to rhetoric and language, Derrida could appear unduly "literary," and it is no accident that Derrida, for better and for worse, was more readily embraced by teachers and students in departments of literature, as well as other cognate areas of the humanities, and not just because he happened to write and think a good deal about poetry and literature and any number of objects of study "proper" to disciplines other than philosophy. (Philosophy, of course, now and then thinks of itself as the master discipline, the discipline of disciplines, able to take up absolutely any object or subject matter.) Yet Derrida's primary responsibility in thinking and writing was not to the protocols of any institutionalized discourse, in the university or beyond, but to the matter itself whose thinking could never entirely be considered apart from the language in which that matter is articulated—which is still a far cry from saying that everything is language. Indeed, Derrida argued indefatigably against logocentrism and the fetishization of language.

Derrida's most insistent preoccupation, early to late, has been the matter—the matters—and the idea of difference. Yet this constant attention, of its own logic, demanded that it be engaged differently: indeed, the later work continues to think difference differently. In *The Gift of Death* Derrida explores difference and otherness via perhaps the most extravagant formulation of his thinking along these lines: "*tout autre est tout autre.*" The formula can be translated in several ways: most neutrally, if perhaps tautologically, as "every other is every other," or more pointedly, if infinitely, "every other is every bit other," that is, absolutely other. In the context of a reading of Søren Kierkegaard's *Fear and Trembling*, Derrida predictably links this otherness to the absolute other so often conceived of as "God." The topic and the scene, we recall, is the harrowing near-sacrifice of Isaac by his father Abraham, which prompts Derrida at one point to a wider meditation on sacrifice in religious and religion-based doctrine and ideology, including what was then the present of the text, published in 1992. Remarking on the "sacrifices" caused or occasioned by war, Derrida comments:

> We are not even talking about wars, the less recent or most recent ones, in which case one can wait an eternity for morality or international law (whether violated with impunity or invoked hypocritically) to determine with any degree of certainty who is responsible or guilty for the hundreds of thousands of victims who are sacrificed for what or whom one knows not, countless victims, each of whose singularity becomes each time infinitely singular, every other (one) being every

(bit) other, whether they be victims of the Iraqi state or victims of the international coalition that accuses the latter of not respecting the law. For in the discourses that dominate during such wars, it is rigorously impossible, on one side and the other, to discern the religious from the moral, the legal from the political. The warring factions are all irreconcilable fellow worshipers of the religions of the Book. Does that not make things converge once again in the fight to the death that continues to range on Mount Moriah over the possession of the secret of the sacrifice by an Abraham who never said anything? Do they not fight in order to take possession of the secret as the sign of an alliance with God and to impose its order on the other, who becomes for his part nothing more than a murderer?[4]

This passage—which hardly sounds like a "turn to religion"—today has a strange resonance, given yet another war against Iraq, though the repetition comes with its difference, since the phrase "international coalition" rings far more hollow today. Derrida's concern here is for singularity, absolute singularity, which we might think of as the most different of differences. The sacrifice of Isaac, it seems, is not over until it's over, and indeed it is not exactly over. Far from being an utterly discrete event shrouded in the mists—or misty texts—of antiquity, the sacrifice of Isaac, seemingly so singular an event, can, almost against all odds, be repeated. At least, after a fashion. And this singular but not merely singular event has its massive, mediated effects, including the singular, infinitely singular, deaths of the victims of (religious) wars.

The *singular* takes manifold forms in Derrida's work, from early to late, but there seems to be a greater insistence on this motif in the later and latest work. The emphasis on singularity in the later work tends to cluster around these motifs: the other, the subject, death, justice, the event.[5] They are, one can see without too much difficulty, not unrelated. But the singularity of those singularities is perhaps threatened by language, the medium in which they all get articulated, for language is relentless in its generality, its inevitable abstraction: even a seemingly "concrete" word such as *tree* is only a very general term for a host of related particulars. And no amount of deictics—the pointing power of language, most evident in words such as "this" or "now," fraught with difficulties when written down, as Hegel made clear in *Phenomenology*—can guarantee singularity of reference, however much one can and even, to Derrida's mind, should attempt to do just that.

Yet if in some respects language obviates against singularity, it also always enacts and is predicated on difference: ceaseless, thoroughgoing difference. In his *Monolingualism of the Other* Derrida meditates on the fraught situation of his speaking (colonial, non-native) French in his native Algeria (which he did not leave for the first nineteen years of his life) and follows an analysis by Abdelkebir Khatabi of the problem of bilingualism (Arabic-French) and a certain dialectic of their crossing alienation and inalienation by commenting on the situation, which included Derrida's having only one language, which was nonetheless not "his":

> In spite of appearances, this exceptional situation is at the same time certainly exemplary of a universal structure; it represents or reflects a sort of originary "alienation" which institutes every language as language of the other: the impossible propriety of a language. But that should not lead to a sort of neutralization of differences, to the misrecognition of determinate expropriations against which a war can be waged on very different fronts. On the contrary, that is what allows one to repoliticize the stakes. Where natural property does not exist, nor property rights in general, where this de-propriation is recognized, it is possible and it becomes more necessary than ever to identify—sometimes in order to combat them—movements, fantasies, "ideologies," "fetishizations" and symbolics of appropriation. Such a reminder allows one both to analyze the historical phenomena of appropriation and to treat them politically, avoiding in particular the reconstitution of what those phantasms were able to motivate: "nationalistic" (always more or less "naturalistic") aggressions, or monoculturalist homo-hegemony.[6]

The intellectual recognition of difference or otherness hardly leads, of its own accord, to a politics of recognition, or a politics of respect for the other, and certainly not to a politics that would be ethically admirable. The old philosophical problem of the relation between the "is" and the "ought" is acknowledged by Derrida to entail a leap. The epistemological realization or recognition of difference does not *necessarily* lead to politics, and even less necessarily to good politics. Indeed, the most disastrous sorts of politics are founded on hierarchies and systems of oppression or exclusion that turn on perceived or postulated differences, as, say, phallocentrism, ethnocentrism, or Eurocentrism, to name but a few. Such political institutions of difference can be arbitrary in the worst sense. Derrida calls, rather, for a *political* leap to the political and to a politics that would be just. The originary alienation (even one's "own" language is not exactly one's "own") "allows" for a "re-politicization" of the stakes, a politicization that must be engaged, for it is certainly not given in advance.

In confronting the singular death of Derrida one is tempted, as a number of our contributors do so appropriately and poignantly, to think the matter through Derrida's own extensive writings on death and mourning. One of Derrida's best-known works from his latest years is *The Work of Mourning*, a collection of eulogies, funeral orations, and other memorial writings for many of the great thinkers of Derrida's time. For reasons that need not be rehearsed here, the collection appeared first in English, though the texts were written in French and usually "delivered" in France. The French version of the collection (expanded a little) appeared, rather preposterously, only after the English. In the later French version, Derrida offers a brief reflection on the status of the world and worlds in relation to death. In a passage that, I believe, has not yet appeared in English, Derrida writes: "Death declares each time *the end of the world in totality*, the end of every world, and *each time the end of the world as unique totality, thus irreplaceable and thus infinite.*"[7] He goes on to resign himself to the possibility that each farewell [*adieu*] or salute [*salut*] to his dead friends must face the possibility of there being no return, and of the end of the world as the end of all and all resurrection (11). This future envisioned is neither that of classical resurrection nor that of the *anastasis* (also usually translated as "resurrection") analyzed by Jean-Luc Nancy in his *Noli me tangere*. This latter, Derrida notes,

> postulates both the existence of some God and that the end of *a* world [*la fin d'un monde*] will not be the end of *the* world [*du monde*]. "God" means: death can put an end to *a* world [un *monde*], it would not signify the end of *the* world [du *monde*]. A world, one world [un *monde*] can always survive another. There is more than one world. More than one possible world [or: more than one world possible—*un monde possible*]. That is what we would wish to believe, as little as we believe or believe to believe in "God." But death, death itself, if there is such a thing, leaves no room, not the least chance, neither for replacement nor survival of the sole and unique [*seul et unique*] world, of the "sole and unique" which makes of each living being (animal, human, or divine), a sole and unique living being. (11)

For all of its extravagance, the rhetoric of this passage—and these passages—stop short of adopting an apocalyptic tone, insisting, in the end, on *a* world rather than *the* world. Derrida's affirmations in the face of death—death as such, if there is such a thing, the deaths of his friends, the deaths of countless war victims, and his own death, impossible to conceive, impossible not to conceive—are risked in the absence of any necessity of a possible return, of the end as (just) the end. There is no apocalypse, not now. Not even now.

Notes

1   Does "9/11" mean the same for American Muslims as for the Bush administration? Does it mean the same thing for all American Muslims? To say nothing of millions of Iraqis implicated after the fact in 9/11, despite their nation having nothing, per se, to do with it?

2   Derrida had, long before "9/11," offered a searching reflection on "the date" in his essay on the work of Paul Celan, "Shibboleth," now reprinted with his other writings on the poet in *Sovereignties in Question: The Poetics of Paul Celan*, ed. Thomas Dutoit and Outi Pasanen (New York: Fordham University Press, 2005), 1–64. The French original is *Shibboleth: Pour Paul Celan* (Paris: Galilée, 1986). On the relation of "suspension" to Derrida's responsibility, see Elisabeth Weber's essay in this volume.

3   Jacques Derrida, *Apprendre à vivre enfin: Entretien avec Jean Birnbaum* (Paris: Galilée, 2005), 23–25; hereafter cited parenthetically in the text as *Apprendre*. An English translation of the interview can be found on the Studio Visit Web site, at www.studiovisit .net/SV.Derrida.pdf. I have modified the translation somewhat. For reflections on the central concern of this portion of the interview, see David Clark in this volume as well as Judith Butler, "On Never Having Learned How to Live," in a special issue of *differences*: "Derrida's Gift," *differences* 16.3 (Fall 2005): 27–34.

4   Jacques Derrida, *The Gift of Death*, trans. David Willis (Chicago: University of Chicago Press, 1995), 86–87. The French original is *Donner la mort in L'éthique du don: Jacques Derrida et la pensée du don* (Paris: Transition, 1992).

5   In his essay on Walter Benjamin's "Critique of Violence" (scrutinized and critiqued in this volume by David Lloyd), Derrida sounded the theme of the singularity of justice in relation to the generality of law, perhaps his most thoroughgoing elaboration of the topic. See "Force of Law: The 'Mystical Foundation of Authority,'" in Jacques Derrida, *Acts of Religion*, ed. Gil Anidjar (New York: Routledge, 2002), 228–98.

6   Jacques Derrida, *Monolingualism of the Other, or the Prosthesis of Origin*, trans. Patrick Mansah (Stanford, CA: Stanford University Press, 1998), 63–64 (translation slightly modified). The French original is *Le monolinguisme de l'autre ou la prothèse d'origine* (Paris: Galilée, 1996), 121–22.

7   Jacques Derrida, *Chaque fois unique, la fin du monde*, ed. Pascale-Anne Brault and Michael Naas (Paris: Galilée, 2003), 9. The earlier English volume that almost entirely corresponds to the later French one is *The Work of Mourning*, ed. Pascal-Anne Brault and Michael Naas (Chicago: University of Chicago Press, 2001).

J. Hillis Miller

Performativity as Performance /
Performativity as Speech Act:
Derrida's Special Theory of Performativity

My hypotheses: (1) Performativity in the sense of the way a dance, a musical composition, or a part in a play is performed has practically nothing to do with performativity in the sense of the ability a given enunciation can function as a performative speech act. "He gave a spectacular performance of Hamlet" does not exemplify, nor does it refer to, the same use of language as does saying, "He gave his solemn promise that he would be here at ten," even though both are forms of enunciation, of speaking out, of uttering words, even of doing something with words. (2) Jacques Derrida's late work proposes a special theory of performativity, a theory that is without antecedent in previous theorists of speech acts.

A hypothesis, such as the ones I have just proposed, *is* a genuine performative. A hypothesis fits the standard definition of a performative in traditional speech act theory. Proffering a hypothesis is like a bet. "I bet you I can show that performativity as performance style and performativity as the felicitous operation of a speech act have almost nothing to do with one another. Considerable confusion, I hypothesize, has resulted, in some quarters, from thinking the two

South Atlantic Quarterly 106:2, Spring 2007
DOI 10.1215/00382876-2006-022   © 2007 Duke University Press

kinds of performativity are the same, or almost the same." These pages are an extended version of what the admirable online encyclopedia Wikipedia[1] calls a "Disambiguation Page," that is, a page that discriminates among the various more or less incompatible meanings of a given term. Wikipedia, for example, distinguishes nine different referents for "catastrophe." I hold that it would be a catastrophe to blur different meanings of "performativity."

A hypothesis is something set down underneath as a foundation on the basis of which further inquiry may be carried out, from Greek *hupo* (under) and *tithenai* (to place). A valid scientific hypothesis must be capable of being falsified if it is mistaken. That is why the religious fundamentalists' claim that God created the world in 4004 B.C. or that the "creation" manifests "intelligent design" is not a valid hypothesis. It can neither be proved true nor be proved false. You have to take it on faith. If I hypothesize that the moon is all made of green cheese, my hypothesis can be proved false by a trip to the moon and the bringing back of moonrock, no cheese, or indeed proved true if green cheese turns up there. My hypothesis about the more or less complete disjunction between the two kinds of performativity will, I hope, be confirmed by the investigation of some examples.

First, however, a word about the words "performative" and "performativity." Neither word exists in the *American Heritage Dictionary of the English Language*. My computer draws red lines under both words when I type them on the screen, even though many people, mostly academic people, now use both words all the time, in the most natural way possible. "Performance" is a word all right. Here are the three relevant meanings of the five given in the *American Heritage Dictionary*: "the act of performing, or the state of being performed," "the act or style of performing a work or role before an audience," and "a presentation, especially a theatrical one, before an audience." That seems clear enough. "Performativity," though it is not a word but a neologism, must mean the quality of a performance, or the condition of someone who is capable of performing or, perhaps, the object of investigation in "performance studies." Here is what Wikipedia says under "Performativity." (I am using Wikipedia here, and in what I say about Judith Butler later, as the best source I know for highly informed received opinion about a given topic or writer.) My interest here, at first at least, is in what people think about "performativity," or about Judith Butler's *Gender Trouble*. In particular, I am interested in figuring out how a certain confusion in the "academic mind" came about:

Performativity is a concept that is related to speech acts theory, to the pragmatics of language, and to the work of John L. Austin. It accounts for situations where a proposition may constitute or instaurate the object to which it is meant to refer, as in so-called "performative utterances."

The concept of performativity has also been used in science and technology studies and in economic sociology. Andrew Pickering has proposed to shift from a "representational idiom" to a "performative idiom" in the study of science. Michel Callon has proposed to study the performative aspects of economics, i.e. the extent to which economic science plays an important role not only in describing markets and economies, but also in framing them.

Other uses of the notion of performativity in the social sciences include the daily behavior (or performance) of individuals based on social norms or habits. Philosopher and feminist theorist Judith Butler has used the concept of performativity in her analysis of political speech.

Wikipedia's entry for "performance studies" contains no references whatsoever to speech act theory, to performatives, or to performativity. "Performance studies," the reader is told, was created as an academic discipline in the 1960s by Richard Schechner, Victor Turner, Brooks McNamara, Michael Kirby, and others—all men, I note. It was first institutionalized at New York University and at Northwestern University. "This field of study," says Wikipedia, "engages performance as both an object of study and as something to be experienced, practiced, enacted. Events are more than their face value. A sporting event, a ceremony, a protest are all performances in their own right. Events have specific actors, costumes, settings and audiences. Within these performances are more minute performances of self: of gender, of societal role(s), of age, of disposition(s). Examining events as performance provides insight into how we perform ourselves and our lives." Though performance studies have an anthropological component, as Victor Turner's role as a founder indicates, they center on performances in dance, music, and drama, as well as on the performance of roles in daily life. If "performance studies" was created in the 1960s, it precedes the work or the wide influence of Foucault, Derrida, and Butler. It even precedes, I believe, any substantial academic influence of Austin's speech act theory. The first edition of *How to Do Things with Words* appeared in 1962, but it was not, I suspect, widely noticed at the time. Foucault's *Les mots et les choses* dates from 1966. "Performativity theory," I suggest, is a somewhat later hybrid combining speech act theory, Foucault, and performance studies. The lines of filiation here, to use a sexist word, are complex and inextricably entangled, as is the case with modern theory generally.

So how does one get from "performance studies" to "performativity"? As I suspected when I began thinking about the genesis of "performativity," Judith Butler's work is the missing link. When I click on the link to "Judith Butler" in Wikipedia's entry for "performativity," I get a little closer to the heart of the matter or to the root of the confusion. The reader will remember that I am more interested here in what people think Butler said than in what she may actually have said:

> The most widely read and misread move in *Gender Trouble* (1990) is the redeployment of Derrida's reading of (1) J. L. Austin's theory of the "performative statement," and (2) Franz Kafka's story, "Before the Law"; both in convergence with Butler's readings of Foucault's *Discipline and Punish* and *History of Sexuality, Volume 1*. This convergence is the crucible of Butler's famous "performative theory of gender," in which "gender" is a kind of repeated, largely "forced" (Foucault's "discipline") enactment or "performance" that in that very repetitive performance produces the imaginary fiction of a "core gender," as well as the distinction between the surface/exterior of "the body" and the "interior core." Paradoxically, it is a kind of forced, repetitive "doing" of gender that itself produces the *fiction* that an individual "has a" stable "gender" that "she/he" is just "expressing" in "her/his actions." And this imaginary fiction crucially produces an equally fictive distinction between an "interior" of "the body" and an "exterior" of "the body."

The concept of performativity is, Wikipedia holds, at the core of Butler's work. It extends beyond the doing of gender and can be understood as a full-fledged theory of subjectivity. Indeed, if her more recent books have shifted focus away from gender, they still rely on performativity as a theoretical matrix. Those more recent books, *Bodies That Matter* (1993) and *Excitable Speech: A Politics of the Performative* (1997), do some disambiguating of their own. They make amends, to some degree, for the confusion between performativity as performance and performativity as speech act that *Gender Trouble* can be read as fostering, if Wikipedia is to be believed. *Gender Trouble*, and its account of a certain performativity, has remained, however, immensely influential.

The genealogy I have been tracing is complicated, however, by the way Jean-François Lyotard was already in 1979, in *La condition postmoderne: Rapport sur le savoir* (English translation: *The Postmodern Condition: A Report on Knowledge*, 1984), using "performativity" as a key word and a key concept. Examples are two chapter titles: "Research and Its Legitimation through Performativity," and "Education and Its Legitimation through Performativity." Lyotard meant by "the performativity criterion" more or less that science, technology, education, and other social enterprises, in the postmodern period, do not depend on preexisting principles of legitimation. They produce their own grounds through the performance of research, or education, or other such "language games," as Lyotard calls them.[2] The rules or principles depend on a social contract or bond. We agree to abide by certain rules in playing a game, or in deciding what counts as new "truth" in science, and so on. Speaking of the way technology "masters" "reality," Lyotard affirms:

> This is how legitimation by power takes shape. Power is not only good performativity, but also effective verification and good verdicts. It legitimates science and the law on the basis of their efficiency, and legitimates this efficiency on the basis of science and law. It is self-legitimating, in the way a system organized around performance maximization seems to be. Now it is precisely this kind of context control that a generalized computerization of society may bring. The performativity of an utterance, be it denotative or prescriptive, increases proportionally to the amount of information about its referent one has at one's disposal. Thus the growth of power, and its self-legitimation, are now taking the route of data storage and accessibility, and the operativity of information. (47)

This is an amazingly prophetic statement, when one reflects that it was written in 1979. Think, if you can remember that far back, what was the state of computing in 1979. Wikipedia, as a self-generating and self-regulating online encyclopedia, collectively created, is a splendid example of the self-legitimating databases that Lyotard so presciently foresaw.

Though space here does not permit detailed demonstration, I think it can be shown that Lyotard's use of the term "performativity" is an example of the confusion I am attempting to disambiguate. Lyotard begins with a more or less orthodox account of performative speech acts à la Austin (9). He then shifts by way of Wittgenstein's theory of language games (10) to the "pragmatic" (his word, 23) notion of performativity as know-how (21) and, as the extract above indicates, to performativity as legitimation by an exercise of power, whether by denotative or prescriptive utterances. By this final shift, Lyotard has come a long way from Austin. It is not unreasonable to assume that Lyotard's celebrated work may have had some influence on Butler and certainly on general received ideas about performativity in the 1980s and 1990s. To put this another way, it almost seems as if Butler's theory of performatively produced gender in *Gender Trouble* is a special (often unfortunate, in her view) case of the "legitimation by power" Lyotard describes as a central feature of the postmodern condition.

Blessings on you, Wikipedia, and on you too, Judith Butler! To say that is to utter another performative utterance, though an odd one, since it invokes God to shower blessings, and, as we know, prayers may or may not be answered. Nevertheless, my sentence constrains even God, since He, She, It, assuming God exists, must either respond to my invocation, my incantation, my conjuration, my prayer, or, as the case may be, not respond.

The three entries in Wikipedia, plus what I have found in Lyotard, succinctly tell a story, the story of how university disciplines wandered away from Austin's quite definite concept of performative utterances in *How to Do Things with Words* to the institutionalizing of something called, on Butler's example, "performativity" or even "performativity theory." Here is the little genealogical story: Judith Butler appropriated Derrida's modification of Austin's speech act theory and married it, under the impetus of feminism and nascent queer theory, to something more or less alien to Derrida's work, namely Foucault's *Discipline and Punish* and his *History of Sexuality: Volume 1*, with Lyotard probably hovering in the background. On that basis, Butler invented a new and immensely influential theory called performativity, that is, the notion that gender is not inherent but is engendered by disciplinary pressures that coerce us into performing, that is, behaving, in a way society assumes is appropriate for a certain gender. "That very repetitive performance," says Wikipedia, with eloquent succinctness, as you will remember, "produces the imaginary fiction of a 'core gender,' as well as the distinction between the surface/exterior of 'the body' and the 'interior core.' Paradoxically, it is a kind of forced, repetitive 'doing' of gender that itself produces the *fiction* that an individual 'has a' stable 'gender' that 'she/he' is just 'expressing' in 'her/his actions.'" This notion of what has come to be called "social construction" was so powerful and so attractive, it explained so much, that it has been appropriated, as Wikipedia tells us, under the name "performativity," in a variety of disciplines, in science and technology, sociology, economics, anthropology, drama studies, and in the study of the "performances" of everyday life, as in, "My son put on quite a performance when I tried to get him to do his homework." Performativity theory has now, it seems, become a discipline or an interdisciplinary project (for example, at the conference where this essay was originally presented). It has become, it seems, an alternative name for what used to be called "performance studies."

"Performativity," it now appears, means, among other things, the assumption that human beings have no innate selfhood or subjectivity but become what they are through more or less forced repetition of a certain role. It is as though someone who plays the role of Hamlet or Ophelia on the stage is in danger of becoming Hamlet or Ophelia, or perhaps no one at all, as the antitheatrical tradition from the Renaissance to Henry James's *The Tragic Muse,* and beyond, feared.[3] That's what "social construction" means. You play the role of being straight, or gay, or an English professor long enough and you become straight, or gay, or an English professor. This is both a depressing and at the same time a tremendously attractive notion, something in the social world akin to what Freud called the "family romance," that is, the child's belief that he or she is not really the offspring of his or her parents but a princess or prince in disguise. Though I am not Prince Hamlet nor was meant to be, I am not really an English professor either. I have been forced to become one by surrounding social circumstances and by playing at being an English professor for so long that it finally has come to seem like what I really am, at my heart's core. This is a depressing theory because it assumes I am not innately anything. It is an exhilarating theory because, apparently, it blows the gaff on the familial, social, ideological, and political forces that have made me what I now think I am by forcing me to repetitive performances of that role. Once I understand that, the way is open to change society so I can be different, or even, so it appears, to take my identity into my own hands and "perform" myself into becoming some other person, some other gender, or some mixture of genders, or one person or gender today and another person or gender tomorrow.

I find this genealogy of performativity theory fascinating. Its wide influence shows the performative force of a theoretical formulation whose time has come. Of course Butlerian performativity has drifted pretty far away from what either Austin or Derrida meant by a performative utterance.

That in itself, one might argue, is no great matter. We can make words mean whatever we like. "It's a question of who is to be master," as Humpty Dumpty said. Intellectual life moves forward widdershins, through creative misinterpretation or exappropriation. It does matter somewhat, however, I believe, if performativity theory, the theory that we are nothing but potentiality initially and perform ourselves, under external discipline, into what we become, is identified too closely, and, I believe, illicitly, with Austin's or Derrida's theories of performative utterances. It *is* important not to confuse kinds. It is important not to be misled by the multiple incompatible uses of the same word, its heterogeneity or plurisignificance, into seeing identities where there are essential differences. We must disambiguate. Austin, Derrida, and Butler have radically different concepts of "performativity," though one can see how the first, Austin, evolved into the others.

Just what are those differences?

J. L. Austin's *How to Do Things with Words* is one of the most important philosophical works of the Anglo-American analytical or "ordinary language" school. It is a wonderfully witty, intelligent, and disarmingly complex book. Its essential claim, however, seems simple enough. Certain intelligible sentences, Austin claims, are not constative statements that can be proved to be either true or false but are what Austin calls, in a made-up word, a neologism, "performatives." He considered at first calling them "performatories" or "operatives," or "contractuals," or "declaratories," but decided, in a performative decision, to call them "performatives." A performative is an utterance "in which to *say* something is to *do* something; or in which *by* saying something we are doing something."[4] A performative speech act is a sentence in "the first person singular present indicative active form" (150) that, uttered by the right person in the right circumstances, brings about what it says. Examples would be "I pronounce you man and wife," or "I promise to finish this essay in twenty-five pages," or "I bequeath my watch to my brother," or "I christen thee the *Queen Mary*," or "I bet you sixpence it will rain tomorrow," or "We may christen those infelicities where the act *is* achieved ABUSES" (16). Such sentences do not make statements of fact that may be true or false. They bring something about, for example that the couple is married or that the ship is now named the *Queen Mary*.

All this seems simple enough and straightforward enough, though it was a revolutionary idea in philosophical thinking. The Austinian performative has, so far as I can see, almost nothing whatsoever to do with the idea that I am disciplined into becoming such and such a person or gender by performing that role repeatedly. Austin's theory, as critics of it have noted, presupposes a preexisting, stable, and perdurable selfhood as a condition of what he calls a "felicitous performative." That enduring selfhood allows me to say "I," as in "I promise," and to be held responsible for fulfilling that promise tomorrow or whenever, without any possibility of saying, "Well, that was yesterday. I am now a different person. You can't be so naive as to hold me to a promise I made when I was a different 'I.'" Austin, moreover, far from thinking that "performance," in the sense of a performance of Hamlet in *Hamlet* or a performance of the prima ballerina's role in *Swan Lake*, can be an efficacious performative, has an ingrained distaste for playacting or for pretending of any kind. *How To* repeatedly stresses this distaste. "I must not be joking, for example, nor writing a poem," avers Austin (9), linking the hollowness of joking with a similar triviality and lack of seriousness in poetry. "[A] performative utterance," he roundly asserts, "will, for example, be *in a peculiar way* hollow or void if said by an actor on the stage, or if introduced in a poem, or spoken in soliloquy. This applies in a similar manner to any and every utterance—a sea-change in special circumstances. Language in such circumstances is in special ways—intelligibly—used not seriously, but in ways *parasitic* upon its normal use—ways which fall under the doctrine of the *etiolations* of language" (22). Etiolation means whitening, enfeebling, as in etiolated asparagus, which is bred in dark straw away from sunlight and so remains white, tender, and never turns green. So much for the idea that "performativity theory" in "performance studies" or in Butler's theory of gender has any consonance with, any resonance or *Stimmung* with, Austin's theory of performative speech acts! One might even claim that Butlerian performativity theory is the opposite of Austinian theory of performatives.

Matters are not by any means so simple with Austin, however, though a full explanation of that complexity would take me far more than my allotted space. The essential complications can, however, be stated succinctly. Austin himself describes the series of lectures that makes up *How To* as a process whereby he "bog[s], by logical stages, down" (13). This bogging down happens by way of the investigation of examples. These show the idea that we sometimes do something by saying something getting more and more complex and even contradictory. The bogging down also happens through a proliferation of terms. Constative versus performative becomes the tripartite distinction among locutionary, illocutionary, and perlocutionary utterances, and those three further divide into five names for classes of speech acts: verdictives, exercitives, commissives, behabitives, expositives. The mind boggles! Moreover, the apparently firm and clear "dichotomy" between constative and performative utterances breaks down almost completely. It "has to be abandoned in favor of more general *families* of related and overlapping speech-acts" (150). All constatives, Austin is forced to recognize, by examination of examples from ordinary language, are a little bit performative, and all performatives are a little bit constative. This bogging down is an extraordinary example of a great philosopher forced by his own thinking to qualify radically what he thought he was going to demonstrate. Moreover, in spite of Austin's stern, even puritanical, assertion that we must not be joking or writing a poem, *How To* is full of jokes and of that form of poetry we call narration or storytelling. All of his examples are, when you think of it, little miniature stories, or synecdoches for implicit stories, for example, "I give and bequeath my watch to my brother" (5). But many memorable Austinian examples are more extended stories, often ironic or joking stories, such as the example of the way you can accuse a woman of adultery "by asking her whether it was not her handkerchief which was in X's bedroom, or by stating that it was hers" (111). This is an allusion to *Othello,* by the way. *How To* is full of allusions, many of them Shakespearean, as in "sea-change," quoted above, an allusion to *The Tempest.* Another story is the example of an infelicitous performative when someone without authority and in the wrong circumstances breaks a bottle over a great new British warship and says, "I name this ship the *Mr. Stalin*" (23), or the disproof of the necessity of a first-person singular pronoun with a present active indicative verb for a felicitous performative. If you want to warn someone a ferocious bull is in the field and about to charge, you do not say, "I warn you that a ferocious bull is in the field about to charge." You just say, "Bull!" (59)

Austin cannot proceed with his argument without using, over and over, in a serious way, the mode of language he calls etiolated, nonserious, parasitic on normal uses. No doubt he would say he is just mentioning these examples, not using them, but, as anyone knows who has thought a bit about this distinction, it no more holds up than the constative/performative distinction. You cannot mention a performative utterance without to some small degree using it.

I make two conclusions from this spectacular bogging down: (1) Austin's philosophical argumentation is not systematic and consistent, but heterogeneous, just as is Butler's performativity doctrine, which is simultaneously distressing ("I am not innately anybody or anything") and liberating ("I can therefore, perhaps, become anything I like"). (2) It follows that Austin is, perhaps unwillingly and unwittingly, granting some performative felicity to performances, such as the performance of a wedding on the stage and in a play. After all, a "real" wedding too is the repetition of a script that has been performed countless times before. This iteration does not disqualify a wedding, in Austin's eyes, from being felicitous, from being a way to do things with words—far from it, since iterability is what makes a wedding ceremony "a conventional procedure having a certain conventional effect" (14). Butler's exappropriation (to borrow a word from Derrida) of Austinian speech act theory in her performativity theory is, after all, not entirely unfaithful to its progenitor, even though, so far as I remember, Austin never uses, nor would have been likely to use, the word "performativity."

What then about Derrida, whom Wikipedia sees, correctly, I believe, as the intermediary between Austin and Butler? Derrida is an essential stage in the progress toward present-day performativity theory. His concept of performatives is, however, fundamentally different not only from Austin's but also from Butler's. The bare facts of Derrida's own exappropriation of Austin are easy enough to specify. Derrida published in 1972 a strong critique of Austin's speech act theory entitled "Signature Event Context." A hapless American philosopher named John Searle then published an incautious attack on Derrida's essay entitled "Reiterating the Differences: A Reply to Derrida." I say "hapless" and "incautious" because Searle's essay called forth a long, often funny, and certainly violently polemical response from Derrida entitled "Limited Inc a b c . . ."[5]

The gravamen of Derrida's accusation of Austin is the following, delivered with Derridian panache but not without respect for Austin, though hardly for Searle: Since any form of words used in a performative utterance (e.g., "I pronounce you man and wife") can be used in more than one, indeed in innumerable, situations, what Derrida calls "iterability" is a fundamental feature of performatives. This iterability has more than one consequence. I shall name the three most important. For one thing, iterability means that, as Derrida puts it, the context of a performative can never be "saturated," whereas it is a feature of felicitous performatives, in Austin's theory, that they occur in the correct "circumstances," so those circumstances must, in a given case, be capable of exhaustive inventory. That, says Derrida, is impossible. Therefore the distinction between felicitous and infelicitous performatives, so important for Austin, breaks down. Second: iterability means that those parasitical or etiolated performatives, writing in a poem, acting on the stage, uttering a soliloquy, or making a joke, and so on, that Austin wants to "exclude," in a resolute anathema, cannot be excluded. No such thing as a fully "serious" performative utterance exists, as a unique, one-time-only event in the present. The possibility of the abnormal is an intrinsic part of the normal. Iterability, finally, disqualifies the requirement that a felicitous performative depends on the self-consciousness of the ego and its "intentions," the "I" who says, "I promise" and means to keep that promise. In case you do not believe me, here are Derrida's own words, in "Signature Event Context":

> For, ultimately, isn't it true that what Austin excludes as anomaly, exception, "non-serious," *citation* (on stage, in a poem, or a soliloquy) is the determined modification of a general citationality—or rather, a general iterability—without which there would not even be a "successful" performative? So that—a paradoxical but unavoidable conclusion—a successful performative is necessarily an "impure" performative, to adopt the word advanced later on by Austin when he acknowledges that there is no "pure" performative.
>
> . . . Given that structure of iteration, the intention animating the utterance will never be through and through present to itself and to its content. The iteration structuring it a priori introduces into it a dehiscence and a cleft [*brisure*] which are essential. The "non-serious," the *oratio obliqua* will no longer be able to be excluded, as Austin wished, from, "ordinary" language. . . . Above all, this essential absence of intending the actuality of utterance, this structural unconsciousness, if you like, prohibits any saturation of the context. In order for a context to be exhaustively determinable, in the sense required by Austin, conscious intention would at the very least have to be totally present and immediately transparent to itself and to others, since it is a determining center [*foyer*] of context. The concept of—or the search for—the context thus seems to suffer at this point from the same theoretical and "interested" uncertainty as the concept of the "ordinary," from the same metaphysical origins: the ethical and teleological discourse of consciousness. (17–18)

This seems a clear enough more or less complete rejection of the whole theoretical scaffolding that Austin so elaborately constructs (only himself to dismantle it) in *How to Do Things with Words*. Why then does Derrida go on, in the long years after publishing "Signature Event Context" and "Limited Inc a b c . . . ," using, as an essential feature of his own philosophical argumentation, the notion of performatives? The idea of the performative speech act appears in many, perhaps most, of Derrida's many essays, seminars, and interviews after 1977. The performative is an essential aspect of Derrida's ideas about the secret, about literature, about friendship, about hospitality, about perjury, about decision, about sovereignty, about politics, about responsibility, about justice, about death, about temporality, about religion, and so on. Performativity permeates every corner of the late Derrida's late work. Why? The answer lies in the quite special and even scandalous concept of the performative that Derrida developed in his late work by exappropriation, that is, through a taking over by way of creative distortion, of Austin's ideas. Exappropriation names the heterogeneity of Derrida's relation to speech act theory. On the one hand, he ferociously ridicules it, "deconstructs" it. On the other hand, his own later work would be impossible without it.

In all the regions of his thought I have named, a more or less similar and quite un-Austinian paradigm of the performative utterance is an essential ingredient. The performative is seen as a response made to a demand made on me by the "wholly other" [*le tout autre*], a response that, far from depending on preexisting rules or laws, on a preexisting ego, I, or self, or on preexisting circumstances or "context," creates the self, the context, and new rules or laws, in a way that is anticipated by Austin's extraordinary statement: "As official acts, a judge's ruling makes law; a jury's finding makes a convicted felon" (154). Derridean performatives are essentially linked to his special concept of time as "out of joint," as *différance*. A Derridean performative creates an absolute rupture between the present and the past. It inaugurates a future that Derrida calls a future anterior, or an unpredictable "à-venir," as in Derrida's iterated phrase in his late work: "la démocratie à venir," the democracy to come. My response to the call made on me is essentially a reciprocal performative saying "yes" to a performative demand issued initially by the wholly other. My "yes" is a performative countersigning or the validating of a performative command that comes from outside me, as in Derrida's analysis, in *Ulysse gramophone: Deux mots pour Joyce*, of Molly Bloom's "yes I said yes I will Yes," or as in Derrida's extraordinary two-hour seminar on the French locution "Je t'aime." To say "je t'aime," said Derrida, is not a constative statement of fact. It is a performative that creates my condition of being in love and thereby makes me into a new person, the one who is in love with someone. That other person, in turn, has no access to my interiority and therefore no way of knowing whether I am lying or telling the truth. My performative utterance, "je t'aime," must be endorsed by your return performative, though you have no certain evidence that I mean what I say: "I swear that I believe that you love me." Another example of this saying yes, analyzed at length by Derrida in *Donner la mort*, is Abraham's response to Jehovah's demand that he sacrifice Isaac. Jehovah says, "Abraham," and Abraham answers, "Behold, here I am." The admirably eloquent final pages of "Psyché: Invention de l'autre" turn on the following sentences: "The very movement of this fabulous repetition can, according to a crossing of chance and necessity, produce the novelty of an event. Not only by the singular invention of a performative, since every performative presupposes conventions and institutional rules; but in turning these rules in respect for these very rules in order to let the other come or announce itself in the opening of this dehiscence. That is perhaps what one calls deconstruction."[6]

I conclude this brief discussion of performativity in Derrida with a passage from *Specters of Marx* in which the word "performativity" actually appears, the only time I have noticed it used by Derrida. The passage admirably encapsulates the Derridean paradigm I have been identifying:

> It is a matter there [in our relation to Marx's works and for Marx himself in relation to what enjoined him to write] of an ethical and political imperative, an appeal as unconditional as the appeal of thinking from which it is not separated. It is a matter of the injunction itself [*l'injonction même*]—if there is one.
>
> What also resonates in "Marx's Three Voices" [the Blanchot essay Derrida is discussing] is the *appeal* [*l'appel*] or the political injunction, the pledge or the promise (the oath, if one prefers: "swear!" [a reference to the ghost scene at the beginning of *Hamlet*, a constant presence in *Specters of Marx*]), the originary performativity [*cette performativité originaire*] that does not conform to preexisting conventions, unlike all the performatives analyzed by the theoreticians of speech acts, but whose force of *rupture* produces the institution or the constitution, the law itself [*la loi même*], which is to say also the meaning that appears to, that ought to, or that appears to have to guarantee it in return. *Violence* of the law before the law and before meaning,

violence that interrupts time, disarticulates it, dislodges it, displaces it out of its natural lodging: "out of joint" [in English in the original; another citation from *Hamlet*]. It is there that différance, if it remains irreducible, irreducibly required by the spacing of any promise and by the future-to-come that comes to open it [*l'à-venir qui vient à l'ouvrir*], does not mean only (as some people have too often believed and so naively) deferral, lateness, delay, postponement. . . . The pledge [*Le gage*] is given here and now, even before, perhaps, a decision confirms it. It thus responds without delay to the demand of justice. The latter by definition is impatient, uncompromising, and unconditional.[7]

The reader will see how far both from Austin's performative and from Butler's performativity is this concept of the political performative as a response to an injunction that comes from the other, as in the ghost's injunction to Hamlet in Shakespeare's play. What is a bad thing for Butler, being solicited and coerced by society to perform a certain gender role, is a good thing for Derrida, when it takes the form of an injunction that comes from the wholly other. I conclude that one must discriminate quite sharply among different notions of performativity. We must disambiguate them in order to avoid confusion of thought. We must resist thinking that gender socially constructed by performativity is like an Austinian promise or that either is like a Derridean performative response, a saying yes to the wholly other, or that the performance of a Mozart piano sonata is like any of these.

And yet . . . And yet . . . And yet—after all my efforts of disambiguation, I must nevertheless assert that these various forms of performativity, different as they are from one another, have a family resemblance, in the Wittgensteinian sense of that phrase. The social construction of gender is somehow a little bit like my first falling in love by saying "I love you." Both of these are a little bit like the way I am changed by playing Mozart and change Mozart's music too in the same performance of performativity. All of these examples show the power of words or other signs to do something, to act.

If I had more space I would analyze in detail two moments in George Eliot's *Daniel Deronda* that demonstrate both the fundamental usefulness of performativity theory for understanding what happens in literary works and, at the same time, for seeing the essential function of literary study as a way of understanding what is at stake in performativity studies. In one of those passages the heroine, Gwendolen Harleth, betrays the shallowness and inauthenticity of her selfhood, the person her society has coached her into becoming, by the way she sings an aria by Bellini. Both her performance and the aria itself are sharply criticized by the true musician in the novel, Klesmer, modeled on Liszt: "Yes, it is true; you have not been well taught. . . . Still, you are not quite without gifts. You sing in tune, and you have a pretty fair organ. But you produce your notes badly; and that music which you sing is beneath you. It is a form of melody which expresses a puerile state of culture—a dangling, canting, see-saw kind of stuff—the passion and thought of people without any breadth of horizon."[8]

In the other passage, which comes much later in the novel, the hero, in this double-plotted novel, Daniel Deronda, utters a solemn promise to the dying Jewish scholar, Mordecai. Daniel promises to carry on his work after Mordecai's death: "Everything I can in conscience do to make your life effective I will do" (600). This looks at first like an Austinian performative, but I claim it can be shown to fit the Derridean paradigm of political, ethical, and religious commitment better. Deronda's promise is a response made to a demand made on him by the wholly other, by the Judaic Jehovah, operating by way of Mordecai as intermediary. Daniel at this point has no idea that he is actually a Jew, so the promise is made without the context that knowledge would provide. It is a Derridean leap in the dark, a fortuitous commitment, a proof that, as Kierkegaard said, in a passage Derrida more than once cited, "The instant of decision is a madness."[9] Deronda's promise makes a sharp rupture or break in his life. It makes him henceforth in a sense a different person, a proto-Jew. Daniel's promise is proleptic of his eventual discovery that he *is* a Jew and of his commitment to the cause of Zionism that forms the dénouement of the novel. What grounds and justifies his decision comes after the decision, not before, metaleptically, or, one might say, the decision seems magically to produce its own ground and justification.

Which kind of performativity does *Daniel Deronda* itself exemplify, if either? I claim it is an example of both kinds of performativity. *Daniel Deronda* is a performance, or reading it is a performance, like performing a Mozart sonata, or, in this case, since the novel is long, complex, and *echt* Victorian, like performing a Liszt piano concerto. *Daniel Deronda* is also an extended performative utterance of a peculiar kind. It generates a virtual literary reality that can be "accessed" only by way of the performative efficacy of the words on the page as I read them. Those words call or conjure into existence, like specters in broad daylight, Gwendolen, Daniel, all the other characters, their "worlds," and all that they do and say.

Notes

This essay was originally prepared, as an exercise in "disambiguation," for a conference titled "Performativity in Music and Literature" at the University of Oslo, on May 3–5, 2006. I am grateful to Professor Christian Refsum for giving me an opportunity to think through these issues.

1   See www.wikipedia.org.

2   See Jean-François Lyotard, *The Postmodern Condition: A Report on Knowledge*, trans. Geoff Bennington and Brian Massumi (Minneapolis: University of Minnesota Press, 1984), 9–11. Subsequent citations are given parenthetically by page number in the text.

3   For a discussion of the latter see my "The Aftermath of Victorian Humanism: Oscar in *The Tragic Muse*," in *Renaissance Humanism — Modern Humanism(s): Festschrift for Claus Uhlig*, ed. Walter Göbel and Bianca Ross (Heidelberg: C. Winter, 2001), 231–39; reprinted as "Oscar in *The Tragic Muse*," in *The Importance of Being Misunderstood*, ed. Giovanna Franci and Giovanna Silvani (Bologna: Pàtron Editore, 2003), 49–61.

4   J. L. Austin, *How to Do Things with Words*, 2nd ed., ed. J. O. Urmson and Marina Sbisà (Oxford: Oxford University Press, 1980), 12. Subsequent citations are given parenthetically by page number in the text.

5   All these (except Searle's essay, which he, for some unstated reason, but one can guess why, refused to have included) were collected, in English translation, with a new "Afterword: Toward an Ethic of Discussion" by Derrida, in *Limited Inc*, ed. Gerald Graff (Evanston, IL: Northwestern University Press, 1988). A subsequent citation is given parenthetically by page number in the text.

6   My translation, from this original: "Le mouvement même de cette fabuleuse répétition peut, selon un croisement de chance et de nécessité, produire le nouveau d'un événement. Non seulement par l'invention singulière d'un performatif, car tout performatif suppose des conventions et des règles institutionnelles; mais en tournant ces règles dans le respect de ces règles mêmes afin de laisser l'autre venir or s'annoncer dans l'ouverture de cette déhiscence. C'est peut-être ce qu'on appelle la deconstruction" (Jacques Derrida, *Psyché: Inventions de l'autre* [Paris: Galilée, 1987], 58–59).

7   Jacques Derrida, *Specters of Marx*, trans. Peggy Kamuf (New York: Routledge, 1993), 30–31; Jacques Derrida, *Spectres de Marx* (Paris: Galilée, 1993), 59–60.

8   George Eliot, *Daniel Deronda*, ed. Barbara Hardy (London: Penguin, 1986), 79. A subsequent citation is given parenthetically by page number in the text.

9   See, for example, Jacques Derrida, "Force of Law: The 'Mystical Foundation of Authority,'" trans. Mary Quaintance, in *Deconstruction and the Possibility of Justice*, ed. Drucilla Cornell, Michel Rosenfeld, and David Gray Carlson (New York: Routledge, 1992), 26.

Rei Terada

Scruples, or, Faith in Derrida

Scruple, hesitation, indecision, reticence (hence modesty [*pudeur*], respect, *restraint* before that which should
remain sacred, holy or safe: unscathed, immune)—
this too is what is meant by *religio*.
—Jacques Derrida, "Faith and Knowledge"

Like many of Derrida's later works, Derrida
and Vattimo's *Religion* begins with the difficulty
of speaking. In his introduction to the text of the
1994 Séminaire de Capri, published in 1996, Vattimo observes that "to write to colleagues request-
ing lectures 'on religion' was a step that was
more problematic than ever."[1] Derrida phrases
the problem in the indirect discourse of imagined critics: "How dare we speak of [religion]
in the singular without fear and trembling, this
very day?"[2] Although neither Vattimo nor Derrida specifies the reason for the nervousness, Vattimo notes "the phenomenon, known rightly or
wrongly as the 'religious revival,'" which he sees
as stronger "in parliaments, terrorism and the
media" than in the churches of Europe;[3] Derrida mentions "the religious whose return is
proclaimed in every newspaper" (2). Both refer
loosely to conflicts between particular religious
cultures and between the religious and the secu-

South Atlantic Quarterly 106:2, Spring 2007
DOI 10.1215/00382876-2006-023   © 2007 Duke University Press

lar altogether, the heightened atmosphere of which could make it difficult to discuss religion in abstract terms as well as intensify the appeal of doing so. In the rhetoric of the seminar, the participants take up bold but hesitant speech against a background of distant threat. Verbal hesitation is more than a mannerism: Derrida thematizes reticence as a religious matter. Reticence enacts the preservative impulse of scruple, which "stop[s] short of that which must or should remain safe and sound, intact, unscathed, before what must be allowed to be what it ought to be" (50). Ideal reticence would be beyond even silence, as in the logic of the secret in late Derrida;[4] within language, reticence is partial and stops and starts, going around obstacles but going on. Scruple is not an entirely nonviolent phenomenon, as Derrida's reflections on Abraham in *The Gift of Death* make clear;[5] my topic is only one association, within the logic of scruple, to preservation, in connection to Derrida's presentation of faith. Eventually, I hope to suggest that for Derrida "religion," sheltering in reticence or in the preservation of "what must be allowed to be," is (most of all?) the idea that verbal scruple preserves value and ultimately life—an idea that is knowingly figurative and nonetheless thinks magically. If Derrida did not practice this verbal animism of the preserving and destroying word, he would be a less religious philosopher.

Early in his contribution to *Religion*, "Faith and Knowledge: The Two Sources of 'Religion' at the Limits of Reason Alone," Derrida raises the question of religion's relation to what he calls, in italics, *"arrachement radical"* (*"radical extirpation"* in the English translation) (2). We soon come to see that "religion"—in quotation marks in Derrida's subtitle—has both an active and a passive role to play with regard to this action of tearing something out by the roots. *"Déracination,"* a near synonym that Derrida uses more often in "Faith and Knowledge" than *"arrachement,"* connotes not only removal from one's home, but, in the context of political systems and institutions, suppression or even elimination. Not only have particular religions sought to eliminate conflicting impurities (hence, sometimes one another), but strands of Enlightenment in the wake of Nietzsche and Freud, or so the narrative goes, have hoped to eliminate the religious altogether from the modes, if not the objects, of philosophical inquiry: extirpating religion in hopes of extirpating motives for extirpation, at times. Derrida remarks that the so-called "'return of religions' . . . particularly astonish[es] those who believed naively that an alternative opposed Religion, on the one side, and on the other, Reason, Enlightenment, Science, Criticism (Marxist

Criticism, Nietzschean Genealogy, Freudian Psychoanalysis and their heritage), as though the one could not but put an end to the other [*ne pouvait qu'en finir avec l'autre*]" (5).[6] Although the phrasing is mutual and religion practices its own aggressions, religion appears in the essay primarily as something to be saved, even as it is itself characterized in part as the action of saving by stopping.

The years since Derrida's lecture have seen growth not only in attention to religion as an object of study but in advocacy of religious perspectives within critical theory.[7] Among the many plausible reasons for this renewal are the heightened public discourse noted in 1996 by Vattimo and Derrida; the ethical project of understanding of the other, often the non-Western other, in terms that approach the other's; recognition of the growing political power of religion in general (and Christianity in particular in the Americas); and the rediscovery of Schmittian political theology as an analytic tool in wartime.[8] In fact, it is now almost as astonishing to find scholarship praising the secular at the expense of the religious as it was (if it was) to witness the so-called "return of religions" in 1994.

This exchange of surprises helps mark the era of "late Derrida." Introducing *Derrida and Religion: Other Testaments*, a collection of lectures drawn from a 2000 meeting of the American Academy of Religion and the Society of Biblical Literature that featured a lecture by Derrida, editors Yvonne Sherwood and Kevin Hart note: "That we can even venture the conjunction 'Derrida and Religion' testifies to a certain move beyond the reception of Derrida in the 1970s and 1980s, partly characterized by a deconstruction of Christian theology."[9] They observe that the "and" between "Derrida" and "religion" was "once timid" but is "now increasingly confident."[10] The quotation marks that Derrida placed around "religion" in 1994–96, too, are literally and figuratively dispensed with by 2000. If theorists formerly shrank from examining religion for fear of being taken for religious, in *Derrida and Religion* they do indeed celebrate religion in and through their investigations of the field. Sherwood and Hart describe their book as a collection of testaments, and characterize Derrida's contribution to the philosophy of religion with ardor for its capacity to inspire: "Resisting the classical antitheses, he ventures the view that religious revelations and Enlightenments *cross* around metaphors of light, elucidation, and revelation and around a desire for the most promising, fervent concepts (such as 'rights,' 'democracy,' and 'truth') that have an inbuilt messianic quality, a striving for perfection that is always yet to come."[11]

I agree with Sherwood and Hart that the associations in such a passage reflect a development exclusive to Derrida's recent reception. The prominent texts of 1970s and 1980s thought on Derrida and religion, such as *Deconstruction and Theology* (1982) and the work of scholars such as John Caputo and Mark C. Taylor,[12] did not then significantly shape the course of critical theory, which remained preoccupied with linguistic and textual theory understood in radically secular terms. In contrast, more recent work associates religion, as Sherwood and Hart do metaphorically in the passage above, with philosophical values (truth, perfection, futurity) and political concepts (rights, democracy) that stir desires for a more ethical world, and in conjunction with ethics and moral philosophy has had more impact on theory. Commitment to connection between religious and ethical thought is reasonably attributed to Derrida's late work, texts like "How to Avoid Speaking" (1987), "Circumfession" (1991), *The Gift of Death* (1992), *On the Name* (1993), "Faith and Knowledge" (1996), *Cosmopolitanism and Forgiveness* (1997), and *Of Hospitality* (1997) standing behind the attribution. In retrospect, "Faith and Knowledge" stands near the beginning of a renaissance of religious studies in theory that replaces the presumed fear of divisive religious debate with a religious studies launched against division. The idea of a nexus of messianism and enlightenment, unecumenically figured by Sherwood and Hart in their textual *"cross,"*[13] is marshaled to countermand the possibility that either religion or one of its alternatives might "put an end to the other" (5).

What counts as putting an end to something? The word *arrachement* occurs rarely in "Faith and Knowledge," but its first occurrence, in the third paragraph, leaves an impression:

> Eventually, we would therefore like to link [*relier*] the question of religion to that of the evil of abstraction. To radical abstraction. Not to the abstract figure of death, of evil or of the sickness of death, but to the forms of evil that are traditionally tied to *radical extirpation [arrachement radical]* and therefore to the deracination of abstraction, passing by way—but only much later—of those *sites of abstraction* that are the machine, technics, technoscience and above all the transcendence of tele-technology. . . .
>
> In order to think religion today *abstractly,* we will take these powers of abstraction as our point of departure, in order to risk, even-

tually, the following hypothesis: with respect to all these forces of abstraction and dissociation (deracination, delocalization, disincarnation, formalization, universalizing schematization, objectification, telecommunication etc.), "religion" is *at the same time* involved in reacting antagonistically and reaffirmatively outbidding itself [*la sur enchère réaffirmatrice*]. (2)

Derrida remains reserved about what may be encompassed by *"arrachement radical"*—the reader might think of genocide, accomplished by misemployed technology, but Derrida does not use genocide as a paradigm. He notes that he is not concerned, for the occasion, with "the figure of death," and he declines to exemplify "evil." Since the phrase remains abstract, it stresses the general imaginary of extirpation and the implausible desire it implies. The word of the English translation, "extirpation," refers literally to stump removal, and conveys the measure of factive struggle involved. Similarly, in French an "arrachement" is also a remnant, a ruin, as of an old tower or wall. "Déracination"—which, again, is stronger in French than in English—also encompasses would-be elimination. As a philosophical instance, Derrida offers up Heidegger in *Being and Time*, whose insistence on "originary conscience" "would in principle allow for the repetition of the Nietzschean genealogy of morals, but dechristianizing it whenever necessary and extirpating [*déracinant*] whatever Christian vestiges it still might contain" (12). To add another example to this one, let's also remember Nietzsche's effort to hold open the possibility that the human being might become better than it is, in part by figuring out through actual struggle what can be changed and what cannot. "And if this moral judging and dissatisfaction [*Ungenügen*] with actuality were in fact, as has been suggested, an ineradicable instinct [*unausrottbarer Instinkt*], might this instinct not be one of the ineradicable stupidities and immodesties of our species [*unausrottbaren Dummheiten, auch Unbescheidenheiten unsrer Spezies*]?"[14] This effort to find out what is *"unausrottbaren"* by actually pulling is the pathos of "extirpation." *Déracination/arrachement* approaches contradiction, since nothing that could in the first place be so planted would be likely to be eliminable. To eliminate it would be to "put an end" to it, but we only want to extirpate things whose ends are hard to find.

On a continuum with *déracination/arrachement*, in "Faith and Knowledge," is "reduction [*réduction*]," a less dramatic word. Idiomatically, reduction may distill rather than eliminate, and whether a particular reduction has concentrated or lost the heart of the matter is always up for debate.

Just after Derrida posits the amazement of those who thought, regarding religion and its alternatives, that "the one could not but put an end to the other," he goes on: "On the contrary, it is an entirely different schema that would have to be taken as one's point of departure in order to try to think the [phrase] 'return of the religious.' Can the latter be reduced [*se réduit*] to what the *doxa* confusedly calls 'fundamentalism,' 'fanaticism' or, in French, 'integrism'?" (5) We don't want to reduce to stereotypes: the idiom entails loss of truth with loss of detail. But it also encompasses the careful isolation and preservation of the significant and its rescue from obfuscation. From the start, with his early analyses of Husserl's transcendental reduction, Derrida argues against the truth claims of rarefaction, stressing the roles played by the particular and marginal in the production of truths. Yet there's room within such a project to question the collapse in "Faith and Knowledge" of *"arrachement"* (often literal) and *"réduction"* (often verbal), which recurs in the lecture and performs its labor in the shadow cast by the threat of conflict and even annihilation; and, consequently, the role of the scruple that is to preserve the life of meaning. In French, *"réduction"* also sets a bone or limb back in place. *Arrachement/déracination* and *réduction* are both ways of approaching sources, the first to tear away and the second to restore, distill, or condense in order to transport—a pairing of interest in "Faith and Knowledge," an lecture about the "two sources" of "religion."

Now, the question of the religious and the secular—even, in a cruder version, of the soul and the body—is the classic test case for how one feels about reduction. In philosophy, "reduction" is a term of art for handling relationships between definitions in competing discourses. Thus, an atheist might believe that everything religion describes can be anchored in definitions provided by psychology, politics, and so on, and in that sense "reduced to" them, and would not believe it also worked the other way around. From such a perspective, religions exist, yet religious terminology as definitive discourse will seem to explain with terms that beg explanation. The same complaint has been directed at Enlightenment explanations. Not surprisingly, the ambitious projects of philosophical reduction—logicism's effort to reduce mathematics to logic and logical positivism's effort to reduce speculation to a vocabulary of observation—have been no match for the generative ambiguities of language. Historically, the major projects of reduction have broken down in semantic problems: in any given instance two terms instead of one may be left standing, representing two interpretations of the same entity. Partly in response to this problem, Donald Davidson began using the term *supervenience* to describe relations that were supposedly dependent but not reductive.[15] For example, a religion may be said to "supervene on" a set of cultural practices and sociological motives, or rely on these practices and motives as its "supervenience base," without this requiring that we think of it as reducing to nothing more than those practices. Philosophers largely saw Davidson's softening of the claim that can be made about competing definitions as necessary because they had come to believe that no system of definitions can determine what counts as an instance of something across all contexts and interpretations.

Although Derrida's projects unfold at a distance from this debate, it frames some of the stakes in "Faith and Knowledge"—for example, Derrida's observation that the discourse of scruple *"goes on* in what can no longer be isolated as a *religious vocabulary"* (31), or his assertion that "the experience of faith" is "of a credit that is irreducible [*irréductible*] to knowledge" (18). The language of irreducibility promotes preservation, even to the end of time: its tropes are figures of residue, excess, and rebound, on one hand, and ellipse, elusion, and secret, on the other. In some of the associations of Derridean negative theology, religion is that which stands in need of preservation and is preserved by being found or rendered irreducible. And it is preserved in its irreducibility, in Derrida's figurations—as are other dualities in the Derridean corpus—by the fact that the event of reduction cannot be *told*: both in the idiomatic sense in which (in English) one "cannot tell" what's going on in obscurity and in the sense that even if one did know, one wouldn't be telling. Thus reticence, secrecy, and denegation respond to the fear of reduction. In "How to Avoid Speaking," for example, Derrida remarks, "Every time I say: *X* is neither this nor that, neither the contrary of this nor of that, neither the simple neutralization of this nor of that with which it has *nothing in common*, being absolutely heterogenous to or incommensurable with them, I would start to speak of God."[16]

In "Faith and Knowledge" the "irreducible duality" on which Derrida insists is that of "the experience of *belief*" and "the experience of the unscathed [*indemné*], of *sacredness* or of *holiness*" (36). "In principle," he points out, "it is possible to sanctify, to sacralize the unscathed . . . without bringing into play an act of belief . . . [and] the acquiescence of trust still does not in itself necessarily involve the sacred" (33). These two experiences of belief and sacredness are aligned in turn with messianicity and *chora*: belief is figured in nonteleological messianicity, and sacredness in the utter exteriority of *chora*. These comprise the "two sources" of the lecture's subtitle, and according to Derrida "should never be confused or reduced to one another as is almost always done" (33). In Derrida's early essay "Ellipsis" (1967), a duality of sources—for instance, two centers of gravity—triggers the differentiality of what revolves around them.[17] In "Faith and Knowledge," the irreducible duality of sources for "religion" assures both its differentiality and its inextricability from its supposed others: "It is to the ellipse of these double Latin foci that the entire modern (geo-theologicopolitical) problematic of the 'return of the religious' refers" (37–38).

Among the materials I've been assembling so far, we now have many pairs: the two perspectives that philosophical reduction often cannot get beyond (for example, "pile of wood" and "Eeyore's house"); two means of approaching sources, both rejected by Derrida, reduction and *arrachement/ déracination* (which, in Derrida's prose, seem to converge); and, within Derrida's argument in "Faith and Knowledge," the "two sources" of religion within the limits of reason alone—messianicity and *chora*, the experience of belief and the experience of the unscathed—that cannot be reduced one to the other and that will therefore serve the function in "Faith and Knowledge" of causing faith and knowledge, the religious and the secular, to contaminate each other. The dual sources of the categories Derrida cares to protect close in on one other in a secluded space—the far end of the ellipse, where we cannot tell what happens. Because we cannot see, know, or tell whether they converge, their reducibility or irreducibility is a matter of guesswork, desire, and/or faith; and, something, for Derrida, is preserved or kept safe autoimmunely by this objective reticence of terms he wants to call "irreducible."

Since reduction is not extirpation of living things, but a way to redescribe things in language, the dread of it in Derrida's texts is interestingly intense. This dread often surfaces in contexts dealing exclusively with competing languages—definitional and logical operations on the page—and may inform Derrida's late style of hesitation.[18] The scruple would be obligatory if words could really extirpate—if a living thing died when one term reduces to another. At times, as in "Faith and Knowledge," the fear of reduction rises amid a flurry of allusions to potential physical violence or the memory of it. Whatever happened to the enjoyment of aggression, discernible in Derrida's earliest writing, that peaks in the responses to John Searle collected in *Limited Inc* (1977) only to vanish from the late writings of infallible generosity, in which Derrida is always hesitating and stopping? The former style may not have been any less animistic about language; it may have simply allowed itself occasional license to enjoy destroying. Similarly, Derrida's discussion of Abraham in *The Gift of Death*, mentioned above, shows the animism of speech and silence in the mode of destruction. Following Kierkegaard's account, Derrida stresses Abraham's refusal to divulge his secret pact with God and hence his preservation of his absolute responsibility from the general accounting requested by language and community. The violent sacrifice of Isaac is the other side of the protection of Abraham's responsibility from "the violence that consists of asking for accounts and justifications."[19] Although I can't explore at length here the intensity with which Derrida animates the question of reductive language, and don't dispute the unlikeliness of ever adjudicating between the religious and the secular in a way that satisfies everyone, I do want to ask, first, what impact this conclusion has on the terms—"faith," "knowledge," "'religion'"—Derrida leaves us with: how should we regard them after reading "Faith and Knowledge"?—and, second, how to begin interpreting the reticence that is the rhetorical mode of the irreducible and that Derrida imagines as an autoimmune defense to threats carried by linguistic as well as bodily harm.

The subtitle of "Faith and Knowledge," in which "religion" appears in quotation marks, "The Two Sources of 'Religion' at the Limits of Reason Alone," echoes Kant's *Die Religion innerhalb der Grenzen der bloßen Vernunft* and Bergson's *Two Sources of Morality and Religion*. Derrida names his own two sources of "religion" "the 'messianic'" and "the *chora*" (17).[20] Later, these names are aligned with the experience of belief and of the unscathed (*indemné*), as mentioned above, so that finally there are two pairs of names to consider, while watching how Derrida sets the duplicity of sources to work against settling the accounts of faith and knowledge.

 1. The "messianic." As a "messianicity without messianism," that is, "without horizon of expectation," forgoing any messianic figure or event (17), Derridean messianicity resonates with the Kantian notion that, as Derrida phrases it, the fully moral person "must act as though God did not exist or no longer concerned himself with our salvation" (11). For Kant, expectation corrupts and personalizes and so underrepresents the self-sufficiency of moral law. In "Faith and Knowledge," messianicity without goal or content—parallel to purposiveness without purpose—"stripped of everything" and prepared "for the best as for the worst" (18), is "linked," Derrida writes, to "an invincible desire for justice" even as it "cannot be contained in any traditional opposition, for example that between reason and mysticism" (18).[21] Messianicity is as unparsable and deeply internal as Kant's law, and expresses a desire for justice inexhaustible by any particular content. Derrida finds this desire for justice inscribed "in the act of faith or in the appeal to faith that inhabits every act of language and every address to the other" (18). Messianicity and the desire to which it is linked find their representation not in any theme but in the continuous performance of linguistic acts as acts of faith or as appeals to faith. We perform these acts and addresses *not* because words have a "minimal trustworthiness" (3) (as in Jürgen Habermas's theories of communication), it is important to note, but even though we *cannot* assume their minimal trustworthiness.[22]

2. *Chora.* The second source of "religion" at the limits of reason, *chora*, "situates the abstract spacing, place itself, the place of absolute exteriority" (19) and "infinite resistance" (21). The function of *chora* in relation to messianicity is complementary, almost as deduction is to induction, or as the irrecoverable past is to the drive toward the future. In *Dissemination*, Derrida develops the *chora* of Plato's *Timaeus* into the notion of "a matrix . . . that is never and nowhere offered up in the form of presence, or in the presence of form."[23] As such, *chora* is "absolutely impassible and heterogeneous to all the processes of historical revelation or of anthropo-theological experience, which at the very least suppose its abstraction. It will never have entered religion and will never permit itself to be sacralized, sanctified, humanized, theologized, cultivated, historicized" (20–21). Derrida channels the abstraction of *chora* into a counterdrive toward reticence, a desire not to be named or presented. *Chora* hesitates, he writes, between "the order of the 'revealed' and the order of the 'revealable'": "the indecisive oscillation, that reticence (*epoché* or *Verhaltenheit*) already alluded to above (between revelation and revealability, *Offenbarung* and *Offenbarkeit*, between event and possibility or virtuality of the event)" (21). "Tolerance" draws on *chora* in that it assumes respect for "the distance of infinite alterity as singularity" (22). For Derrida, this respect would again "still be *religio, religio* as scruple or reticence, distance, dissociation, disjunction." In complementary ways, then — as desire and withdrawal, performance and reticence — messianicity and *chora* support between them "every social or communitarian link" (22).

Finally, Derrida aligns messianicity and *chora* — philosophical names for two sources of religion—with "two experiences that are generally held to be equally religious":

> (1) the experience of *belief*, on the one hand (believing or credit, the fiduciary or the trustworthy in the act of faith, fidelity, the appeal to blind confidence, the testimonial that is always beyond proof, demonstrative reason, intuition); and (2) the experience of the unscathed, of *sacredness* or of *holiness*, on the other. (33)

The duplicity of sources derails reduction, as in the elliptical figure— an internally differential errance from circular perfection that remains obscure to classical perspective, recessed from view, as a result. The difference within "religion," difficulty getting the religious into perspective— its reticence—makes it difficult to distinguish the difference between the religious and the nonreligious, and vice versa. "To determine a war of religion *as such*"—for example, to complain that others commit violence in the name of religion—"one would have to be certain that one can delimit the religious. One would have to be certain that one can distinguish all the predicates of the religious (and, as we shall see, this is not easy: there are at least *two* families[)]" and one of these two "is precisely the drive to remain unscathed" by any determination (25), including that of religion. I quote from §28 of "Faith and Knowledge," an example of Derrida's rejection of the logic of isolation worth reading at length:

> **Religion?** *In the singular?* [*La* religion? *Article défini au singulier?*] Perhaps, *may-be* (this should always remain possible) there is *something else*, of course, and other interests (economic, politico-military etc.) behind the new "wars of religion," behind what presents itself under the name of religion, beyond what defends or attacks in its name, kills, kills itself or kills one another and for that invokes declared stakes, or in other words, names *indemnity* in the light of day. But inversely, if what is thus *happening to us*, as we said, often (but not always) assumes the figures of evil and of the worst in the unprecedented forms of an *atrocious* "war of religions," the latter in turn does not always speak its name. Because it is not certain that in addition to or in face of the most spectacular and most barbarous crimes of certain "fundamentalisms" (of the present or of the past), *other* over-armed forces are not *also* leading "wars of religion," albeit unavowed. Wars or military "interventions," led by the Judaeo-Christian West in the name of the best

causes (of international law, democracy, the sovereignty of peoples, of nations or of states, even of humanitarian imperatives), are they not also, from a certain side, wars of religion? The hypothesis would not necessarily be defamatory, nor even very original, except in the eyes of those who hasten to believe that all these just causes are not only secular but *pure* of all religiosity. To determine a war of religion *as such*, one would have to be certain that one can delimit the religious. One would have to be certain that one can distinguish all the predicates of the religious (and, as we shall see, this is not easy: there are at least *two* families, two strata or sources [*souches ou sources*] that overlap, mingle, contaminate each other without ever merging; and just in case things are still too simple, one of the two is precisely the drive [*pulsion*] to remain unscathed, on the part of that which is allergic to contamination, *save by itself, auto-immunely*). One would have to dissociate the essential traits of the religious as such from those that establish, for example, the concepts of ethics, of the juridical, of the political or of the economic. And yet, nothing is more problematic than such a dissociation. The fundamental concepts that often permit us to isolate or to *pretend* to isolate the *political*—restricting ourselves to this particular circumscription—remain religious or in any case theologico-political. (25; original emphasis)

The passage is immersed in the problem of competing definitions. "The religious" and "the political" may describe equally the features of a single set of practices: by this reasoning, it is exactly because "behind what presents itself under the name of religion" *do* lie "other interests (economic, politico-military etc.)" that these other interests—"for example, the concepts of ethics, of the juridical, of the political or of the economic" (25)—cannot be considered nonreligious. Because Derrida sees the explanatory discourses as mutually explanatory (each lies "behind" the other from different perspectives), he rejects the idea that religion reduces to politics, society, and so on, and vice versa. At one point, Derrida asserts that since "one of the two responses ought always to be able to contaminate the other," "it will never be proven whether it is the one or the other, never in an act of determining, theoretical or cognitive judgment" (29). No system of definitions will ever be stable enough to render a determination acceptable to points of view both inside and outside this system.[24]

Within this frame, for about two-thirds of the lecture Derrida specifies varieties of reasoning by each of which religion contaminates its alternatives, often via its sources. Here I'd like to review briefly the means by which Derrida evidences religion's presence in and for its others, in order later to take account of the conclusions of the analysis. Derrida's reasoning takes

1.   A historically and culturally genetic form: as when, in the continuation of §28 above, Carl Schmitt is "obliged to acknowledge" that his "ostensibly purely political categories were the product of a secularization or of a theologico-political heritage"; when the Western idea of democracy is "inherited in truth from a determinate religious stratum" (26); when hermeneutics develops from religious exegesis (7); or when "religion" derives from *religio*, scruple (31).

2.   An implicative cultural and institutional form and

3.   A crypto-logical form, both of which are exemplified when "technoscientific reason, far from opposing religion, bears, supports, and supposes it [*la porte, la supporte et la suppose*]" (28)—"supports" it and "supposes" it, respectively. The claim that technoscience "supports" religion deploys a social logic of the effects of public statements and acts. In the claim that technoscience "supposes" religion, a cryptic, ideal, or virtual concept of religion is back-projected by technoscience. A similar implicative form emerges through performance, as when their common use of promise shows that "religion and reason have the same source" in reliance on testimony (28). Religion and reason act out faith in testimony; the assumption here is of an unconscious dependence, shown when not said.

4.   A Kantian, negative form that bases the possibility of religion on the fact that our knowledge cannot be complete and that our philosophy is undogmatic: as when the utter abstraction of messianicity without messianism is too sheer to deny faith (19), since it does not involve assertion or denial of any content.

5.   An associative, linguistic form, as when Derrida refers responsibility to "what is called belief, trustworthiness or fidelity, the fiduciary, 'trust' [*la fiance*] in general, the tribunal [instance] of faith" (29). Or when words and phrases are bound in antithesis: "*In this very place, knowledge and faith, technoscience ['capitalist' and fiduciary] and belief, credit, trustworthiness, the act of faith will always have made common cause, bound to one another by the band of their opposition*"

(2; original emphasis). "Contamination" is Derrida's privileged figure for the promiscuity of language by which "religion" suffuses its would-be others: "by ineluctable contagion, no semantic cell can remain alien, I dare not say 'safe and sound,' 'unscathed,' in this apparently borderless process" (29). The only thing that remains outside this process is *chora*, by definition radical exteriority; hence for us respect for *chora* is again related—via its very unrelatability!—to the unscathed or holy.

"Faith and Knowledge" deflects the wish for *pure* secularity by the repleteness of dissemination. What is odd is that it isn't enough that the discourses of culture, technology, or politics include the religious each within themselves, so that it would be impossible to expunge religion from the explanatory vocabularies that vie with one another in arguments about reduction. In "Faith and Knowledge" there is, so to speak, not a moment's secularity apart from religion, not a moment of language or memory that is not inscribed in a structure of faith. Further, semantic and living cells are implicitly continuous. The assumption of the lecture is that the analysis of language tells something about faith and knowledge because faith and knowledge don't exist except in and through language. At the same time that these are inextricable, however, *chora*, the radically unscathed, remains unassimilable;[25] and *chora* is linked to the sacred because it is the only thing that cannot be assimilated, not only to the secular or to the religious, but to anything. No semantic cell remains unscathed; therefore, what *is* unscathed is what is not named in any semantic cell in the first place and remains unaffected by linguistic movements. As in *Feu la cendre*, "pure difference, different from (it)self, ceases to be what it is in order to remain what it is."[26] Thus the irreducibility of religion's two sources is determined from the beginning by the selection of *chora* as one of them and is analytic to *chora*, since *chora* is irreducibly different from anything at all.

What should follow from the saturation of the secular with the religious, on one hand, and the irreducible duality of the sources of religion, on the other?

If there's not to be something totalizing about Derrida's description of contamination, then the contamination, as far as it goes, needs to be two-way, differential in itself and divided against itself. As Derrida writes, "Instead of opposing" faith and knowledge, "as is almost always done, they ought to be thought *together, as one and the same possibility*" (48); "we are constantly trying to think the interconnectedness, albeit otherwise, of knowledge *and* faith, technoscience *and* religious belief, calculation *and* the sacrosanct" (54). Derrida describes myriad self-divisions of the sources of religion (e.g., in §49: "this source can collect or scatter itself, rejoin or disjoin itself," etc. [64]). Each source, however, creates more of itself, and the effect is to multiply the modes of belief and sacredness to the point of incorporating fully unbelief and the profane. What is notable is that the internal division and differentiality of belief and sacredness allow them to assimilate their others without much disturbing belief or sacredness. We might have expected the implications of mutual contamination of faith and knowledge and self-division of the sources of religion to be distributed mutally, or, if not evenly, to some significant degree, across all the former oppositions that are subject to the forces of contamination, including faith, belief, and sacredness themselves. They should all be un-self-sufficient, compromised to some extent, from the point of view of the more capacious possibility of faith and knowledge "thought *together.*" For example, faith might be shown by virtue of its contamination in every cell by knowledge to be not the same "faith" that once seemed to exist outside knowledge. In the lecture, however, "knowledge" appears as the bad faith of faith, but "faith" does not appear as the bad faith of knowledge. The effects of contamination bear disproportionately on the integrity of the secular.[27]

When Derrida states, for example, that the religiousness of secular causes is uncontroversial unless one needs to believe that they are "not only secular but *pure* of all religiosity"—the hypothesis that wars of sovereignty, for example, are also "wars of religion" "would not necessarily be defamatory, nor even very original" unless we already believed that we *knew* what is and is not religious (25)—he implies that secularists are naively disturbed at the religiousness of the secular; no corresponding passage points out that it is naive for fideists to be disturbed at the appearance of "knowledge" in the safe houses of "faith"—as though knowledge merely usurped the roles of faith, instead of being something to be understood anew in its intimacy with it. Even in more extended examples whose purpose is explicitly to recognize symmetries, the lecture remains pointed at secularists. Even while Derrida observes, for example, that there is "no faith, therefore, nor future without everything technical, automatic, machine-like supposed by iterability. In this sense, the technical is the possibility of faith" (47)— where "the technical," according to alliances set up earlier in the lecture, does some of the work of rationality and knowledge as well as some of the work of writing—no shift in the content or significance of faith is remarked in light of its thorough reliance on its supposed alternative. Rather, technology as alternative has already shifted its content in light of its reliance on faith, so by the time faith is returned to technology, there is no tension within faith as a result of the dynamic. Similarly, Derrida states many times that since technoscience enlarges the religious realm even in opposing it, its secular culture is a religious culture, without dwelling on the other possible implication that arises here—that there is no religious culture that is not secular through and through. Carl Schmitt is "obliged to acknowledge" (26) that his concept of pure politics draws from a theologico-political heritage; we are not at this point obliged to acknowledge what Derrida states at the outset of the lecture, that "what presents itself under the name of religion" is often generated by and composed of political, economic, psychological, and other interests (25). And if "the experience of disenchantment, however indubitable it is, is only one modality of this 'miraculous' experience" [of "even the slightest testimony concerning the most plausible, ordinary, or everyday thing"], then we might not only expect that "the experience itself of non-relationship" will be found in every linguistic social bond (64), but will want to ask how the newfound recognition of nonrelation in every bond may affect our opinion of both nonrelation and linguistic social bonds. Over the years, the idiom *certain* has indicated a word or notion that has passed through a productive contamination; thus, in the present instance, we continue with "a certain faith" (65). It is for Derrida's readers to explore what the addition of that word, *certain*, indicates, in each case. In the case of "faith," the change is too minimal to observe. Any degree of faith, even when placed in knowledge itself, interrupts the purity of the secular and fractures the concept of secularity. Knowledge within faith—calculability in the example above—does not fracture the concept of faith: "no calculation, no assurance, will ever be able to reduce [*réduire*] its ultimate necessity, that of the testimonial signature" (45). The demonstration of contamination, in a way, has gone to argue that faith can open itself up to all of its others and in and through that opening remain an "ultimate necessity."

It might be different. Even though it may not be necessary to require exact reciprocity wherever we discover co-contamination, this story could be written in another way. The co-contamination of faith and reason might show not only that we don't know the boundaries of "religion"—how "pure reason" banks on itself in a way that exceeds calculation—but that we don't know the upper boundaries of rationality, how inexhaustibly it returns (for a time) to explain and quantify the formerly inexplicable and unquantifiable. "The limits of pure reason"—what are they? When Kant gives the formal and circular answer that the limits of reason must also be its transcendental conditions, for the very reason that his answer is formal it does not pretend to say where that limit is, that is, *how much* reasoning structured by space and time can accomplish. Only experience can answer that question, and we are not standing at the end of time—a perspective to which any claim of reducibility *or irreducibility* must leap. And as soon as we return from the empirical to the formal again, then regardless of where the limits of faith and knowledge may be, the mutual contagion described in "Faith and Knowledge" cannot extend the sphere of religion without extending the sphere of the secular. Derrida's deepest acknowledgment of the two-way consequences of co-contamination is in his subtitle, in the quotation marks around "religion." This is an important feature of the lecture, one that its reception tends to pass over. *"Religion" is religion. And religion is "religion"*—that should be one implication of the semantic cell division described in "Faith and Knowledge."

≡≡≡

Why is this not the story that "Faith and Knowledge" itself emphasizes? Why have implications for faith had so small a part to play in conversation about "Faith and Knowledge" since 1996?

Unlike strategic attacks on systems, structures of significantly mutual distribution feature a relativization of value that can be alarming and an equanimity of tone that can sound like indifference or even irony. And equanimity about whether something is religious or secular is not the desire of late Derrida, of resurgent religious studies, nor, it almost goes without saying, of almost anybody. Such an attitude can be breathtakingly anticlimactic and uninspiring (and therefore inspiring to the Socratic ironist—it is one of the favorite stances of de Man). This attitude is also that of the implacable, neutral symmetry of the Kantian architectonic, including the place held in it by Kant's religion within reason alone. Derrida asks, "What would a book be like today which, like Kant's, is entitled, *Religion within the Limits of Reason Alone?*" (8).[28] It would not, I suggest, be like "Faith and Knowledge." The implications of Derrida's stance on religion can be clarified by comparing it with the discomfiting neutrality of Kant's symmetrical world and the minimal, if crucial, nature of Kant's affirmations of it.

In the passage of *Religion within the Limits of Reason Alone* Derrida is citing when he brings up Kant's idea that the moral person "must act as though God did not exist," Kant asks the reader to suppose that "a human being of such a truly divine disposition had descended, as it were, from heaven to earth at a specific time."[29] We would "not . . . absolutely deny that he might indeed also be a supernaturally begotten human being," writes Kant; we are disinterested on this point. It is, first of all, for pragmatic reasons that we should act as though he isn't: an assumption of holiness could discourage our moral efforts by placing the exemplar beyond reach, beyond point. "The elevation of such a Holy One above every frailty of human nature would rather, from all that we can see, stand in the way of the practical adoption of the idea of such a being for our imitation."[30] Kant's philosophical reasons, however, are the ones that use Kantian disinterest to suggest the deep irrelevance of divinity. Maurizio Ferraris, writing in *Religion*, approaches some of the potential outrage of what Kant is up to when, in a discussion of how "the key point in this theandric affair is whether or not Christ is exemplary," he cites the passages in which Kant argues the irrelevance of example and asks, "What is Christ for, then?"[31] Answer: for Kant "the need for a Messiah is for a representational limit of the soul" (in Kant's words, "a *schematism of analogy*, with which we cannot dispense").[32] Ferraris notes that "the inappropriateness of the divine genesis of Christ is what most obviously follows from this basic perspective";[33] further, one can never derive the existence of an object from its use in an analogy. To Kant's way of thinking, the object of divinity is simply beyond the capacity of reason to ascertain, and hence neither to be asserted nor denied, while the idea of divinity already contains all of the relevance to human beings that divinity itself could have. Even more to the point, however, according to moral law as distinct from its exemplification, and as a direct result of its reasonlessness—a territory beyond reason and unreason in much the way Derrida wants to encourage religion to be—it is a matter of *total indifference* to us whether the person of maximally "divine disposition" is supernatural *or not*. Religion is not a question of the actuality of the divine; the actuality of the divine, that is, the actuality of an idea that is by definition merely intelligible, is a contradiction. I bring up this passage of Kant's text because it too contains the structure of possible convergence at the far end of the ellipse—the humanity and the divinity of Christ do or do not meet—to point out the difference between a religion capable of encompassing the humanity and/or divinity of Christ and Kantian religion, which rejects the question of the humanity or divinity of Christ as unintelligible.

Derrida's paraphrase of Kant in the passage below, "We must act as though God did not exist or did not concern himself with our salvation," doesn't capture Kant's implication: "in order to conduct oneself in a moral manner, one must act as though God did not exist or no longer concerned himself with our salvation. This shows who is moral and who is therefore Christian, assuming that a Christian owes it to himself to be moral: no longer turn towards God at the moment of acting in good faith; act as though God had abandoned us" (11). "We must act as though God did not exist" conveys the obligation to discover morality within; the suggestion to "act as though God had abandoned us" is different, and moves toward objectifying God. Even the first phrase, however, differs greatly from Kant's version, in which it is clear that as good Kantians, we cannot really care whether God exists or whether he is concerned with our salvation. It is not so much God who may be unconcerned about us, but we who are unconcerned about God, who can never be as important to us as our own idea of him; this is different from the continued importance, in Derrida, of lack of assurance about the existence and concern of God. For Derrida, lack of assurance furnishes the necessary and significant condition for meaningful faith. "The entire question of religion comes down, *perhaps*, to . . . lack of assurance" (3), much as linguistic acts are faithful because one cannot assume the minimal trustworthiness of words. Kant, in contrast, questions not only whether assurance is given, but whether it is relevant. If we did possess assurance, the moral law would still be above it: the question of God's existence is trivial, since it can never drive one's free moral action. That if the Messiah came, and we knew it, *it would be a matter of total indifference* from the perspective of Kant's moral law—this is the sort of possibility, raised all the time by Kant's work, that made Kleist think he was the most wicked ironist ever. Kant's precise distribution of obligations as rights, his boundaries that leave to each only what it already has and cannot not have, a "justice" so even that no one can triumph in it and that has already been entirely given out in the mere formation of the living consciousness and its world—these are the anticlimactic qualities of the world within the limits of reason alone, shared by the Kantian religion of that world.

In Derrida, in contrast, faith and knowledge will not have their names spoken, nor define their realms, whether these are to be considered separate, shared, or both. They withdraw from formal and empirical efforts of disposition alike. The two sources of "religion" are irreducible, each saved from inundation by the other, through reticence: "'religion' figures their *ellipse* because it both comprehends the two foci but also sometimes shrouds their irreducible duality in silence, in a manner precisely that is secret and *reticent*" (36). As long as this reticent moment veils the action of the two, an action that might otherwise seem to lose one in the other or each in the other, we cannot conclude that the terms of the opposition are fictive. In contrast, the time often comes in de Man or Nietzsche when after a long period of interaction, terms such as *religious* and *secular* give up the ghost and are recast as nominalist fictions. Derrida has a scruple about that moment. If it occurs at all, it happens out of sight, at the far end of the ellipse, where we can't see and don't know; it occurs, if at all, in the ellipsis of the sentence, something untold. "And what if the ellipsis, the silent figure and the 'keeping quiet' of reticence were precisely, we will come to that later, religion?" (39).

Late in "Faith and Knowledge," in a passage I've already cited, Derrida associates "keeping quiet" with letting live, "stop[ping] short of that which must or should remain safe and sound, intact, unscathed, before what must be allowed to be what it ought to be" (50). Reticence itself could be "precisely . . . religion," stopping short in a protective gesture, even as this gesture is itself one of the sources of religion. Religion therefore comes to have a self-protective, "autoimmune" dimension. In a section of "Faith and Knowledge" on "the absolute respect of **life**, the 'Thou shalt not kill'" (50; original emphasis), "absolute respect" is placed in relation to the self-sacrificial auto-immunity of the living being's impulse to self-preservation. If verbal reticence expresses in part the preservational impulses of the living being, then linguistic reduction—in contrast to the ellipse—begins to look like a figurative transgression of the commandment not to kill, not even in words.

In Bernard Stiegler's reading of "Faith and Knowledge," repeated figures of the irreducible and the given are interpreted as having to do with dependence, affirmation, and what it means to want to live. Stiegler argues that when Derrida "deconstructs the metaphysics of subjectivity insofar as it ignores the irreducibility of passive synthesis—and of the already-there qua the ground of *all* belief,"[34] passive synthesis performs dependence: "arche-writing means that what is alive cannot be sufficient unto itself."[35] Stiegler identifies faith with involuntary affirmation of life in the passive synthesis ongoing in and beyond the personal body, such that its absence is held to be impossible in the living being:

> [Derrida] thereby sets out the *fallibility* of the subject, putting in question both the "trustworthiness" [*fiabilité*] of its "en-gagement" ["*fiance*"] and the conditions of that trust [*confiance*] without which there would be no longer be life (or *différance*). The living is what *wants* to live, and wanting to live, *what believes unconditionally* in life in that, having access to the "gramme as such," it only believes in life insofar as it is haunted by the dead qua the non-living, by the dead in the sense of those who have lived, and by death as that to which life testifies.[36]

Derrida's "Sauf le Nom," "How to Avoid Speaking," "Passions: An Oblique Offering," and *Rogues*, among other texts, explore autoimmune affirmation as a matter of belief and *bio*.[37] In Derrida's slightly earlier miniature "'Che cos'è la poesia?'" (1988), the autoimmune impulses of the poetic are represented in the figure of the hedgehog [*hérisson*] which rolls up to protect itself "and for that very reason . . . may get itself run over."[38] The poetic, Derrida argues, demands to be remembered and so asks the reader or hearer to maintain its very existence: "learn me by heart, copy me down, guard and keep me, look out for me."[39] In the allegory, the poetic is the hedgehog and the road is "named translation";[40] but the literal level is even more relevant for the question of *bios*—in Stiegler's words, of "what *wants* to live, and, wanting to live . . . *believes unconditionally* in life."[41] The hedgehog figure suggests that in the poetic realm, the secret is nothing more or less than mortality: when the hedgehog does get hit, its secret runs out. Derrida's prescriptive phrasing in "Faith and Knowledge"—"*restraint* before that which should remain sacred, holy or safe: unscathed, immune [*halte* devant ce qui doit rester sacré, saint ou sauf: indemne, immun]" (31)—associates scruple and the sacred not with the safe but with what "should" be and therefore isn't (and so needs our restraint).

Most important for my purposes, however, Derrida connects the verbal level of the threat and fulfillment of translation—perhaps, worse, reduction, the ending of an idiom in its subsumption by another—and the literal level of clinging to and letting go of life:

> *Literally*: you would like to retain by heart an absolutely unique form, an event whose intangible singularity no longer separates the ideality, the ideal meaning as one says, from the body of the letter. In the desire of this absolute inseparation, the absolute nonabsolute, you breath[e] the origin of the poetic. Whence the infinite resistance to the transfer of the letter *which the animal, in its name*, nevertheless calls out for [*D'où la résistance infinie au transfert de la lettre que l'animal, en son nom, réclame pourtant*]. That is the distress of the *hérisson*.[42]

Derrida animates the letter while analyzing the magical, poetic desire to safeguard something by "confid[ing it] like a prayer—that's safe—to a certain exteriority of the automaton, to the laws of mnemotechnics,"[43] and also by disguising it or "render[ing it] indeterminate."[44] He writes that "you would like" to protect the singular and hence would like to believe it is united with ideality in the body of the letter, even as "the animal" calls out for the "transfer of the letter" "in its name." For a moment, it is unclear whether the animal calls (in the name of, i.e., on behalf of, the letter), or whether the calling is done in and through the name of the animal, that is, by its being named *"hérisson"* (from *hérisser*, to bristle or spike). The prose obscures the distinction between life and the letter, between animal cry and linguistic animation. Derrida notes that (self-destructive) life is characterized by an element of amnesia;[45] this element of amnesia, I'd like to suggest, is figured in Derrida's prose in the persistent animation of language. In the rhetoric of the essay, focus on a transfer within language—the submission of the singular verbal act to the transfer of the letter—obsures a second transfer between life and the letter. Only the letter connects us to the past that exceeds the sum of living memory, as Stiegler puts it.[46] But its being a prosthesis of life's memory of itself does not transmit life to or from it. Much as de Man points out that we are "quite powerless to convert even the smallest particle of nature into something human,"[47] we could say that however much the letter is a prosthesis of life, we are powerless to convert it into something alive itself or possessed of the power in itself to give, preserve, or destroy life. This second figure of transfer from letter to life is more dramatic than any transfer between letters, and informs fundamentally the concepts of both the poetic and the religious—the figure of the spirit of the letter is *their* shared source. In the heresy of paraphrase we refind resistance to reduction as a religious question of scruple.

The detranscendentalized figures of "'Che cos'è la poesia?'" allow us to explore operations of reticence and reduction aside from the heightened discourses of the religious, even while animation as a source of the poetic, as it emerges in the essay, leads soon enough to the origins of religion again. In light of this essay's treatment of "life," the threat of extirpation that hangs over the conversation about religion reflects an anxiety about turning against life or becoming indifferent to it, as well as the lucid fantasy of being able to destroy life with language and preserve it by being careful with language. I don't mean to claim that the figurative animation of the letter in Derrida's texts, specifically, necessarily indexes conviction. But Derridean respect for the quasi-existence of linguistic and logical entities such as binaries and arche-structures is another matter, and does exceed the binary of belief and disbelief in order to stop before disbelief. Whatever the distance "Faith and Knowledge" takes from religion beyond Kantian limits, the quality that makes Derrida a more religious writer than he might be is his implication that we not only participate involuntarily in the generation of binaries, arche-structures, and, in general, "specters," but that that participation constitutes a significant affirmation that whatever they are, their quasi-existence—their not being nothing—is enough to call for the suspension of inquiry into their possible reducibility to other, more robust terms.[48] Kant's affirmation of the ideas of reason at parallel moments is, in contrast, so circumscribed as to remove all of their glamour and most of their significance. Another alternative procedure is represented by most of Nietzsche's career, in which ineradicability needs to be tested by experience and, even when confirmed, does not, especially in the case of ideas, solve the question of what deserves respect.[49] It is peculiar to Derrida that the affirmation of an irreducible distinction or an ineradicable idea is circumscribed yet substantive and crucial: substantive and crucial enough that we should have a scruple about pushing the point. Although Derrida radicalizes the secret so that it is what cannot be told, it may be more important that there are things that Derrida does not wish to say. Derrida raises the question of neurotic scruple in "Fors," his preface to Nicolas Abraham and Maria Torok's work on the Wolf-Man. Abraham and Torok argue that the Wolf-Man had a "magic word" that crystallized his psychic secrets and was unspeakable; Derrida identifies himself with the Wolf-Man, describing himself as writing only the word that comes before words: "I'll stop here . . . setting down on the edge of the crypt the little blank stone of a scruple, a voiceless word for the thought alone, on the sole path, in order to engage others to it, of a crypt."[50] But shouldn't the Wolf-Man have spoken? Didn't he suffer needlessly from the imaginary weight he carried by believing in the impact of the magic word?

What is left to say is that I've had a hard time saying *this*, because, wanting to preserve my imagination of Derrida, I wish that whatever Derrida did not know, he did not have things that he didn't wish to know. Writing this essay has been nothing but stopping short and going on with difficulty, as though to preserve a Derrida that lives in me, as though to imagine that I could possibly animate or deanimate anything that is still alive about Derrida — as though, finally, to imagine that there is something still alive about Derrida. This specter of a Derrida who can still use our protection, even if it should prove resilient, is for me a kind of error that I feel obfuscates my feelings about Derrida, my gratitude for his epochal work and my admiration for the person he was. All of those feelings can remain while I wish his late work had been different. I think it would have been more helpful to contemporary conversations about ethics if Derrida had been more interested in telling the difference between what is and what is in thought, between what should not be done and what should not be said; but my preference among these options will necessarily appear to some readers to insist on a difference that won't be told.

Notes

1 Gianni Vattimo, "Circumstances" [1996], in *Religion*, ed. Jacques Derrida and Gianni Vattimo, trans. David Webb (Stanford, CA: Stanford University Press, 1998), x. Throughout these notes, dates in brackets indicate original publications and dates in parentheses indicate translation publications.

2 Jacques Derrida, "Faith and Knowledge: Two Sources of 'Religion' at the Limits of Reason Alone" [1996], in *Religion*, ed. Jacques Derrida and Gianni Vattimo, trans. Samuel Weber (Stanford, CA: Stanford University Press, 1998), 1. All parenthetical citations in the text are from "Faith and Knowledge."

   Derrida's apology for the fact that the seminar includes no women and no scholars of religions outside the Judeo-Christian (5) may implicitly identify part of the audience of critics he imagines.

3 Vattimo, "Circumstances," ix.

4 See especially Jacques Derrida, "Sauf le Nom (Post-Scriptum)" [1993], in *On the Name*, ed. Thomas Dutoit, trans. John P. Leavey Jr. (Stanford, CA: Stanford University Press, 1995), 35–88; and Derrida, "Passions: 'An Oblique Offering'" [1993], in *On the Name*, ed. Thomas Dutoit, trans. David Wood (Stanford, CA: Stanford University Press, 1995), 3–34.

5 Jacques Derrida, *The Gift of Death* [1992], trans. David Wills (Chicago: University of Chicago Press, 1995), 58–65. Thanks to Bernard Richter for ideas about Abraham and many other matters, and to Eyal Amiran and David Lloyd for additional suggestions.

6   For an extended discussion of a similar cultural narrative, see Bruno Latour, *We Have Never Been Modern* [1991], trans. Catherine Porter (Cambridge, MA: Harvard University Press, 1993). However reasonable it may be to assume that religion is a long-term human project, it would be problematic to offer its persistence as a reason for affirming it, as I've occasionally heard its advocates do.

7   A few of the many relevant philosophical works since 1994 are: Giorgio Agamben, *The Time That Remains: A Commentary on the Letter to the Romans* [2000], trans. Patricia Dailey (Stanford, CA: Stanford University Press, 2005); Alain Badiou, *Saint Paul: The Foundation of Univeralism* [1997], trans. Ray Brassier (Stanford, CA: Stanford University Press, 2003); the first English translation of Jacob Taubes, *The Political Theology of Paul*, trans. Dana Hollander (Stanford, CA: Stanford University Press, 2004); and Jacques Derrida, *Acts of Religion*, ed. Gil Anidjar (New York: Routledge, 2002). Works of critical theory since the Capri seminar that inhabit and promote forms of religious thinking include: Eric Santner, *On the Psychotheology of Everyday Life: Reflections on Freud and Rosenzweig* (Chicago: University of Chicago Press, 2001); Slavoj Žižek, *The Fragile Absolute: Or, Why Is the Christian Legacy Worth Fighting For?* (New York: Verso, 2001) and by the same author *The Puppet and the Dwarf: The Perverse Core of Christianity* (Cambridge, MA: MIT Press, 2003); the continuing work of Jean-Luc Marion, especially, in this period, *Being Given: Toward a Phenomenology of Givenness* [1997], trans. Jeffrey L. Kosky (Stanford, CA: Stanford University Press, 1992), and, by the same author, *The Crossing of the Visible* [1996], trans. James K. A. Smith (Stanford, CA: Stanford University Press, 2004). This period has also seen the English translation of Hent de Vries, *Minimal Theologies: Critiques of Secular Reason in Adorno and Levinas*, trans. Geoffrey Hale (Baltimore: Johns Hopkins University Press, 2005). It would be difficult to imagine most of these texts being discussed so widely in the 1980s, when religion in theory tended to be filtered through Benjamin or Levinas and cast as interpretation of their idiosyncratic thought. Some of these later texts are "atheistic" in a mode that conforms to Derrida's assimilation of atheism into negative theology and the sources of religion. On the former see especially de Vries, *Minimal Theologies*, 631–57, especially 650–57.

8   The most plausible reason, however, is the relationship between religiousness and humanism which is part of commitment to the category of the human per se and ingrained in the culture of the humanities and especially literature.

9   *Derrida and Religion: Other Testaments*, ed. Yvonne Sherwood and Kevin Hart (New York: Routledge, 2005), 11.

10   Ibid., 11.

11   Ibid., 13.

12   See especially John D. Caputo, *The Mystical Element in Heidegger's Thought* (Athens: Ohio University Press, 1978) and by the same author *Heidegger and Aquinas: An Essay on Overcoming Metaphysics* (New York: Fordham University Press, 1982); and Mark C. Taylor, *Deconstructing Theology* (New York: Crossroad Publishing, 1982); *Erring: A Postmodern A/Theology* (Chicago: University of Chicago Press, 1984); and *Altarity* (Chicago: University of Chicago Press, 1987).

13   Sherwood and Hart note that by the publication of *Derrida and Religion* in 2005 "there is still no Hindu, Buddhist, or representative of any other religious group [but the Judeo-Christian]. . . . here, too, there is no Muslim" (15). Rather than apologizing, they go on,

"Without in any way wanting to deny or qualify the important and solid fact of our Abrahamic, Judeo-Christian particularity, it is clear that there is more than enough difference, and far more than we can begin to take account of, in the complex space that is the 'Judeo-Christian'" (16). For fairer representation see *Religion and Media*, ed. Hent de Vries and Samuel Weber (Stanford, CA: Stanford University Press, 2001).

14   Friedrich Nietzsche, *The Will to Power*, ed. Walter Kaufmann, trans. Walter Kaufmann and R. J. Hollingdale (New York: Vintage, 1968), §331, trans. modified.

15   Donald Davidson, "Mental Events" [1970], in *Essays on Actions and Events* (New York: Oxford University Press, 1980), 207–25.

16   Jacques Derrida, "How to Avoid Speaking: Denials" [1987], in *Languages of the Unsayable: The Play of Negativity in Literature and Literary Theory*, ed. Sanford Budick and Wolfgang Iser, trans. Ken Frieden (New York: Columbia University Press, 1989), 13.

17   Jacques Derrida, "Ellipsis" [1967], in *Writing and Difference*, trans. Alan Bass (Chicago: University of Chicago Press, 1978), 294–300.

18   Derrida approaches his horror of extirpation perhaps most directly in *Of Spirit: Heidegger and the Question* [1987], trans. Geoffrey Bennington and Rachel Bowlby (Chicago: University of Chicago Press, 1989), and *Feu la cendre* [1987], trans. as *Cinders* by Ned Lukacher (Lincoln: University of Nebraska Press, 1991), texts on the borderline of "late Derrida." *Feu la cendre* is among other things a meditation on "animadversion" commissioned "for *Anima*, a now defunct journal" (22). On the figural animation of words in this text, "the cinder within a sentence," see especially 49, 53.

19   Derrida, *The Gift of Death*, 62.

20   On the figure of "sources" see Jacques Derrida, "Qual Quelle: Valéry's Sources" [1971], in *Margins of Philosophy*, trans. Alan Bass (Chicago: University of Chicago Press, 1982), 273–306. Here, part of the discussion uses the prosaic context of mineral water production.

21   In Kant, contemplation of the sublimity of one's own inner moral law provides, in the inspiring prospect of self-sufficiency, the one legitimate motive force external to morality itself for being a moral person. The only thing that supplements the moral law is the *very idea* of the moral law: on this alone one can get high without undermining the power of the law itself.

22   I'm not sure this point is well understood, and it is useful in distinguishing Derrida's argument from the linguistic arguments of Habermas, Stanley Cavell, or ordinary language philosophy. A little earlier in "Faith and Knowledge" Derrida rejects the view that common use of the word "religion" presupposes common bases for understanding what religion means: "We believe we can pretend to believe—fiduciary act—that we share in some pre-understanding. We act as though we had some common sense of what 'religion' means through the languages that we believe (how much belief already, to this moment, to this very day!) we know how to speak. We believe in the minimal trustworthiness of this word. Like Heidegger, concerning what he calls the *Faktum* of the vocabulary of being (at the beginning of *Sein und Zeit*), we believe (or believe it is obligatory that) we pre-understand the meaning of this word, if only to be able to question and in order to interrogate ourselves on this subject. Well—we will have to return to this much later— nothing is less pre-assured than such a *Faktum* (in both of these cases, precisely!) and the entire question of religion comes down, *perhaps*, to this lack of assurance" (Derrida, "Faith and Knowledge," 3).

23 Jacques Derrida, *Dissemination* [1972], trans. Barbara Johnson (Chicago: University of Chicago Press, 1981), 160; see also by the same author "Khora" [1993], in *On the Name*, ed. Thomas Dutoit, trans. Ian MacLeod (Stanford, CA: Stanford University Press, 1995), 89–127.

24 It is worth pausing to observe that, even in the context of the impossibility of proof one way or the other, "Faith and Knowledge" never mentions agnosticism. Although the semantic boundaries of agnosticism wouldn't hold up any better than that of "religion," it seems fair to say that agnosticism in the mode of indifference is more of a challenge to Derrida's argument than atheism, with its declarative content. We cannot tell what reduces to what, because we're not at the end of all the trials of all reductionist projects: isn't this a reason not to use the word *irreducible*?

25 On the problematic of remaining, see Jacques Derrida, "Demeure: Fiction and Testimony" [1998], in *The Instant of My Death/Demeure: Fiction and Testimony*, Maurice Blanchot/Jacques Derrida, trans. Elizabeth Rottenberg (Stanford, CA: Stanford University Press, 2000), 13–103.

26 Derrida, *Feu la cindre/Cinders*, 44.

27 The effects are mainly newly produced modes, and it is hard to tell from "Faith and Knowledge" how significant a shift in mode should be taken to be—to what extent the discovery of a new mode affects one's view of that of which it is a mode.

28 He does not claim that his own stance is like Kant's, although the comparison has been pursued elsewhere, for instance in Bernard Stiegler, "Derrida and Technology: Fidelity at the Limits of Deconstruction and the Prosthesis of Faith," in *Jacques Derrida and the Humanities: A Critical Reader*, ed. Tom Cohen, trans. Richard Beardsworth (Cambridge: Cambridge University Press, 2001), 238–70.

29 Immanuel Kant, "Religion within the Boundaries of Mere Reason," in *Religion and Rational Theology*, ed. and trans. Allen W. Wood and George di Giovanni (Cambridge: Cambridge University Press, 1996), 106.

30 Ibid.

31 Maurizio Ferraris, "The Meaning of Being as a Determinate Ontic Trace," in *Religion*, ed. Jacques Derrida and Gianni Vattimo, trans. David Webb (Stanford, CA: Stanford University Press, 1998), 179.

32 Kant, "Religion within the Boundaries of Mere Reason," 107n.

33 Ferraris, "The Meaning of Being as a Determinate Ontic Trace," 178.

34 Stiegler, "Derrida and Technology," 256.

35 Ibid., 253–54.

36 Ibid., 256.

37 It would be interesting to look for differences between Derrida's writings on "life" before and after the autoimmunity motif comes to the foreground. Robert Smith's relatively early discussion of Derridean *bios* is interesting in this respect. See Smith, "The Book of Zoë," in *Derrida and Autobiography* (Cambridge: Cambridge University Press, 1995), 97–191.

38 Jacques Derrida, "'Che cos'è la poesia?'" in *A Derrida Reader: Between the Blinds*, trans. Peggy Kamuf (New York: Columbia University Press, 1991), 223.

39 Derrida, "'Che cos'è la poesia?'" 223. At stake in the distinction between poetry and the poetic is reduction: "with the *poetic* . . . you intend to speak about an *experience*, another

word for voyage, here the aleatory rambling of a trek, the strophe that turns but never leads back to discourse, or back home, at least is never reduced to poetry—written, spoken, even sung" ("'Che cos'è la poesia?'" 225). The poem ends, but the poetic never does.

40 Derrida, "'Che cos'è la poesia?'" 227.

41 Stiegler, "Derrida and Technology," 256.

42 Derrida, "'Che cos'è la poesia?'" 230–31 (my italics).

43 Ibid., 231.

44 Ibid., 227.

45 Ibid., 233.

46 Stiegler, "Derrida and Technology," 254–55.

47 Paul de Man, "The Rhetoric of Temporality," in *Blindness and Insight: Essays in the Rhetoric of Contemporary Criticism*, 2nd ed. (Minneapolis: University of Minnesota Press, 1983), 214.

48 Derrida's major statement of the necessity for respecting that which can best be described as "not nothing" is *Specters of Marx: The State of the Debt, the Work of Mourning, and the New International* [1993], trans. Peggy Kamuf (New York: Routledge, 1994). On the relation of the spectral, the religious model, and the ideological, see especially, e.g., 148.

49 On the irreplaceability of actually trying things in Nietzsche, see Avital Ronell, *The Test Drive* (Urbana: University of Illinois Press, 2005).

50 See Jacques Derrida, "Fors," trans. Barbara Johnson, foreword to Nicholas Abraham and Maria Torok, *The Wolf-Man's Magic Word: A Cryptonomy*, trans. Nicolas Rand (Minneapolis: University of Minnesota Press, 1987), xiii.

David E. Johnson

As If the Time Were Now: Deconstructing Agamben

> This small word, "as," might well be the name of the true problem, not to say the target, of deconstruction.
> —Jacques Derrida, "The University Without Condition"

> Whence its always monstrous, unpresentable character, demonstrable *as* un-monstrable. Thus never as such.
> —Jacques Derrida, *Rogues*

> One can always act as if it made no difference.
> —Jacques Derrida, "Différance"

With the exception of a brief comment in *Rogues*, Derrida seems to have ignored Agamben's work.[1] The same cannot, however, be said of Agamben, who throughout his career has consistently situated his work in relation to Derrida's. In multiple texts Agamben honors Derrida, but he also challenges and ostensibly corrects Derrida's understanding of phonocentrism, of authenticity and inauthenticity in Heidegger, and of the status of divine violence in Benjamin.[2] More recently, in *The Time That Remains*, he distinguishes his interpretation of the messianic event from Derrida's and reinscribes the trace as if it were a frustrated *Aufhebung* incapable of "seiz[ing] hold of itself" or of "catch[ing] up with

South Atlantic Quarterly 106:2, Spring 2007
DOI 10.1215/00382876-2006-024   © 2007 Duke University Press

a void in representation."[3] Although Agamben acknowledges that Derrida "restored philosophical standing to" the Aristotelian concepts of presence and absence by "demonstrating their connectedness to Hegelian *Aufhebung*" (102), he nevertheless claims that Derrida develops these concepts "into an actual ontology of the trace and originary supplement" (102). Agamben concludes, "The trace is a suspended *Aufhebung* that will never come to know its own *pleroma*" (103). Because Agamben conceives the messianic as "the very opening through which we may seize hold of time, achieving our representation of time, making it end" (100), for him, "Deconstruction is a thwarted messianism, a suspension of the messianic" (103).

Insofar as *Aufhebung* operates only through the suspension of time, Agamben effectively accuses Derrida of suspending the suspension of time. He argues that deconstruction, unlike *Aufhebung* or messianic time, is thwarted by its inability to seize time, to take hold of it. For Agamben, the issue is the possibility of dominating time by mastering its representation, which entails abolishing the "as" and the "as if." In order to master representation, time must be suspended, because representation, as opposed to what Agamben calls "pure philosophical presentation" (*Potentialities*, 47),[4] is an effect of constitutive non-self-coincidence. Agamben attempts to overcome representation by suspending temporalization. In opposition to *chronos*, he posits the messianic present of *kairos*, which, he asserts, makes possible the stretching out, the suspension, of infinitely divisible *chronos*. The kairological suspension of temporalization, according to Agamben, allows for the mastery of chronological time. Without *kairos*, Agamben argues, *chronos* remains unfulfilled: "Messianic presence lies beside itself, since, without ever coinciding with a chronological instant, and without ever adding itself onto it, it seizes hold of this instant and brings it forth to fulfillment" (*Time That Remains*, 70–71). In short, Agamben recoils from the possibility that, without *kairos*, which is the time of the end of time, realizing or actualizing ourselves necessarily depends on the "as if" of self-understanding. Without *kairos*, *chronos* exceeds our grasp; it is always beyond our reach, out of touch.

Agamben grounds his understanding of the necessary suspension of time through readings of two of his principal philosophical interlocutors: Aristotle and Hegel. But these texts also provide the resources for another interpretation of temporalization, one that makes clear that time cannot be suspended, that it cannot be mastered; one that makes clear, in other words, that such sovereignty is only ever *as if.*

Aristotle's *Categories* establishes homology, and thus the name and equivocation, as the first problem for thinking *as* categorical and rational: "Things are equivocally named when they have the name only in common, the definition . . . corresponding with the name being different."[5] The example Aristotle gives is instructive, not least because it concerns the status of life and the animal (*zoon*): "For instance, while a man and a portrait can properly both be called 'animals,' these are equivocally named. For they have the name only in common, the definitions . . . corresponding with the name being different" (1a2–3/13). *Zoon* thus means both what is living, a living creature, and the representation, itself inanimate, of what is living; it means life and the representation of life. Between what is living and what is dead, there is equivocation, homonymy; the living and the (dead) representation of the living have the same name, their names are alike, homologous, but their essences—their being, *ousia*—are different. The first principle for establishing the rules for thinking, for determining the categories for thought, therefore, concerns the equivocation—which here means the difference—between name and being (the essence or definition, *ousia*), a difference determined according to reason (*logos*), hence, by correspondence or by analogy. In the *Categories*, Aristotle limits the problem of homonymic indeterminacy to the relation of two things that share the same name; that is, homonymy does not appear to be a problem of the relation of any one thing to its particular name. In other words, for Aristotle the fact that the definition or statement of essence of *zoon* is *gegrammenon* (portrait) is not in itself equivocal. The equivocation arises only insofar as *zoon* also is defined as *anthropos*. The divergence of *zoon*'s *ousia* into *gegrammenon* and *anthropos* is the condition of homonymy. Were *gegrammenon* and *anthropos* both defined as *zoon*, it would be an instance and example of synonymy: "Things are univocally named, when not only they bear the same name but the name means the same in each case—has the same definition corresponding. Thus a man and an ox are called 'animals.' The name is the same in both cases; so also the statement of essence" (1a6–9/13). Whereas whatever is synonymous shares both its name and its definition, whatever is homonymous shares its name with something else but has its own, proper (*idios*) definition or essence.

In homonymy, the same name has a different essence. Hence, in each case the same name refers to something *idios*, unique, proper. The necessary possibility of such idiomaticity results in equivocation. On the one hand, without correspondence, analogy, or the as-structure, there would be no possibility of thought. On the other hand, without homonymy and thus the possibility of equivocation, there would be no possibility of correspondence. In his 1931 lectures on Aristotle and *dunamis*, Heidegger asked, "What would be the point of a sum of fixed definitions with words grafted onto them and thereby made unequivocal? That of course would be the decline and death of language."[6] More recently, Agamben has argued for "a full acceptance of the anonymity of language and the homonymy that governs its field" (*Potentialities*, 46). According to Agamben, homonymy is necessary in order that there be Ideas: "a perfect language purged of all homonymy and composed solely of univocal signs would be a language absolutely without Ideas" (47). Nevertheless, Agamben cautions against the infinite play of reference that homonymy threatens: "If every human word always presupposed another word, if the presuppositional power of language knew no limits, then there would truly be no possible experience of the limits of language" (46). For Agamben, homonymy is both necessary for the possibility of language, that it will have Ideas, and, at the same time, a threat to language, that is, to the possibility of the experience of the limits of language.

The stakes, then, are high: according to Agamben, were language's presuppositional power unlimited, there would be no "true human community," in that community cannot be founded "on the basis of a presupposition—be it a nation, a language, or even the a priori of communication of which hermeneutics speaks" (47). There must, therefore, be a limit to the constitutive power of homonymy and, as its necessary corollary, the possibility of an experience of the limit of language: "What unites human beings among themselves . . . is the vision of language itself and, therefore, the experience of language's limits, its *end*. A true community can only be a community that is not presupposed" (47). "The vision of language itself," Agamben calls the "Idea" of language. The Idea of language is not presupposed because *the Idea neither is and has a name nor is not and does not have a name*. The Idea is not a word (a metalanguage), nor is it a vision of an object outside language (there is no such object, no such unsayable thing); it is a *vision of language itself*. Language, which for human beings mediates all things and all knowledge, is itself immediate" (47). Consequently, language, *as* constitutive mediation, is the only immediacy to which humans have access: "For human beings, such an *immediate mediation* constitutes the sole possibility of reaching a principle freed of every presupposition, including self-presupposition" (47). The "itself" or the being-in-itself of language depends on the limit of presupposition; this limit, however, extends even to the self-presupposition of language *itself.* In other words, language *as such* is not presupposed, not even by *itself.*

On the one hand, presuppositionality is another way to say mediation, and language, according to Agamben, is constitutive mediation. Thus, language must be presupposed; it must be marked by presuppositionality. Consequently, language can never shed the possibility of homonymy and equivocation. Language, then, is always *in name only.* On the other hand, Agamben argues, language *as such* is immediate, therefore it cannot be presupposed. The possibility of "true human community" depends, moreover, on the immediate presentation of language, on the unpresupposed appearance of language *as such*: "Pure philosophical presentation . . . cannot merely be the presentation of ideas about language or the world; instead, it must above all be the presentation of *the Idea of language*" (47). Pure (philosophical) presentation is the immediate presentation of language *as such*; in pure (philosophical) presentation language shows *itself* immediately. But it not only *shows* itself immediately. In Agamben's account, language touches itself and, in so doing, founds "authentic human community and communication": "*The task of philosophical presentation is to come with speech to help speech, so that, in speech, speech itself does not remain presupposed but instead comes to speech.* At this point, the presuppositional power of language *touches its limit and its end* [emphasis added]; language says presuppositions *as* [emphasis added] presuppositions and, in this way, reaches the unpresupposable and unpresupposed principle (*arkhe anypothetos*) that, as such, constitutes authentic human community and communication" (35). The instant language qua "presuppositional power" touches itself at its limit and end, touches itself there where it sees and shows itself as "*a vision of language itself*," it absolves and absolutizes itself *as* "absolute presupposition" (43). Where language sees itself *as* itself touching itself, it affects itself. This is the instant of language's auto-affection, the moment in which absolute mediation comes to itself, to its limit and end, such that, as absolute presuppositionality, it immediately auto-affects itself as the unpresupposed ground of any possible mediation, hence also of any "authentic human community or communication."

In Agamben's argument, language shows itself as "*a vision of language itself*" at the limit or end at which it touches itself. Language experiences itself *as such* immediately. At the same time, however, in this touching auto-affection, language opens itself or is opened to our experience, to communicability: "The thing itself [which is the Idea of language] is not a thing; it is the very sayability, the very openness at issue in language, which, in language, we always presuppose and forget, perhaps because it is at bottom its own oblivion and abandonment. . . . It is what we are always disclosing in speaking, what we are always saying and communicating, and that of which we nevertheless are always losing sight" (35). Immediately in sight of itself, language is nonetheless out of sight, as the condition of possibility of its use. We forget language, its immediacy and unpresuppositionality, in our use of language, in everything we say. In other words, language as such is not temporal; rather, our use of language constitutes "the presuppositional structure of language" (35). Yet only our blindness to language's vision of itself touching itself makes possible all communication. This is, Agamben notes, "the very structure of tradition" (35). In sum, without the instance of language's absolute auto-affection, which is nonetheless forgotten in our use of language, there would be neither inheritance nor passing on; nor would there be the possibility to "speak about something" (35). There would thus be no possibility of representation. In short, language's representational function, its communicative capacity, wholly depends on the always already forgotten instance of its absolute auto-affection, its immediate self-presentation.

In order to explain the possibility of the immediate manifestation of language, Agamben turns to Emile Benveniste's explanation of deixis. "Following an ancient grammatical tradition," Agamben writes, "even linguistics seems to presuppose that, at the limit of the possibility of signification, language can *show* itself, or can *indicate* the present instance of discourse as its own taking place, through shifters" (*Language and Death*, 31). It is not only a question of showing itself; language must also touch itself, must come into contact with itself at its limit. The end of language is the site and the sight of intimate touching at the limit, which already exceeds itself, which already goes beyond the limit, and which makes language come—to itself and to us. Benveniste, however, does not say this; instead, he "bases the indexical nature of the shifter on a 'contemporaneity with the instance of discourse that carries the indicator of the person'" (31).[7] It is the "instance of discourse" that interests Agamben: shifters or the deictic function of language "provide the instrument of . . . the conversion of language into discourse" (Benveniste, *Problems*, 220). Shifters indicate the locutionary possibility of language; without any material reference, deictics *site* language, instantiate it, and thus mark the conversion from a general language that never takes place to the instance of discourse. Prior to any meaningful articulation, then, there is the taking place of language. This is, of course, what deixis means: to show, to manifest.

Agamben wonders, however, what makes possible the indication of the instance of discourse. Benveniste's answer is that shifters are "the discrete and always unique acts by which the language is actualized in speech by a speaker" (217). Furthermore, his consideration of personal pronouns, which constitute a specific set of shifters, leads him to argue for a distinction between the spoken instantiation of discourse and the written one: "A linguistic text of great length . . . can be imagined in which *I* and *you* would not appear a single time; conversely, it would be difficult to conceive of a short spoken text in which they were not employed" (217–18). Because they are uniquely determined in relation to the instance of discourse, shifters are intimately related to the voice, to the presence of the voice. However, the voice as mere audible sound is of little interest to Agamben. Insofar as he is concerned with the end of language and the possibility of an experience of language that would ground "authentic human community," he must in fact locate the taking-place of language in a place that is no longer simple audibility but not yet meaningful. Located in this way, as neither *vox inarticulada* nor *vox* qua significant term, "The voice . . . will then show itself as a pure intention to signify, as pure meaning, in which something is given to be understood before a determinate event of meaning is produced" (*Language and Death*, 33). Agamben also refers to this moment as "a pure event of language before or beyond all particular meaning" (*Potentialities*, 42). Commenting on a passage from Augustine's *De Trinitate* that deals with "the now-familiar idea of a 'dead language'" (*Language and Death*, 33), he remarks, "This passage isolates an experience of the word in which it is no longer mere sound . . . and it is not yet meaning, but *the pure intention to signify*" (33).

Agamben literally capitalizes on this intention in that he designates it the "Voice," which removes the voice qua animal voice or inarticulate sound. Although such pure intentionality opens language to itself, it does so as negativity and thus as temporal: "*The taking place of language between the removal of the voice and the event of meaning is the other Voice. . . .* But inasmuch as this Voice . . . enjoys the status of a *no-longer* (voice) and of a *not-yet* (meaning), it necessarily constitutes a negative dimension. It is *ground*, but in the sense that it goes *to the ground* and disappears in order for being and language to take place" (35).[8] Agamben asserts that this Voice "coincides with the most universal dimension of meaning, Being" (*Potentialities*, 42). Language thus takes place, actualizes itself, negatively, as a vanishing limit between inarticulateness and meaning. It does so, moreover, as the pure intention to signify that no longer and not yet means anything other than the "possibility of thought beyond meaningful propositions" (42). Understood this way, the Voice instances the absolution of language; it marks the place where language absolves itself of itself and thus absolutizes itself *as* language *itself*.

Agamben is aware that he is playing in Hegel's neighborhood: the removal of the voice preserves and institutes—through negation—the Voice. This is the gesture of Hegel's *Aufhebung*. More recently, in *The Time That Remains*, Agamben translates his interest in the *Aufhebung* of voice *as* Voice into the Pauline lexicon of *katargein, hos me* ("as not"), and the relation of *chronos* to *kairos*. "Messianic *katargesis*," Agamben explains, "does not merely abolish; it preserves and brings to fulfillment" (*Time That Remains*, 99). Indeed, Agamben takes credit for "the discovery" of the "posthumous life of the verb *katargein* in the philosophical tradition" (99). Ultimately, Agamben inscribes Hegel's speculative philosophy within the horizon of the Pauline *corpus*, for Luther translates Paul's *katargein* by *Aufheben*, "the very word that harbors the double meaning of abolishing and conserving . . . used by Hegel as a foundation for his dialectic!" (99).

The genealogy of the term is less important, however, than Agamben's determination that the "pure intention to signify" and the joint operation of negation and preservation that come to fulfillment organize the necessary temporalization of language and being. Intentionality and fulfillment: on the one hand, the ground of any possible significance without itself being that significance; on the other hand, the possibility of actualization, of being qua presence without presupposition. They are not unrelated. The pure intention to signify instances language; it gives language to itself as the possibility of discourse. Fulfillment is perfection. As such it is absolute: what is fulfilled is without presupposition, without reference or correspondence, and thus without the possibility of homonymy. The pure intention to signify *is* the fulfillment of language; it is the perfection and actualization of language *as such, in itself*. And the fulfillment of language is the moment, the instant, in which language becomes actual, the moment it sees itself and touches itself at its limit. The end, the *telos*, of language is its perfection, its fulfillment: in touching *itself*, language masters itself, puts itself under its own hand, its own authority. No-longer animal voice and not-yet meaningful, language instances itself as such and touches only itself: language is masturbatory, impotent in its self-actualization. It has no relation to any other, to any excess, to any outside. This is the operation of *katargesis* or *Aufhebung*: the making-inoperative, the preservation of that which is abolished or suspended. Language is actualized and thus perfected in itself qua impotent. In other words, impotence is not the necessary negative possibility of potency, namely, that what has the potential to be no less has the potential not to be. In the case of *katargesis*, impotence is actualized. Consequently, weakness, the lack of power, is power. According to Paul, this is the truth that God will have revealed to him: "My power is made perfect in weakness [*he gar dunamis en astheneiea teleitai*]" (2 Corinthians 12:9). Agamben calls such suspension the messianic vocation or the revocation of all vocations. The messianic vocation actualizes itself in the Pauline "as not," the *hos me*, which, Agamben argues, is not to be mistaken for the nihilistic "as if" that haunts Nietzsche (*Time That Remains*, 35–37). Whereas the "as if" indicates the perspective the subject takes on itself, the "as not" "does not involve a point of view from which we could see a world in which redemption had taken place" (41). This is so, Agamben explains, because "no subject could watch it or act *as if* at a given point" (41). Indeed, the messianic event, the coming of the Messiah, "means that all things, even the subjects who contemplate it, are caught up in the *as not*, called and revoked at one and the same time" (41). For sure, the messianic "as not" dislocates the subject, but it does so by nullifying the "as if" as the necessary analogical structure of the ontological ground for the subject, that is, as the determination of the place or locus of the subject and its enunciation. Agamben notes, for instance, "Karl Barth's thesis that there is no place for the *as if* in the messianic" except insofar as it has already undergone the process of *katargesis* or *Aufhebung* as hope (41). Consequently, the messianic amounts to "the simultaneous abolition and realization of the *as if*" (42). The fulfillment of the "as if" means the end of representation: "the subject wishing to indefinitely maintain himself in similitude (in the *as if*) . . . simply loses the wager" (42). It would be a mistake to think, however, that the "as if" Agamben targets is simply the "as if" of fantasy, illusion, dream narratives, although undoubtedly the "as if" of illusion, of fiction, no less than that of deception, is related to the philosophical "as if." In Agamben, rather, the "as if" signals the difference between signifier (*signum*) and signified (*res significa*). Insofar as the "as if" is the minimal structure of representation, it also marks the analogical structure of thought. It is therefore the very structure of representation that Agamben targets for abolition in the Pauline "as not." As Agamben puts it, "Everything hangs on the moment and manner in which the *as* becomes abolished" (43).

Agamben has already spelled out the "manner" in which the "as," and consequently the "as if," are abolished: it happens through the making-inoperative, the suspension and preservation—the absolution—effected in *katargesis*, which is the Pauline way of saying *Aufhebung*. The analogical structure of thought, however, can only be relieved—according to the logic of Pauline *katargesis* or Hegelian *Aufhebung*—in the "time" of the end of time, in an absolute present or the now. The time of the "as not," then, is no time at all; it is, rather, now. Thus Agamben's recourse to Paul's *ho nun kairos*, which he claims is Paul's technical term for the messianic event (61).

The distinction between *kairos* and *chronos* serves to absolve the problem of the representation of time, which Agamben figures in terms of the difference between representation and thought: "A general problem arises here regarding our representations of time, which are of a spatial order. It has often been noted that these spatial representations . . . generate a kind of falsification that makes unthinkable the lived experience of time. The confusion between *eskhaton* and messianic time is a flagrant example of this: if you represent time as a straight line and its end as a punctual instant, you end up with something perfectly *representable*, but absolutely *unthinkable*. Vice-versa, if you reflect on a real experience of time, you end up with something *thinkable*, but absolutely *unrepresentable*" (64). To address this problem Agamben turns to "the work of a linguist who is perhaps the most philosophical linguist of our century: Gustave Guillaume" (65). For our purposes, a detailed reading of Guillaume's work is unnecessary; it suffices to point out that his attempt to inscribe temporalization within spatial representation hinges on the notion of "operational time," which is the time it takes to realize the representation of time. Operational time describes the necessary recursiveness of any possible representation of time, which means, simply, that it takes time to posit or determine time. Guillaume calls the representation of the time it takes to represent time "chronogenetic time," which affords a three-dimensional representation that "takes into account all the verb forms of a language (aspects, modalities, and tenses) according to a unitary model" (66). The question is, what is the principle of unity that regulates operational or chronogenetic time?[9]

Guillaume's investigations into the representation of time provide the ground for what Agamben calls "one of the most ingenious creations of twentieth-century linguistics, Benveniste's theory of enunciation" (66). Agamben reminds us that in Benveniste's account, "through shifters . . . language refers to its own taking place, to a pure instance of discourse in action" (66). Importantly, "this capacity to refer to the pure presence of enunciation goes hand in hand . . . with *chronothèse*, time-positing (literally, 'chronothesis'), itself the origin of our representation of time" (66). "Time-positing" follows closely Kant's understanding of schematism, which Derrida called "the movement of temporalization."[10] Because schematism and time-positing, both of which name temporal determination, are necessary to the production of any image whatsoever, it stands to reason that there can be no absolute or totalizing schema of the schema. Every instance of temporal determination must also be temporally determined. This structure of irreducible displacement also marks the structure of enunciation: "If each mental operation . . . implies an operational time, then even referring to the instance of discourse in action would imply a certain time, and chronothesis, or time-positing, would contain within itself another time that introduces a disjointedness and delay in the 'pure presence' of the enunciation. Because Benveniste makes enunciation the very foundation of subjectivity and consciousness, this lapse and delay would then be a part of the structure of the subject" (66–67). Despite the insistence that "thought could never coincide perfectly with itself" and that "the self-presence of consciousness consequently would always take on the form of time" (67), Agamben nevertheless argues that time is unified in the taking-place of operational time. Such unity provides for the possibility of self-mastery. Operational time is not chronological time; rather, it is the time of the end, "it is the time we need to make time end" (68). In Agamben's account, operational time, which is another way of saying messianic time and is therefore another name for *kairos*, also *relieves* representation; it instances the *katargesis* or *Aufhebung* of representation: "Whereas our representation of chronological time, as the time *in which* we are, separates us from ourselves and transforms us into impotent spectators of ourselves—spectators who look at the time that flies without any time left, continually missing themselves—messianic time, an operational time in which we take hold of and achieve our representations of time, is the time *that* we ourselves are" (68).

This awareness of ourselves qua temporal suspends our impotence and allows us to "take hold of and achieve our representations of time," which undoubtedly implies the possibility of taking hold of and achieving *ourselves* insofar as we are temporal. We no longer miss ourselves. It is only in messianic time, *kairos*, that, no longer impotent spectators missing ourselves, we are able to realize ourselves. For Agamben, importantly, *kairos* is not another time: "What we take hold of when we seize *kairos* is not another time, but a contracted and abridged *chronos*" (69). *Kairos*, however, does not supplement *chronos*; it is not added on to *chronos*: they are, rather, "coextensive but cannot be added together" (70). Indeed, Agamben explains, "messianic presence [*kairos*, operational time] lies beside itself, since, without ever coinciding with a chronological instant, and without ever adding itself onto it, it seizes hold of this instant and brings it forth to fulfillment" (70–71). Then, in a rather remarkable phrase, Agamben notes that "the messianic event has already happened, but its presence contains within itself another time, which stretches its *parousia*, not in order to defer it, but, on the contrary, to make it graspable" (71). In short, *kairos* is *chronos* held together; it is the name of the possibility of self-presence and thus of the possibility of temporal unity. Following Heidegger, Agamben explains that *kairos* is Dasein's authentic temporality, while *chronos* names Dasein's inauthentic temporality: "The factical link between these two dimensions of Dasein [between its ontical impropriety and its ontological propriety, but also between *chronos* and *kairos*] is so intimate and original that Heidegger writes, '*authentic* existence is not something which floats above falling everydayness; existentially, it is only a modified way in which such everydayness is seized upon'" (*Potentialities*, 197).[11] Agamben insists that such seizure makes all the difference: "Even in proper Being-toward-death and proper decision, Dasein seizes hold of its impropriety alone, *mastering an alienation and becoming attentive to a distraction*" (197, emphasis added). Self-mastery is at stake in Agamben's determination of the "slight adjustment," the "meager difference" that *kairos* makes in the world: "The messianic world is not another world, but the secular world itself, with a slight adjustment, a meager difference. But this ever so slight difference, which results from my having grasped my disjointedness with regard to chronological time, is, in every way, a decisive one" (*Time That Remains*, 69).

The slight adjustment to which Agamben refers in both *Potentialities* and *The Time That Remains* is the effect of a Pauline-Hegelian *Aufhebung*. At stake in both texts is the possibility of dialectical purification and redemption, of absolution in the actualization of the absolute. The only time for the actualization of such redemption is the present, which accounts for

Agamben's insistence that apostolic time is neither prophetic time nor apocalyptic time, which refer to and anticipate an end to come. Agamben's Pauline-Hegelian investment in *kairos* (moment, now, absolute, present) as the solution to *chronos*, which qua infinitely divisible can only be thought *as* the absolute future to come and thus *as* constitutive non-self-coincidence, marks the difference between Agamben's project and Derrida's.

Although Derrida rarely found it necessary to address Agamben's work, he did think it imperative to assess his proximity to Hegel: "If there were a definition of *différance*, it would be precisely the limit, the interruption, the destruction of the Hegelian *relève wherever* it operates."[12] Derrida was well aware, however, that "the double meaning of *Aufhebung* could be written otherwise. Whence its proximity to all the operations conducted *against* Hegel's dialectical speculation" (41).[13] Although in *Positions* Derrida admits that *différance* maintains an "almost absolute proximity" (44) to the operator of speculative dialectics, *Aufhebung*, he nonetheless insists that *différance* can be accommodated neither to Hegel's concept of difference nor to his understanding of *Aufhebung*. This is so because, unlike Hegelian difference and *Aufhebung*, both of which are ultimately absolved—resolved through a movement of raising up—"into the self-presence of an onto-theological or onto-teleological synthesis," *différance* "can never be totally resolved"; as a consequence, its effects "can never be governed by a referent in the classical sense, that is, by a thing or by a transcendental signified that would regulate its movement" (44).

Space and time, in Hegel as in Agamben, are relieved. In the *Philosophy of Nature*, Hegel explains, "The truth of space is time, and thus space becomes time; the transition to time is not made subjectively by us, but made by space itself. In pictorial [i.e., representational] thought, space and time are taken to be quite separate: we have space and *also* time; philosophy fights against this 'also.'"[14] In Hegel's account, philosophy undermines temporal and spatial discretion: it challenges the representational logic that would keep them apart, that would fail to grasp their necessary relation to one another in and through the Hegelian concept. Following Hegel closely, Derrida explains: "At each stage of the negation, each time that the *Aufhebung* produced the truth of the previous determination [truth of the point as line, truth of the line as plane], time was requisite. The negation at work *in* space or as [*comme*] space, the spatial negation of space, time is the truth of space. To the extent that it *is*, that is, to the extent that it becomes and is produced, that it manifests itself in its essence, that it spaces itself, in itself relating to itself, that is, in negating itself, space is time. It temporalizes itself, it relates to itself and mediates itself as [*comme*] time. Time is *spacing*" (*Margins*, 42–43). In order for space to correspond to itself *as* space, time must be at work in space. Space mediates (itself) *as* time. Space, therefore, cannot be thought simply on the basis of the point, *stigmè*, because without temporalizing (itself), the point cannot relate to itself and thus cannot posit itself *as* space. The possibility of space depends on temporalization, but this does not amount to the privilege of time over space. For although there must be temporalization in order that space appear *as* space, which means there must be the negation or mediation of space *as* space in order that space appear, nevertheless, Derrida explains, time is *spacing*.

This follows not only from Derrida's reading of Hegel's *Encyclopedia* but also from the aporetic logic of Aristotle's consideration of the now (*nun*) in book IV of the *Physics*. Derrida recapitulates Aristotle's understanding of the sequence of nows in the following way: "The preceding now, it is said, must be destroyed by the following now. But, Aristotle then points out, it cannot be destroyed 'in itself' (*en heautoi*), that is, at the moment when it is (now, in act). No more can it be destroyed in an other now (*en alloi*): for then it would not be destroyed as now, itself; and, as a now which has been, it is (remains) inaccessible to the action of the following now" (*Margins* 57). Martin Hägglund explains the inevitable effects of this aporia for the metaphysical conception of time: "as long as one holds on to the idea of an indivisible now . . . or . . . to the concept of identity as presence in itself . . . it is impossible to think succession."[15] As we have already seen, Agamben follows Paul and Hegel in arguing that the solution to the aporia lies in positing an absolute now. Through the operation of *katargesis* or *Aufhebung*, the messianic presence of *kairos* supercedes and unifies the infinite succession of *chronos*. Derrida's conception of the trace, far from being a thwarted messianism or a frustrated *Aufhebung*, affords the possibility of thinking through the aporia of time without recurring to an indivisible present. Hägglund provides a lucid account of the operation of the trace: "Given that the now can appear only by disappearing, it must be inscribed as a trace in order to be at all. This is the *becoming-space of time*. The trace is necessarily spatial, since spatiality is characterized by the ability to remain in spite of temporal succession. Spatiality is thus the condition for synthesis, since it enables the tracing of relations between past and future" (43). Nevertheless, as the preceding analysis of Hegel made clear, space *qua* simultaneity "is unthinkable without the temporalization that relates one spatial juncture to another" (43). This is what Derrida calls the becoming-time of space, which is necessary not only for the trace to be related to other traces, but also, as Hägglund argues, "for it to be a trace in the first place" (43). This is so because the trace is legible "only after its inscription and is thus marked by a relation to the future that temporalizes space" (43). The implications of Derrida's understanding of the trace are severe for Agamben's insistence on a kairological solution to the infinite divisibility of *chronos*. Hägglund writes: "If the spatialization of time makes the synthesis *possible*, the temporalization of space makes it *impossible* for the synthesis to be grounded in an indivisible presence. The synthesis is always a trace of the past that is left *for the future*. Thus, it can never be in itself, but is essentially exposed to that which may erase it" (43). It follows from this understanding of the becoming-space of time and the becoming-time of space that neither space nor time is the truth, as Hegel argued, of the other. Space and time are, rather, heterogeneous and indissociable.[16] For our purposes, however, Derrida's account of the trace reveals the dead-end of Agamben's attempt to think the synthesis of temporality, for insofar as *kairos* names the time of the end of time, it literally has no future.

Derrida recalls the importance of spacing at the moment he demarcates the impossibility of democracy: "In both senses of *différance*, then, democracy is differential; it is *différance*, *renvoi*, and spacing. That is why, let me repeat, the theme of spacing, the theme of the interval or the gap, of the trace as gap, of the becoming-space of time or the becoming-time of space, plays such an important role as early as *Of Grammatology* and 'Différance'" (*Rogues*, 38). Derrida's reassertion of *différance*'s importance in this particular context and in these specific terms makes clear that deconstruction has always had implications for how we think of the political. Put simply, as well as being addressed to the authority of the question, deconstruction has always been concerned with the question of authority. Indeed, according to Derrida, the aporetic structure of ipseity is the minimal condition of sovereignty: "By *ipseity* I thus wish to suggest some 'I can,' or at the very least the power that *gives itself* its own law, its force of law, its self-representation, the sovereign and reappropriating gathering of self in the simultaneity of an assemblage or assembly" (11). Ipseity names the "quasi-circular return or rotation toward the self" constitutive "of sovereign self-determination, of the autonomy of the self" (10). There is no sovereignty without the turn (back) toward self that assembles or gathers the self in itself. "The turn makes up the whole and makes a whole with itself; it consists in totalizing, in totalizing itself, and thus in gathering itself by tending toward simultaneity; and it is thus that the turn, as a whole, is one with itself, together with itself" (12). Such totalization is possible, however, only insofar as it is marked by the aporetic logic of spacing. Thus, sovereignty in itself and indivisible is impossible.

At stake in Derrida's interrogation of sovereignty is the impossible gathering of the self, the impossible auto-affection at the heart of all self-determination. For there to be sovereignty, the self must be immediately in touch with itself; it must be simultaneous to itself, which is possible only if time is annulled. Yet despite the necessity of such immediacy, the possibility of sovereignty no less requires a turn (back) on or around itself in order to assemble itself. The turn irreducibly temporalizes, thus divides, the sovereign.

Given Agamben's Hegelian absolution of the subject at the moment it touches itself at the end of language and Derrida's critique of an immediate, self-touching sovereignty, it is worth considering Hegel's conception of the place of touch in the formation of the subject. Importantly, although Hegel posits the constitutive temporality of the subject's self-comprehension, he does so in a way that absolves the effects of time:

> Time is the Notion itself that *is there* and which presents itself to consciousness as empty intuition; for this reason, Spirit necessarily appears in Time, and it appears in Time just so long as it has not *grasped* its pure Notion, i.e. has not annulled Time. It is the *outer*, intuited pure Self which is *not grasped* by the Self, the merely intuited Notion; when this latter grasps itself it sets aside its Time-form, comprehends this intuiting, and is a comprehended and comprehending intuiting. Time, therefore, appears as the destiny and necessity of Spirit that is not yet complete within itself.[17]

Time is necessary for the possibility of the concept's coming to itself, but because time is negation, it cannot be *in itself*, and, therefore, it cannot grasp itself. At the instant the concept grasps itself, time must be—must always already have been—annulled.

The absolute structure of self-comprehension is not limited to the concept's being in and for itself in absolute knowing. In the third part of the *Encyclopedia of Philosophical Sciences*, the *Philosophy of Mind*, Hegel takes up Spirit's return into itself from its self-externalization in and as nature. In the *Philosophy of Mind*'s first part, the "anthropology," Hegel indicates the importance of touch for the soul's coming-to-itself.

In order, therefore, to become fully awake and certain of it, we open our eyes, take hold of ourselves, in short, examine ourselves to find out whether something is, for us, a definite Other, is definitely distinct from us. In this examination we do not relate ourselves directly to the Other, but indirectly. Thus, for example, *touch* is the mediation between myself and the Other, since though it is distinct from these two sides of the opposition, yet at the same time it unites them. Here, therefore, as in sensation generally, the soul by the mediation of something standing between itself and the Other, unites with itself in the content of its sensation, reflects itself out of the Other into itself, separates itself from it and thereby assures itself of its being-for-self. This union of the soul with itself is the progress made by the soul—which in waking had parted itself—by its transition to sensation.[18]

The soul takes hold of itself *as if* it were another; it touches itself and comes to know itself *as* another. Touch, however, is nothing *in itself*. It is mediation. *As* such it is the sense of negativity, of temporalization.

Touch puts the soul in touch with itself *as* another, but it also exposes the soul to the touch of another *as* itself. This necessary exposure to the other leads Hegel to warn, "It is quite inadmissible for anyone to appeal simply to his feelings. He who does so withdraws from the sphere, common to all, of reasoned argument, of thought, of the matter in hand, into his particular subjectivity which, since it is essentially passive, is just as receptive of the worst and the most irrational as it is of the reasonable and the good" (§400 *Zusatz*/75). On the one hand, touch allows the soul to grasp itself *as* itself by mediating its relation to the other. On the other hand, touch's essential passivity opens the soul to whatever or whoever comes and thus threatens it *in itself* with irrationality, hence, with the worst. For this reason Hegel stipulates, "The subjectivity of the sentient soul is one so immediate, so undeveloped, so little self-determining and self-differentiating, that the soul to the extent it *only* feels, does not as yet seize itself as a subject confronting an object. This difference belongs only to *consciousness*" (§400 *Zusatz*/75). According to Hegel, "man . . . raises himself above the singleness of sensation," above sensation's indeterminate immediacy, "to the universality of thought, to self-knowledge, to the *grasp* of his subjectivity" (§381 *Zusatz*/14, emphasis added). The "raising up"—the resurrection—of man is the suspension of the singularity of sensation in and *as* the "I." Hegel figures this raising up as a *grasping*—touching—of subjectivity in which consciousness touches itself *in* and *for itself*. But such touching, *as* touching, singularly exposes the "I" to the other. Thus, consciousness raises itself up only through an auto-hetero-affectivity that suspends, by raising it up, affectivity *in* and *as* thought; yet, in grasping itself, consciousness remains essentially passive and thus absolutely open to the other *in* and *as* itself.

Both Agamben's Pauline *katargesis* and Hegel's Lutheran *Aufhebung* instance attempts to master life by taking hold of time. They are the key figures of philosophies of absolute sovereignty. *Différance*, however, solicits—makes tremble in its entirety—"the domination of beings" by Being. As Derrida explained,

> It is the determination of Being as presence or as beingness that is interrogated by the thought of *différance*. Such a question could not emerge and be understood unless the difference between Being and beings were somewhere to be broached. First consequence: *différance* is not. It is not a present being, however excellent, unique, principal, or transcendent. It governs nothing, reigns over nothing, and nowhere exercises any authority. . . . Not only is there no kingdom of *différance*, but *différance* instigates the subversion of every kingdom. Which makes it obviously threatening and infallibly dreaded by everything within us that desires a kingdom, the past or future presence of a kingdom. And it is always in the name of a kingdom that one may reproach *différance* with wishing to reign, believing that one sees it aggrandize itself with a capital letter. (*Margins*, 21–22)[19]

In *Positions* Derrida more or less repeated the stakes of *différance*: "Nothing—no present and in-*different* being—thus precedes *différance* and spacing. There is no subject who is agent, author, and master of *différance*, who eventually and empirically would be overtaken by *différance*" (28). Deconstruction does not announce or articulate a political position or program in that a position—a locus of enunciation or a determining point—always poses itself *as* a determinable and effective limit, an end, *telos*, and thus *as* a site of mastery. Rather, deconstruction opens the field of all possible determinations. Such determinations, however, cannot be established on any given—whether sensible or intelligible—ground. Hence, they can never be posited in themselves; they can never be secured from the operation and violence of *différance*. Consequently, *différance* makes impossible the possibility of *whatever is*. It undermines, necessarily and incessantly, the ground it opens. The examples of such necessary *impossibility* multiply across Derrida's text. The possibility of justice, for instance, is its *im*possibility, which is another way of saying that justice, the event of justice, only appears *as* justice, which *is not*. The same logic or structural *im*possibility holds for testimony, experience, democracy.[20] They remain "to come."

All claims of mastery, of indivisible sovereignty, are possible only insofar as *différance* (spacing, autoimmunity) is already at work, which means such claims are *im*possible: the master shows himself *as* the master, but in showing himself *as* the master he is not the master *as such*, not even, finally, of himself; yet this is the only possibility of mastery. The sign of mastery is self-control, which both Agamben and Hegel figure as taking hold of one's self. It is clear, however, that to take hold of oneself *as such* is *im*possible: at the moment one touches oneself, the grasp, the touch, is *ex*cessive, *ex*orbitant.

Aristotle already knew this. On the one hand, he argues that touch is the only sense necessary to the living animal: "The primary form of sense is touch, which belongs to all animals"[21] and, later, "It is evident, therefore, that the loss of this one sense alone must bring about the death of the animal" (435b4/602). Consequently, "it is the only one [i.e., sense] which is indispensably necessary to what is an animal" (435b6/602). Yet touch is also the sense of death: "But excess of intensity in tangible qualities . . . destroys the animal" (435b15/602). Whereas an excess of the other senses destroys only the organ of the sense, in the case of touch an excess of "what is tangible destroys touch, which is the essential mark of life; for it has been shown that without touch it is impossible for an animal to be. That is why excess in intensity of tangible qualities destroys not merely the organ, but the animal itself, because this is the only sense which it must have" (435b15–19/603). Touch, therefore, must always be measured; it must always be conditioned or moderated. Despite this, Aristotle claims that "touch takes place by direct contact with its objects, whence also its name. All other organs of sense, no doubt, perceive by contact, only the contact is mediate: touch alone perceives by immediate contact" (435a16–19/602). Herein lies the problem, for inasmuch as touch is immediate, it is also without measure. Without measure, however, touch is necessarily excessive. Because nothing conditions touch, it is always absolutely exposed, overexposed, to the other. This means the condition of possibility of touch, of feeling at all, even of feeling or touching oneself, and thus of auto-affection, is *im*possible, not because there is not touch but because there is always too much touch. Touch is always lethal. The condition of possibility of life, therefore, is also the condition of possibility of death: "An animal is a body with soul in it: every body is tangible, i.e. perceptible by touch; hence necessarily, if an animal is to survive, its body must have tactual sensation. All the other senses, e. g. smell, sight, hearing, apprehend through media; but where there is immediate contact the animal, if it has no sensation, will be unable to avoid some things and take others, and so will find it impossible to survive" (434b11–17/601). But it is also the case that absolute or immediate touch is the absolute foreclosure of touch. Aristotle notes that although touch is immediate and necessary to life, we cannot be sure where touch takes place. "It is also a problem," Aristotle writes, "what is the organ of touch; is it or is it not the flesh (including what in certain animals is analogous [*analogon*] with flesh)? On the second view, flesh is 'the medium' of touch, the real organ being situated farther inward" (422b20–22/577, translation slightly modified). Interestingly but also problematically, Aristotle discounts the probative quality of the fact that "if the object comes into contact with the flesh it is at once perceived" (423a1/577). Against this evidence he points out, first, that were a membrane placed over the skin and then touched, although the touch would be felt, the membrane would not be the organ of touch; second, that were this membrane grown onto the skin, "the report [*aesthesis*] would travel [*diïknoît', diikneomai*, to penetrate, to go through, to recount] still quicker" (423a5/577). These spatial-temporal mediations jeopardize the immediacy of touch. First, touch appears not to take place at the point of contact: the skin is only the "medium" of touch, which means touch is mediated spatially. Second, touch takes time; indeed, touch cannot be distinguished from the account, the report, of touch. Touch is perhaps nothing but this impossible correspondence. The need for such accounting, however, problematizes the immediacy of touch, *as if* it were necessary for touch to get a grip on itself, to grasp or comprehend itself, in order to be touch and touched, and, at the same time, *as if* it were possible for touch *either* to touch itself *or* to delay and defer touching itself without destroying itself.[22]

How, then, to touch oneself, how to touch the *in itself* of itself, whether (of) the sovereign-subject or language or Being? How to master oneself? As the figure of indivisible sovereignty, of an absolute auto-affection or absolute immunity from affection, masturbation, which is self-touching or touching-*itself*, is always already *excessive*. It instances the necessary exposure to the other *as* to oneself. Masturbation is always auto-hetero-affection, a touching *of* the other. *De Anima* touches on the *im*possibility of touch, of touching oneself and of being touched in oneself: touching oneself is touching and being touched *as* (by) the other. It names the impossible possibility of touching the other *as* oneself. There is no self-touching, no auto-affection that does not come *as* from the other. And this means that we touch, that there is touch, *in name only*, homonymically, equivocally, where the possibility of the *homo*nym is proportionality, calculation, accounting, in short, analogy. Likeness, therefore, is conditioned, it is always determined *as* difference that has been accounted for; that which is like another is always like the other *insofar as* their difference has been calculated. The like thus corresponds to itself *as* to the other itself. In every case, the *homo-* corresponds to another. Strictly speaking, then, there is neither *homo* nor *hetero as such* or *in itself*. No matter how quickly, no matter how immediately, the *homo* takes time to report to the other itself *as* itself; and the *hetero* corresponds to the other *as* to itself. The possibility of sameness, of self-identity, therefore, is impossible: the homonym, which is necessary to the possibility of language according to Agamben, and the possibility of which, according to Aristotle, must first be defined and delimited in order to posit the categories of thought *as such*, is necessarily determined *in* and *as* analogy, as the impossible possibility of correspondence, relation, identity. Which is why *whatever is* is *in name only* and thus without any essential unity of being.

De Anima presents Aristotle's most sustained discussion of potentiality. The autoimmune structure of touch, along with the impossibility of locating it, makes touch — and life and the soul — potential. The potentiality of touch, however, cannot be thought in relation to actuality, in which *what is* is actual and therefore privileged over what is *not*. Aristotle's definition of potentiality as that which is as much as it is not sustains the privilege of actuality in that in both cases potentiality is determined in relation to being and to presence. The potentiality of touch is of another order entirely: touch is "to come." Were touch of the order of being, were it *simply* to be, we would already be out of touch, dead, for touch is, if it ever is, according to Aristotle, immediate and excessive, beyond the measure of life. If there were touch, if we could experience touch *as such*, simply, here and now, in the present, we could not survive it. But touch is not of the order of being: on Aristotle's own account, we can never know if we have been touched, which means touch is an impossible experience, an experience of the impossible. Touch is therefore only *as if*, only by analogy. Nevertheless, in *Homo Sacer*, Agamben cites Aristotle's *De Anima* (417b2–16) and then relates what he calls "the most authentic nature of potentiality" to "the paradigm of sovereignty" (46). The sovereign ban, Agamben explains, "*corresponds* to the structure of potentiality, which maintains itself in relation to actuality precisely through its ability not to be. Potentiality (in its double appearance *as* potentiality to and *as* potentiality not to) is that through which Being founds itself *sovereignly* [Agamben's emphasis], which is to say, without anything preceding or determining it . . . other than its own ability not to be" (46, emphasis added). Being is *as* not. Being is sovereignty. It is absolutely sovereign in that it is unpresupposed. Nothing precedes being; nothing determines it. It is, in short, unconditional. These are Agamben's theses.

Two things are clear from this text. First, potentiality remains circumscribed within the horizon of being (to be or not to be, being *as* not being). Thus, potentiality's "most authentic nature" remains of the order of *phusis*, which is to say, of the order of that which determines itself from out of itself. Absolute potentiality, then, is absolute actuality. In Agamben, there is no difference between being and not being, between power and powerlessness, between justice and law. Second, the identity of being and sovereignty instances the nightmare of reason *as* the end, *as* the *telos* of reason, in that it posits being and sovereignty beyond analogy, beyond the *as*, thus beyond all conditions. What would unconditional being, unconditional sovereignty, be?

Despite his reading of Aristotle, Agamben seeks to abolish precisely that which he calls, following Aristotle, "the most authentic way" to say the unity of being, namely, by analogy or *virtually*: being is called *in name only*. Does not equivocation, the *in name only* of homonymy, necessarily condition being and sovereignty? Writing of the "university without condition," Derrida remarks, "if this unconditionality, in principle and *de jure*, constitutes the invincible force of the university, it has never been in effect. By reason of this abstract and hyperbolic invincibility, by reason of its very impossibility, this unconditionality exposes as well the weakness or the vulnerability of the university. It exhibits its impotence, the fragility of its defenses against all the powers that command it, besiege it, and attempt to appropriate it."[23] On the one hand, the university must be without condition, unconditional. Only insofar as the university is unconditional can it be sovereign. On the other hand, such unconditional sovereignty has never been in effect, for if the university were "without condition" it would also be absolutely impotent and thus absolutely vulnerable. An unconditional sovereignty would be incapable of acting, either offensively or defensively, in that any act, whether to impose itself upon others or to defend itself against them, would necessarily condition the unconditional and thus destroy it absolutely. The price of freedom, then, is absolute vulnerability to the other, to whatever or whoever comes.

Sovereignty, therefore, must be conditioned. The sovereign must put up its guard. This is the case whether it is nation-state sovereignty or whether it is the free and sovereign critique of sovereignty or the sovereign defense against such sovereign attacks. Yet no matter how well the sovereign fortifies itself, conditions itself, against the other, it remains exposed to whatever and whoever comes. It is always possible that the sovereign be deposed, and not necessarily by an outside or foreign invader, but by a courtier, by one who would depose the sovereign *in the name* of the sovereign. This is not all bad, either, for an absolutely conditioned or absolutely immune sovereignty, an actualized or present sovereignty, would not be free. Such a sovereign would be always already decapitated, incapable of self-determination and auto-critique. An absolutely conditioned sovereignty, one absolutely protected against whatever or whoever comes, would be an absolutely impotent sovereignty, incapable of either deciding or enforcing its decisions. It would be a sovereignty deposed in itself, unable either to attack or defend itself, whether in its own name or in the name of any other. *In any name, in name only.*

This double bind, this aporia—the heterogeneity and indissociability of unconditional and conditional sovereignty—cannot be relieved; it cannot be absolved. Rather, it is constitutive of sovereignty and thus what defines sovereignty as *im*possible. Hence, the impossibility of sovereignty is not an accident that befalls sovereignty, nor does it mean that sovereignty does not happen, that sovereign decisions are not made. On the contrary, impossibility marks sovereignty's only possibility; indeed, that sovereignty is impossible is necessary in order that there be the possibility of "the sovereignty that touches a *unique* place in the world—today, here now."[24] Sovereignty is only ever the promise of sovereignty. *As if* it were possible.

What conclusion can be drawn from this? There cannot be a limit at which language touches itself beyond presupposition. Were language ever to touch itself at its proper limit, and thus to touch itself *in itself*, there would no longer be language, or anything else. Agamben's dream of the abolition of the *as* and of the absolute unity of signifier and signified in a now without temporalization, in a messianic present, is the dream of an absolute sovereignty. It is only the most recent articulation of an ontotheology that misunderstands the aporia of temporalization, for as the solution of the aporetic structure of *chronos, kairos* names the absolute immunity from whatever comes. Without exposure to the other and to the future, which is also exposure of and to the *as* and the *as if,* nothing happens: "Without autoimmunity, with absolute immunity, nothing would ever happen or arrive; we would no longer wait, await, or expect, no longer expect one another or expect any event" (Derrida, *Rogues,* 152).

Notes

For their incisive and timely comments on this essay I thank Galen Brokaw, Stephen D. Gingerich, and Martin Hägglund.

1   See Jacques Derrida, *Rogues: Two Essays on Reason,* trans. Pascale-Anne Brault and Michael Naas (Stanford, CA: Stanford University Press, 2005), 24. Subsequent citations are given parenthetically by page number in the text.

2   See Giorgio Agamben, *Language and Death: The Place of Negativity,* trans. Karen Pinkus and Michael Hardt (Minneapolis: University of Minnesota Press, 1991), 39; *Homo Sacer: Sovereign Power and Bare Life,* trans. Daniel Heller-Roazen (Stanford, CA: Stanford University Press, 1998), 57, 64; *Potentialities: Collected Essays in Philosophy,* trans. Daniel Heller-Roazen (Stanford, CA: Stanford University Press, 1999), 205–19; *Remnants of Auschwitz: The Witness and the Archive,* trans. Daniel Heller-Roazen (New York: Zone, 1999), 130. Subsequent citations of these texts are given parenthetically by page number in the text.

3   Giorgio Agamben, *The Time That Remains: A Commentary on the Letter to the Romans,* trans. Patricia Dailey (Stanford, CA: Stanford University Press, 2005), 103. Subsequent citations are given parenthetically by page number in the text.

4   Agamben's assertion of the opposition between "pure philosophical presentation" and "representation," and the possible solution of it, underscores the difference between his project and Derrida's, for Derrida deconstructed this opposition already in his remarkable reading of Husserl. See Derrida, *Speech and Phenomena,* trans. David B. Allison (Evanston, IL: Northwestern University Press, 1973), 52.

5   Aristotle, *Categories, On Interpretation, Prior Analytics,* trans. H. P. Cooke and Hugh Tredennick (Cambridge, MA: Harvard University Press, 2002 [original ed., 1938]), 1a1–2/13. Subsequent citations are given parenthetically by page number in the text.

6   Martin Heidegger, *Aristotle's Metaphysics θ 1–3: On the Essence and Actuality of Force,* trans. Walter Brogan and Peter Warnek (Bloomington: Indiana University Press, 1995), 61. Subsequent citations are given parenthetically by page number in the text. On the analogy of being in Aristotle, Heidegger, and Derrida, see Rodolphe Gasché, *The Tain of the Mirror: Derrida and the Philosophy of Reflection* (Cambridge, MA: Harvard University Press, 1986), 296–307.

7   Agamben quotes from Emile Benveniste, *Problems in General Linguistics,* trans. Mary Elizabeth Meek (Miami, FL: University of Miami Press, 1971), 219. Subsequent citations from Benveniste are given parenthetically by page number in the text.

8   This is also the meaning of revelation for Agamben: "The most original logical dimension at issue in revelation is therefore not that of meaningful speech but rather that of a voice that, without signifying anything, signifies signification itself" (*Potentialities*, 42).

9   There is nothing new about this problem, nor anything special, per Agamben's description, about Guillaume's solution. Kant, for one, understood the necessity of temporal unity and recursivity for representation and, as a consequence, for conceptualization. See Immanuel Kant, *Critique of Pure Reason*, trans. Paul Guyer and Allen W. Wood (Cambridge: Cambridge University Press, 1998), 230. For a discussion of schematism, time, and transcendental apperception, see David E. Johnson, "Kant's Dog," *Diacritics* 34.1 (Spring 2004): 19–39.

10 Jacques Derrida, *Margins of Philosophy*, trans. Alan Bass (Chicago: University of Chicago Press, 1982), 79. Subsequent citations are given parenthetically by page number in the text.

11 Agamben cites from Martin Heidegger, *Being and Time*, trans. John Macquarrie and Edward Robinson (New York: Harper and Row, 1962), 224/G179.

12 Jacques Derrida, *Positions*, trans. Alan Bass (Chicago: University of Chicago Press, 1981 [French original, 1972]), 40–41. Subsequent citations are given parenthetically by page number in the text.

13 See also Derrida, *Positions*, 77–78. For an example of reading Hegel otherwise, see Jean-Luc Nancy, *Hegel: The Restlessness of the Negative*, trans. Jason Smith and Steven Miller (Minneapolis: University of Minnesota Press, 2002).

14 G. W. F. Hegel, *Philosophy of Nature*, trans. A. V. Miller (Oxford: Oxford University Press, 1970), §257 *Zusatz*/34.

15 Martin Hägglund, "The Necessity of Discrimination: Disjoining Derrida and Levinas," *Diacritics* 34.1 (2004): 40–71; here 42. Subsequent citations are given parenthetically by page number in the text.

16 Derrida uses the phrase "heterogeneous and indissociable" (and variants) more recently to describe the aporetic relation of unconditional and conditional hospitality as well as the relation between law and justice. See Derrida, *Of Hospitality*, trans. Rachel Bowlby (Stanford, CA: Stanford University Press, 2000), 25–27, 79–81.

17 G. W. F. Hegel, *Phenomenology of Spirit*, trans. A. V. Miller (Oxford: Oxford University Press, 1977), §801/487.

18 G. W. F. Hegel, *Philosophy of Mind*, trans. William Wallace and A. V. Miller (Oxford: Oxford University Press, 1971), §399*Zusatz*/72–73. Subsequent citations are given parenthetically by page number in the text.

19 This passage is not often cited, and when it is, as for instance by Gasché, it is deployed to recall the nonontological, nonexistential "status" of *différance*; see Gasché, *Tain*, 149.

20 Among other texts, see Jacques Derrida, *Demeure: Fiction and Testimony* (2000); "The University without Condition" (2002); *The Other Heading* (1992); *Rogues* (2005). On the structure of the "to come" and the necessary opening to the future, see Hägglund, "The Necessity of Discrimination."

21 Aristotle, *De Anima*, trans. J. A. Smith, *The Basic Works of Aristotle*, ed. Richard McKeon (New York: Random House, 1941), 413B5/557. Subsequent citations are given parenthetically by page number in the text.

22 For a reading of touch and touching that takes Aristotle's *De Anima* as a point of depar-

ture, see Derrida, *On Touching—Jean-Luc Nancy*, trans. Christine Irizarry (Stanford, CA: Stanford University Press, 2005).

23 Derrida, "The University without Condition," *Without Alibi*, trans. Peggy Kamuf (Stanford, CA: Stanford University Press, 2002), 206.

24 Jacques Derrida, "Provocation: Forewords," in Derrida, *Without Alibi*, xxii.

David L. Clark

Bereft: Derrida's Memory and the Spirit
of Friendship

> If you press me to say why I loved him, I feel that it can
> only be expressed by replying: "Because it was him:
> because it was me."
> —Michel de Montaigne, *On Affectionate Relationships*

At the point of assembling the "four guiding threads" with which the argument of *Of Spirit: Heidegger and the Question* will be knitted, Jacques Derrida pauses to recall some of the felicitous intellectual circumstances and personal affiliations out of which his book arose.[1] Why reconstruct this somewhat circuitous path leading to the book's ostensible beginnings? For Derrida there are debts to be acknowledged, thanks to be given, and above all friendships to be affirmed, although it is not until the book's second chapter that he chooses to speak of these things in so many words. A faint but discernible genealogy or perhaps "destinterrancy"[2] for *Of Spirit* thereby emerges, with Derrida tracing his thoughts to a scene which, if not primal in nature, is important enough not to be relegated to the book's prefatory matter (where dedications are more usually made), but delayed until its argument can be more fully marshaled. The suggestion is that the argument and the acknowledgments are con-

South Atlantic Quarterly 106:2, Spring 2007
DOI 10.1215/00382876-2006-025   © 2007 Duke University Press

nected in unusually significant ways. According to Derrida's telling, at least three colloquies, staged in three overdetermined locations in the history of his reception—France, England, America—pace *Of Spirit*'s wayward and bilingual development. Published as the edited (and translated) transcript of a lecture delivered at the closing session of "a conference organized by the *Collège international de philosophie* in Paris, entitled 'Heidegger: Open Questions'" (*OS*, vii), *Of Spirit* reproduces "remarks" delivered at an earlier colloquia—"another conference on Heidegger," Derrida tells us, this one "at the University of Essex," organized by David Farrell Krell (*OS*, 8). But those comments themselves required "preparation," he remembers, and it is the scene of that labor to which he finally turns, with gratitude. At least "four threads" in Martin Heidegger call for rigorous consideration, he repeats: "the privilege of the *Fragen*," "the essence of technology," "the discourse of animality," and "the thinking of *epochality*" (*OS*, 12). Together, these "motifs of worry," as he elsewhere characterizes them,[3] his language registering a certain concernful identification with Heidegger, together these filaments of thought and feeling point to "a Heideggerian thinking that is multiple and that, for a long time to come, will remain provocative, enigmatic, still to be read" ("HP," 183, 182). What led him to these open-ended considerations, he admits in a subsequent interview, "goes back a long way" ("HP," 183), leaving it unclear whether the source he evokes is remote in time or located at some unknown psychic depth. But in *Of Spirit* he traces their initial articulation to a remarkably modest setting—not a scholarly symposium, not as such, but an informal "conversation" that he held in the United States with a small group of familiars—the *philia* of philosophy and the philosophy of *philia* being concepts and phenomena that he more than anyone has taught us to respect and to interrogate. We will not stray far from that lesson here. "I held at Yale a sort of private seminar with some American friends" (*OS*, 8), he recalls, before graciously remembering their names. It is during the course of "replying to their questions or suggestions" that Derrida reiterates the importance of the unforeseen other that will form the interpretive horizon of his subsequent work on Heidegger, work that culminated—without being completed—in the publication of *Of Spirit*. In the company of his friends, and unfolding his sentence with great care, he confides, "I tried to define what appeared to me to be left hanging, uncertain, still in movement and therefore, for me at least, *yet to come* in Heidegger's text" (*OS*, 8).

Like a dear one whose loss is ambivalently yet keenly felt, the *arrivant* in Heidegger overtakes Derrida, and it does so in the shape of something from which he finds he cannot turn away, even if he is unable and unwilling to grasp it either. Heidegger's archive, which for Derrida is neither a single thing nor self-contained, is for this reason "unbearable and fascinating" ("HP," 182), as he remarks, speaking again in an affective register that more closely resembles the rhetoric of love and loss than the discourse of philosophical history. In the *tableau vivant* that Derrida briefly stages in *Of Spirit*, he remembers giving the *arrivant* the opportunity to come, and to be heard, even if what arrives and what is being said leaves him to this day "actively perplexed" ("HP," 183). The fact that he calls attention to the specific time and place in which he affirms this ghostlike "appearance," deeply uncertain as its self-showing nevertheless is, would seem to suggest that the timing is important. What is the estimated time of arrival of the Heideggerian *arrivant*, we might ask? Can one ever know with confidence where and from where it will come, to whom or for whom? Is *Of Spirit* any more that place than the seminar in New Haven where Derrida dreams of the book's beginnings, or of one of its beginnings?

In a single paragraph, *Of Spirit* joins the aloofness of an incalculable future *to* a remembrance of things past, even as it brings the distant summons of the *arrivant* into proximity with a scene of conviviality and scholarly sociality. Among close friends something far away comes; in memory of the intimacy those friends afforded me, Derrida suggests, I found myself promised to the future. What does this gathering together of nearness and farness say about Derrida's difficult colloquy with Heidegger? Elsewhere Derrida associates the dislocation of thinkers and thought with the very nature of intellectual comradeship: "What holds me here in life holds first of all in friendship," Derrida writes, referring to another symposium, this one in Cerisy, "by the grace of friendship of thought, of a friendship itself to be thought."[4] A friendship of thought, at once unexpected—hence full of grace—and as yet, perhaps forever, "un-*gedacht*": the wager of this essay is that Derrida's work offers up a language with which to reconsider his writing about and thinking with Heidegger as a posthumous gift of *l'amitié*, a friendship *without* friendship that is characterized by interruption, asymmetry, and, above all, unrequited generosity. "Posthumous gift" is in fact the evocative way in which Maurice Blanchot describes his friendship with Michel Foucault, in a text whose analysis forms the culminating argument of Derrida's *Politics of Friendship*. "In bearing witness to a work demanding study (unprejudiced reading) rather than praise," Blanchot says, "I believe

I am remaining faithful, however awkwardly, to the intellectual friendship that his death, so painful to me, today allows me to declare to him . . . '*Oh my friends, there is no friend.*'"[5] What I want to suggest is that Derrida encounters Heidegger belatedly and under the aegis of an analogously radicalized notion of philosophical fraternity, in which the conventional meanings of *l'amitié* are all but nullified; friendship is here about promising to do justice to the other and expecting nothing—no friendship—in return, rather than a condition of reciprocality and nurturing familiarity. This reframing of the work done in texts like *Of Spirit* will help us understand why, in an intellectual environment of sometimes hyperbolic certainty about the German philosopher and his legacy, a certainty matched, perhaps, only by a similarly dreamy confidence about what to do with Marx (Marx and Heidegger—such apparently different sorts of ghosts for the Right and the Left, respectively, to put to rest, to have *done* with, but with the same vehemence, the same lack of hospitality and friendship, the same sureness about who the "enemy" is, and thus who is the "friend"),[6] Derrida insists that nothing about Heidegger's thought is assured in advance, not even, it seems, the experience of being promised to a future of readings. Hence the marked tentativeness with which he warily approaches the memory of what happened in class on that day in New Haven: "I tried to define what appeared to me to be left hanging, uncertain, still in movement and therefore, for me at least, *yet to come* in Heidegger's text." "For me at least": it will take a great deal to unpack what Derrida leaves "hanging, uncertain," and "still in movement" in this inconspicuous turn of phrase. But for now we should note that conjectural steps around ambiguous forms of knowledge characterize these early moments in the prehistory of *Of Spirit*; the old school setting confirms that we have been returned to the unforgettable condition that Deborah P. Britzman evocatively calls "theory kindergarten," a place of immemorial beginnings and unusually powerful psychic investments whose withdrawal from thought sets us on the path of education even as it marks its irrevocable limits.[7] Derrida rightly treats the object of his recollections as if their evidentiary status were in question, both to his fellow seminarists and even to himself. In the end, is it Derrida's memory or that which he "tried to define" that is "left hanging [and] uncertain"? Nothing in his sentences lets us decide one way or the other. Can he even be certain of this approaching uncertainty in Heidegger's text? Far from a *fait accompli*, what he recalls is at best an *attempt*—"I tried to define," he says—at specifying something "still in movement" in Heidegger's writings, an undertaking whose success he is reluctant to claim even in retrospect. Derrida is careful not to speak too quickly for others (of the other), not without certain caveats. He does not presume that his "friends" will have had the same uncanny encounter with the *arrivant* that he discerned or thought he discerned coming out of the experience of the seminar.

The apprehension of the *arrivant* would never be assured, not without transforming the "yet to come" into one Heideggerian theme or question (like *"Dasein"* or *"die Seinsfrage"*) among others. But is the chance of that transformation ever absolutely preventable? How to seal up the radical idiomaticity of the "yet to come" *for* Derrida from the becoming-general of its conceptuality, a conceptuality that would thereby become a pedagogical theme, the repeatable subject matter or assigned question? For the "yet to come" to remain as absolutely uncertain as Derrida uncertainly claims, it must be "yet to come" to "Heidegger," or to a certain teaching and reading of "Heidegger," as well. The secret of the "yet to come" would here need to be understood as something other than a privation, as Derrida's qualification—"sort of private"—faintly suggests. One wonders if there could be a "seminar," an event-like gathering involving contingent questions and replies worthy of those names, if it were not for this secrecy, this withdrawal from thought. As Thomas Dutoit suggests, "What Derrida teaches is that without an unteachable we cannot teach and are not teachers."[8] How then to teach *that*? How to orient thinking in the classroom toward the (utopic) other, before which the classroom is nevertheless situated, and in whose memory it is always held? In the classroom of permanent parabasis in which the lesson is the "yet to come," there can be no overcoming this resistance to teaching, since teaching is itself this resistance, this self-secrecy at the heart of pedagogical disclosure. Kant is exemplary for Derrida as a philosopher who wrestled with these paradoxes, a philosopher who hated secrecy and called for the publicity of reason, but who also grasped the importance of respecting the thought that one withholds from others and that which withholds itself from thought.

Derrida's lesson is that he cannot respond to the *arrivant* in another's writings without his own work being exposed to something analogously futural, no more, as he says in his commemorative essay on Louis Marin, than he can write a work *about* mourning that is not also a work *of* mourning. What is unstable or "uncertain" in Heidegger is so *"for me* at least," he notes, his inconspicuous qualification signaling, among other things, that his thinking not only welcomes the "yet to come," it also in some sense interiorizes it, makes it his own, with all the terrific ambiguities, not to say unexpected indignities, that attend such incorporative labor. What feels at first like a haunting of Heidegger's "text," as he indeed puts it, the singular noun seeming for a moment to localize the *arrivant* with more precision than it can possibly have, is a complication and an acceding to thought that troubles and inhabits Derrida's writing as well. The "yet to come" is a wavering alterity that is available to his thinking but also part of that thinking, "for me at least" here marking the intimacy of the relationship Derrida here shares with Heidegger, even the privacy and singularity of his receptivity to him.[9]

The "for me" registers not possession, much less self-possession, as it does sometimes in Hegel, but the trial, exposure, and *surprise* of the encounter with that which remains difficult because unthought in Heidegger. In Derrida's allegory of reading, Heidegger's text, and in particular that which remains "in movement" in it, is a problem and an opening to thought that uncertainly interpellates him into a condition of permanent *extemporization*. Derrida responds to Heidegger, *engages* him, but his pledge to his text and to his future is nakedly "out there," as it were, because it is made without the expectation of anything like a definitive answer, without even recognizing from where or to where he makes his pledge or addresses the other that comes. "For me at least" affirms this condition of having acceded to a certain isolation, liability, contingency, and asymmetry vis-à-vis the other text; it means reading Heidegger is a "*salut* without return."[10] The phrase nicely captures Derrida's association of reading with uneconomizable imperilment and finitude. But is there any other kind of reading? Wouldn't reading that wasn't always also a "*salut* without return" be the death of reading, or the reduction of reading to a kind of decoding without remainder? As Derrida says, this greeting before the expectation of an answer "signs the very breathing of the dialogue" ("R," 140).

The "for me at least" remembers the concomitantly singular nature of Derrida's oath to continue to bear witness not only to Heidegger's text but also, as important, to intellectual relationships—to legacies, philosophical histories, interpretive communities, and individual readings, assuming these terms name discrete things—that respond and that continue to respond, "for essential reasons," to its peculiarly heterogeneous and aleatory character. One must do justice to Heidegger's text, yes, but "before" that happens one must already have promised oneself to justice—to reading for the sake of the other *and* for the sake of reading otherwise. The "me" of "for me at least" quietly remembers this pledge *to* reading—to the mortal one who reads—that limns every particular reading. To be this reader, to live on and even to flourish in the wake of these writings, one must effectively be the subject presumed *not* to know, the subject who cultivates a "passion for non-knowledge," as Derrida says in another context.[11] We would then need to consider this turn of phrase, this *turning*, in terms of an *epoché*, an inhibition or bracketing, a modest withdrawal and respectful sacrifice or desertification, a "suspension of certainty" that Derrida identifies as elemental to the work of testimony, witnessing, and prayer—the irony being that it is Heidegger who argues "with force and radicality the assertion that belief *in general* has no place in the experience or the act of thinking *in general*."[12] Beyond or before any constative knowledge *of* Heidegger, there is a pledge, a bare affirmation and expectation: "I promise truth and ask the other to believe the other that I am, there where I am the only one able to bear witness and where the order of proof or of intuition will never be reducible to or homogeneous with the elementary trust, the 'good faith' that is promised or demanded" ("F," 63). Perhaps the subtlest autobiographical reference of Derrida's "me" and "for me at least" can be found here, his affectation of a certain modesty and solitude signaling not self-assertion (in the mode of falsely modest self-effacement) but rather a kind of reserve, a passivity-before or giving-over-to the other that for obvious reasons Derrida cannot and will not presume is the same for any other. In the shadow of the "yet to come," we could say, Derrida sequesters himself, slightly contracts himself, this, in the name of an analogous reserve in Heidegger's text, the abyss of possibilities that call for a hearing even as they recede from sight, from the theoria of vision. In this gesture of hospitality, not unrelated to the "state of being drained" or "without force," that Derrida explores (in memory of Marin), we sense the importance of a certain cordiality toward reading, not in narcissistic and self-confirming reclusiveness but with others and exposed to otherness. The phrase names, in other words, the burden of a complex fidelity—rather than fealty—to Heidegger's text, even a kind of "friendship" with it. At this very moment in this work where I am, Derrida in effect says: "'I am addressing you, and I commit myself, in this language here; listen how I speak in my language, me, and you can speak to me in your language.'"[13]

Looking back, Derrida declares that it was always his intent, from that day in New Haven, to resist calls for Heidegger's summary arrest, and instead to find ways to respond to Heidegger's endless insurgency, all those elements in his texts which threaten to rise up unexpectedly and from who knows where. "What he leaves us is . . . the gift of an ordeal, the summons to a work of reading, historical interpretation, ethico-political reflection, an interminable analysis."[14] Derrida says this of his friend, de Man, in the name of friendship; could the same receptivity to the burden and the possibility of the future be claimed for Heidegger? A responsible engagement with the German philosopher's work means reckoning not only with what is imagined to be publicly known and settled about him—his political assignations, for example, or his ethical failures, what he said or did not say, and when, not to mention all the various paths marking his turn to "the worst"—but also with what remains irreducibly private about his texts, all that is held there in reserve, withdrawn in some instances even from his own thought, or from the thought that Heidegger might have signed with his name. In reading Heidegger otherwise, Derrida no doubt takes his cue from the magister, who, it should be remembered, distinguished between two ways of responding to another thinker. As he argues in *What Is Called Thinking?* one can proceed contrarily with respect to the other, whether through critique or polemic; or one can proceed by "going to their encounter," what David Wood usefully characterizes as "entering, or trying to approach, the space of the other's relation to alterity."[15] It is this hospitality to the other thinker that Derrida brings to Heidegger, although it should be noted that for him there is no generosity that is not contaminated by a certain hostility, no welcome of or "going to" the other without the allergic reassertion of the same.

Heidegger troubles Derrida in the manner of a ghost: "The concept of the other in the same . . . the completely other, dead, living in me."[16] A ghostly friend? In all rigor, is there any other? In the presence of his intimates, to whom he has patiently listened and replied, Derrida calls for another kind of audition and response: who could say that the aptness for and giving over to Heidegger that he quietly claims for himself is entirely different from the teachability his self-described friends demonstrate toward him, or he toward them? In a richly detailed footnote in *Envois*, Derrida speaks of his relationship with Heidegger as one that is under constant scrutiny: "What will he do with the ghost or Geist of Martin?" unnamed others ask, perhaps not altogether generously, as if in expectation of either a confirmation of an open secret, or of the disclosure of some hitherto closeted truth between men. It cannot be an accident that Derrida explores this question on the margins of a text that is otherwise almost entirely taken up with letters between a philosopher—who signs his name "J.D."—and a lover whose name is never spoken, letters that wax passionate about a relationship that is absolutely singular in its sentiments, everydayness, hopes, and fears, at the same time that it is available for all to read. *Envois* at once archives and shares the secrets of these lovers. Because Heidegger's writings are so often the implied philosophical referent of these *billets-doux*, it is hard not to think that he is the obscure object of their author's desire—that they are love letters for and to "Heidegger." Playful though he was said to be in those days, Derrida will not play this particular "truth" game and offer up a simple answer to the questions about his relationship with Heidegger. He will not accept the charge that he is simply possessed or seduced by the man. But neither will he phobically disavow him: "All this must not lead you to believe that no telephonic communication links me to Heidegger's ghost as to more than one other. Quite the contrary, the network of my hookups . . . is on the burdensome side, and more than one switchboard is necessary in order to digest the overload. It is simply . . . that my private relation with Martin does not go through the same exchange."[17] The push and pull of this complex account is worth remarking, as is its emphasis on "speaking" *to* Heidegger rather than *of* him,[18] not least because these features register a relationship with the dead that Derrida ordinarily reserves for intimate acquaintances, for those he might have called his contemporaries. In the wake of Jean-François Lyotard's death, for example, he speaks of the importance of turning both toward and away from the one who speaks: "A double injunction, then, contradictory and unforgiving. How to leave him alone without abandoning him?" (*WM*, 225). This is the question that Derrida asks of himself in the presence of Heidegger, in opposition to those who would instead ask how he could stay with him without thereby in some sense *becoming* him. Derrida calls for a kind of loving patience and for a certain slow reading, a labor of deliberation at odds with the confessional impulses and the commitment to speediness that the latest age of telecommunication otherwise encourages and demands—especially around the work of mourning. Derrida's encounter with Heidegger is in plain sight, he says, but for that no less obscure or interminable: "There are witnesses and a postal archive of the thing," he writes; "I call upon these witnesses (these way stations between Heidegger and myself) to make themselves known" (*E*, 21).

Derrida's language suggests that his kinship with Heidegger is at once "private" *and* available to be read, indeed, requiring a certain supplementary verification by go-betweens. Although Derrida does not quite say it this way, not yet, he calls here for friends to testify to a friendship, and for intimates to affirm the burdensome closeness he shares with this aloof likeness of Heidegger. To the question "[What will] he do with the ghost or Geist of Martin?" Derrida offers up some questions of his own (these, from *Politics of Friendship*): "Why would love be only the ardent force of attraction tending toward fusion, union and identification? Why would the infinite distance which opens respect up, and which Kant wished to limit by love, not open love up as well?" (*PF*, 255). "Martin" is interiorized by Derrida in the manner that a dead friend might be interiorized, even cherished, but this inwardness is also a condition of exposure, because, as Derrida's telephonic rhetoric insists, it is circulated through already existing and still unfolding networks, some of them profoundly obscure rather than obscurantist. As fast, efficient, or direct as some of those telecommunication providers claim to be, Derrida insists, there is always a delay or lag, in which the potential for interference, dropped or missed calls, and other "performative" infelicities looms large. Whatever "Martin" is *for* Derrida, he is not reducible to these philosophical exchanges, the philosopher's phrasing puts to us; but he is not separate from them either. Derrida incorporates Heidegger, to be sure; he readily admits to having a "private relation" with the man and his thinking; others will be in a position to make analogous claims and will have witnessed what happened between Derrida and Heidegger, even if they perhaps did not fully understand it. Yet what he or they interiorize is in excess of any inwardizing or purely "private" memory, individual or collective. A loving memory might remember this cohabitation of inwardness and uncontainability, this siting of the expanse lying at the heart of the closeness that the philosopher shares with his ghostly familiar. That the "yet to come" in Heidegger is yet to come "for me at least" figures forth this strange convocation of privacy and publicity in which the assertion of oneself is also the affirmation of the other. As Derrida argues in a discussion of Augustine, the arduous indeterminacy of friendship after the death of the friend is the expression of this very question: "Do you desire to survive for yourself *or* for the person whom you are mourning, from the moment the two of you are as one?" (*PF*, 187; emphasis mine).

There was something about being in the presence of intimates that encouraged Derrida to celebrate his treatment of Heidegger's "text" not as a closed book but as a kind of philosophical postcard, or perhaps as "the remainders of a recently burned correspondence" (*E*, 3), as he describes his radically experimental writing in *Envois*. Heidegger is not likely to have approved; as Derrida notes, the philosopher "would doubtless see in the postal determination a premature imposition of *tekhnē* and therefore of metaphysics" (*E*, 65). Strictly speaking, for Heidegger, the sending of Being demands a much more elevated rhetoric. But what about other kinds of transmissions, those involving something otherwise than Being? As Derrida suggests, what is subversive about the idea of postcards or fragmentary letters is that they become "found" texts at the moment they are "lost." While they remain in circulation, they are "open for anyone to read," rather than legible only to the appointed addressees, whether the keepers of the archive, or the archons who claim to mediate a philosopher's texts, who tell us, for example, to forget him, or who reduce reading him to playing the roles of either the "prosecution" or the "defence" (*PF*, 183). The scandal of the postcard is the scandal of *écriture*: as he explains, what makes the postcard or "found" text troublesome is its potential indifference to such regulatory regimes, its contingent exposure to a proliferation of readings, none of them intended or otherwise determined in advance: in Hillis Miller's formulation, "if an example either happens to fall under my eye . . . I can magically make myself or am magically made into its recipient."[19] Just so with Heidegger, whose "text"—Derrida does not say "work"—momentarily passes before his gaze *as if* he were the intimate addressee (we recall here what Derrida calls "the deconstructive ferment" and the virtualizing effect of the Kantian *als ob*),[20] as if Heidegger's writings were available to being read otherwise—for example, as missives that were en route rather than as having definitely arrived. Derrida's gamble: to read a range of texts, from the *Rectorship Address* to the *Gespräch* with Trakl, as postcards "from" Heidegger, but stamped, as it were, either "Sender Unknown" or "No Such Address."

Something "uncertain" in Heidegger troubled and activated Derrida, setting him on the path of which *Of Spirit* is said to be the working result. Yet depending on how much attention we pay to Derrida's little phrase "for me at least," the appearing of this appearance to him (and thus possibly to him alone) can suddenly feel oddly inward, isolating, and even hallucinatory because it lacks the firm corroboration of others. In *Envois* Derrida calls upon "witnesses . . . to make themselves known," whereas in the face of the "yet to come" in the classroom memory in *Of Spirit*, Derrida is somewhat more circumspect. The *arrivant*: could its coming have gone unwitnessed? Others in the shape of intimates were unquestionably nearby, yet may have remained at a distance from the phenomenon whose very name, after all, signifies a kind of infinite distance. Although formally occupying the position of witness (his "American friends" were present, in that place, at that time; their names are duly recorded in an accompanying endnote), Derrida gently refuses them that validating role, momentarily holding it away from them without making it inaccessible to them either. Why does he genially if equivocally claim this solitude? In a late essay written in memory of Paul Celan, for example, he suggests that "bearing witness must not essentially consist in proving, in confirming a knowledge, in ensuring a theoretical certitude, a determinant judgment. It can only appeal to an act of faith" ("R," 79). "Bearing witness, if there is such a thing" ("R," 78), he argues, is event-like in nature, at root a pledge or a promise that something happened *to me and before me.* "What distinguishes an act of bearing witness from the simple transmission of knowledge, from simple information, from the simple statement or mere demonstration of a proven theoretical truth, is that in it someone *engages* himself with regard to someone else, by an oath that is at least implicit. The witness *promises* to say or to manifest something to an other, his addressee; a truth, a sense that was or is in some way present to him as a unique and irreplaceable witness" ("R," 82). The *for me* of witnessing is thus not privative in kind but precisely the secret source of a provocation and of an opening toward others—"secret" here signifying the inaccessible singularity (but not indivisibility) of the witness, and of the moment of witnessing. "For me at least" marks the irreducible difference between the witness and those who are called upon to witness witnessing, to hear his or her testimony, which is to say those who are summoned to witness something to which, precisely, they cannot testify, namely that which appeared *to* the other (witness) *as* other. Witnesses to witnessing cannot be found, not as such, but this interdiction in no way prohibits witnesses from witnessing; as Derrida says, the "prohibition imposed on bearing witness" occurs "in the very place where one has to go on appealing to it" ("R," 91).

Before promising others, there is a promise to the other who is oneself, and that in truth is the promise *of* the other insofar as the appeal to belief is not, as Derrida notes, "accessible to the order of thought" ("R," 84). Without this minimal difference, the *retrait* of the *trait,* so to speak, it would be hard to understand how any form of address, and thus communication, teaching, writing, or reading, could happen at all. The "yet to come" in Heidegger may well appear to others, and Derrida no doubt hopes, in the end, that it indeed does (why else hold seminars or write books about Heidegger?), but his point here is that whatever the future holds for his "text," whatever particular courses his legacies take, however his thinking and writing continue to be disseminated, understood, and misunderstood, however Heidegger is perjured or possibilized, in any case, whatever is yet to come in the name of Heidegger, it *begins* with a promise; not so much a knowledge or a form of knowledge about him, although these forms of apprehension remain, on their own terms, important, but a confession of a certain *faith* in knowledge, delicate as it is ineradicable, idiomatic but therefore also always calling for translation. The promise of Heidegger, the opening to thought to which Derrida responds, as if answering a call from nowhere, induces a certain form of faith or perhaps countersignature in the other. "To this act of language, to this 'performative' of testimony and declaration, the only possible response, in the night of faith, is another 'performative' that consists in saying or testing out, sometimes without even saying it, 'I believe you'" ("R," 83), Derrida writes. Heidegger's text *as* a text appeals to belief, which can of course be embraced or profaned, but in each case, as Derrida reminds us, we only confirm that performative's "invincibility." Is belief in general only a matter of "credulity or passivity before authority," as indeed Heidegger claims in his rigorist attempt to draw a bright line between acts of faith and the labor of thinking? Derrida's gamble is that there is a belief or receptivity to the other that is irreducible to thought and to the concept of consent. "For me at least" speaks to that susceptibility, that acquiescence toward the other that isn't thraldom or possession. The future of Heidegger, if there is to be one, starts by taking responsibility for it; but "for me at least" registers not a virile act of self-possession, but an accession to obligation, a pledge to accept the burden that one has already accepted by virtue of being "after" Heidegger, thinking and writing and holding seminars in his text's many wakes. Derrida says yes to Heidegger, accedes to what is yet to come in his text, regardless of whether or in what way he says yes or no to him.

If writing is treated as a sending whose origins, like its addressees, are enigmatic, and in which reading is figured as a chance encounter rather than an act of cognitive certainty, an interruption of something already in progress rather than the reception of a discrete message, who could hope to disentangle Derrida's receptivity to the interminable problems energizing Heidegger's text and the problems "themselves"? Whatever Heidegger's "text" is for Derrida, it is "for" him and him alone to the extent that Heidegger's interminability becomes a constitutive part of Derrida's text. What is "for" Derrida is thus also "for" others, because in memory of others. The friends to whom Derrida refers with such affection are an uncanny figure for the readers whose task it will always have been to "define" what appears "to be left hanging, uncertain, still in movement" in his work, as well as in Heidegger's, and, for that matter, in the writings of any thinker worthy of the name. For them, *at least*, we say again, since of course not all of Derrida's readers are as hospitable to his writing and ideas as those he describes as "friends." (Indeed, as "*American* friends"; "America *is* deconstruction" [*l'Amérique, mais* c'est *la deconstruction*], Derrida once wrote [*M*, 18], hyperbolically evoking the particularity and originality, not to mention the complex forcefulness with which his ideas were being taken up and worked through by thinkers in North America.) Unless we remember that the many futures that await Derrida and that have awaited him since forever necessarily include the chance of what he might call "the worst"—for example, the proclamation that there is no future for "Derrida" and that "Derrida," like "theory," "deconstruction," and "Heidegger," is dead. *Dead*, but not in the way Lacan says somewhere about the dead, whose problem, he points out, is that you "can't shut them up," but "dead" as a grotesque synonym for the putative inertness and illegibility and irrelevance of Derrida's ideas and influence. (In this symmetrically reversed scenario, "America is decidedly *not* deconstruction," not while "theory" is maligned there as a threat to homeland security or, as David Simpson has pointedly argued, as "a synonym for the other, the foreign, and for the foreign that threatens to take up residence within our borders, our classrooms.")[21] We sometimes forget that when Derrida remarks that the letter can always miss its destination and thus "suffer the fatal necessity of going astray" (*E*, 66), he also means that it sometimes really does get delivered, and therefore that the postal system is not wholly "uncertain, still in movement" but, in its own way, remarkably predictable and unwavering. In postal systems, as with intellectual legacies, the foreseen and the unforeseeable, like the "have been" and the "yet to come," activate and trouble each other as each other's other. Today, caught up as we are in the midst of a still-developing discursive environment that is inflected by Derrida's works and legacies, and harassed by valedictions forbidding mourning, it is difficult to determine how the thing is functioning, what either its ends or end is, and this is arguably especially the case when we are speaking of that strand of Derrida's text that is woven so discreetly with Heidegger's.

There are some who arrogate to themselves precisely this naively testimonial position, speaking with confidence from inside the system as if they were safely outside, as if the outside were not merely the inside's figure of its own outside, the fabled, inapparent, and much misunderstood *d'hors-texte*. Without the double possibility of Derrida's future being open-ended and foreclosed, the republic of letters devoted to his work would either be an absolutely totalitarian condition, in which no message—and no intellectual legacy—went astray, *or* an absolutely chaotic state, in which messages were not so much misdirected, read by who knows who, as impossible to discern *as* messages, as legible writing against a background of semiotic noise or static. Two forms of illegibility, two dreams of languagelessness, at once frame and threaten writing and reading. As we well know, Derrida's readers include those who read in the mode of not-reading; these are readers for whom his text is not in flux, in the way that Heidegger remained for Derrida and that he hopes will be the case for others going forward, but dead, quite dead.

Contrary to attempts to put an end to all that is "left hanging, uncertain, still in movement," both in Heidegger and in the "Heidegger" that is "for" Derrida, uneasily incorporated into the body of his work, Derrida's death makes the promise of his work not less but more pressing—if that were indeed possible. But what can "more" or "less" mean here? For what is this quantitative metaphor a metaphor, except to register the fact that the burden of responding to the call of Derrida's work is now both ours and not "ours," which is to say—in sadness—not only *only* ours, but also not in our possession, not while this work of interpellation remains, as it presumably always will, as futural as it is urgent? More than ever, today, we are abandoned to have conversations, write essays, and hold seminars, each of them more or less "private," each of them carried out in his name but without him being able to respond in person to his name, without even the hypothetical possibility of such a response. In that hush, a silence that is admittedly hard to hear amid the irrepressible sounding of his archive, we are *without* Derrida; we suffer a condition in which Derrida's text survives *sans* Derrida, this, without necessarily knowing, without ever having known, what it meant to have been *with* him either. *That* he was once alive is irrefutably a part of all who knew him and knew of him; *what* that meant, how to reckon with it, and thus with its loss, is much more obscure, and, I dare say, yet to come. In any case, mourning *happens*; this is in part what Derrida means by the "force of mourning"; the conventions and performativity of mourning-work, in their reiterative, autonomous, and automatic nature, allegorize this event-like kernel of *Trauerarbeit*; they are a "figure" in the radical sense that de Man gives the term. So the problem at hand is how one endures this force, how one survives its obscurities. As Jean-Michel Rabaté says, "In order to mourn you have to be sure that you are alive, and one is never sure that one is alive." "This is something that Derrida complicated for us," he adds.[22] Today, we have Derrida but in the mode of not-having him, and with that loss, as irrefutable as it is impossible to understand, the world is lost as well. Again Derrida gives us a language with which to think this disaster, even if we remain, as he said of himself, "uneducable about the wisdom of learning to die": "Death takes from us not only some particular life within the world . . . but, each time, without limit, someone through whom the world, and first of all our own world, will have opened up in a both finite and infinite—mortally infinite—way" (*WM*, 95). The definitional work Derrida remembers attempting in New Haven continues to this day, even if Derrida—no more than Heidegger—cannot speak to it and of it himself, cannot speak to it and of it in the precise manner that he recalls doing while he was alive, before his "American friends," namely in the mode of a "reply"—a "reply" that in its finitude awaited death.

When Derrida talked with his friends at Yale, the discussion will have happened before the horizon of that deathly silence and as a condition of the possibility of them speaking together at all. What was left "hanging, uncertain . . . [and] yet to come" among that circle of friends was not only something in "Heidegger's text" but also the demise of one or more of them; so closely overlapped are the two ways of thinking about the *arrivant* that it almost seems as if a textual predicament were a displaced name for death. Far from constituting a scene of communicative transparency or consensus, then, those gathered in New Haven were already pledged elsewhere and otherwise—because they were promised to the death of the other. Responding to their questions and suggestions, in friendship, Derrida and the seminarists spoke on the condition that the day would come in which he could not answer his friends, and, for that matter, in which some of those friends could not respond to him. This is not the same thing as saying that the death of the friend marks the end of friendship, a question put to us with particular forcefulness now, when, in *Of Spirit*, we read of Derrida's friendships after his death, when we read Derrida writing about friends in words that have survived him, and that speak "for" him in his terrible absence. Derrida's wager, consecrated at the moment that he names his American friends "friends," is that friendship survives the passing of the friend, albeit differently or otherwise, this, because it is *already* surviving that loss before the death "*actually* happens, as we say, in 'reality'" (*M*, 29). Not for nothing, but also in the name of a certain nothingness, does Derrida begin the funeral oration for his cherished acquaintance, "For a long time, for a very long time, I've feared having to say *Adieu* to Emmanuel Levinas" (*WM*, 200). In death, in the wake of death, one can say, as Derrida often did, remembering Montaigne, Aristotle, and Kant, among other philosophical intimates, "Oh my friends, there is no friend," which is in part to say that friendship remains, friendship *is* what remains, when the friend is gone, when there is no friend.[23] Friendship is irreducible to living together as friends, perhaps in the same way that education is irreducible to being together in a classroom. In both friendship and education, something dies, but something else lives on. The replies that Derrida gave, and that he recalls in *Of Spirit* as having given, *as* replies, not answers, still less *the* answer, but as irrepressibly contingent expressions of finitude, his, and others', were marked in advance by this muteness about which nothing can be said, and for which therefore there is only more, and yet more, to be said. Gayatri Spivak insists that it is too soon, *too soon*, to know how to mourn Derrida, not in spite but precisely because of the pressure to commit him to memory, whether with tenderness or with derision.[24] Too soon, it is true, but also too late, and never enough. "Speaking is impossible," Derrida says at the memorial for de Man, "but so too would be silence or absence or a refusal to share one's sadness" (*M*, xvi).

We recall Derrida's discussion of Montaigne's dream of perfect friendship as a fraternity of two souls who share secrets with each other and no one else (*PF*, 171–83). When Derrida says that his "private relation with Martin does not go through" readily available "exchange[s]," it is impossible not to think of the same kind of intimacy. Of Heidegger, but in the presence of his fellow seminarists, and as a sign of his *amitié*, Derrida repeats a vow that he makes to and about the work of another "American" friend at Yale: the pledge to "speak of the future, of what is bequeathed and promised to us by the work" (*M*, 19). As the commemorative essays in *The Work of Mourning* attest, Derrida most often remembers and mourns the dead friend in these terms; his fidelity to their memory, his respect for them, is expressed in the form of promising himself to the future of that friend's writing and thinking. With friendship, the future anterior is always already at work; whether dead or alive, the friend is experienced and remembered "as *having been* the one who . . . will have been" (*WM*, 156). Is this not what Derrida also says of Heidegger—remembered, even treasured, after a fashion, not only for all that was said and done, but also for "the yet to come" in what was left behind. To my knowledge, Derrida never describes himself as a friend to Heidegger, or of his writings, not in those words, although in the epilogue of *Politiques de l'amitié* he subsequently explores the question of the friend *in* Heidegger and in particular the puzzling reference, in *Being and Time*, to the "voice of the friend" that dwells within every *Dasein*.[25] We know that there is no book called *Memoires for Martin Heidegger* (unless of course it is entitled *Of Spirit*), and that Derrida was not one of those present at the Messkirch cemetery in Baden-Wurttemberg where, in 1976, Heidegger was interred. But could we therefore say definitively that he was not a friend, or that Heidegger did not, in the manner of friendship, make a claim on Derrida's life and thought, and evoke in him a certain passion, intellectual steadfastness, and magnanimity, without thereby simply overpowering him? That he did not *touch* Derrida and stir a kind of critical generosity in him? What would *Of Spirit* be if not a testament to a certain *amitié* and a certain *politiques de l'amitié*?

Could we then say that "friendship," if there is such a thing, did not in a fundamental way characterize his complicated relationship with the man's bodies of thought, with his writings and his legacies, or that "friendship" does not to this day name the uniquely configured distances and proximities, the multiplying partitions or boundaries, that both join and separate the two thinkers in a kind of endless colloquy—perhaps even in a "sort of private seminar" yet to come? Derrida never shies away from acknowledging the difficulties that marred and energized his friendships, including the silences, unspoken gestures, and "stormy discussion[s]" (*WM*, 81) by which they were characterized. Of Foucault, for example, Derrida recalls the "shadow that made us invisible to one another" and which came "to obscure" their friendship; but as he says, these lacunae are not so much regretful as "part of the story that I love like life itself" (*WM*, 80). Derrida and Heidegger probably never spoke together or communicated directly, but there is no guarantee that this missed encounter precluded at least one of them from being a friend or a kind of friend to the other. For who or what was Heidegger *to* Derrida?—a story yet to be told, or rather, one that is being told in "the postal archive of the thing," in *Of Spirit*, and in all the other writings entrusted to what Derrida calls "the place of this strange dative" (*M*, 33). (Another, but not unrelated question to consider: who was

Derrida *to* Heidegger? *"Ich freue mich, Herrn Derrida kennen zu lernen,"* Heidegger wrote to Lucien Braun in May 1973.[26] For whom did Derrida write if not Heidegger, or a certain "Heidegger"? Was he not the one to whom Heidegger wrote, his reader, yet to come?) Again, the question: of what or whom is Derrida speaking when he speaks of the Heidegger that is important and irrepressible, "for him at least"? If not something irreducibly obscure, "sort of private," and singular, joining them like secret sharers, sharers of a secret from each other and from themselves, does "friendship" also describe, after a fashion, the nature of the larger fraternal philosophical gathering of which Derrida and Heidegger are but one couple?

Heidegger and Derrida: friends? "Collaborators," yes, perhaps, and thus "friendly" in the manner of co-conspirators. A man who fraternized with the enemy. Is that what they wanted Derrida to say when asked about what he was doing "with the ghost or Geist of Martin"? Confess to a certain criminality? But were they friends in the sense that Derrida explores in his book on the phenomenon and the philosopheme and that he modeled with infinite variety in his relationships with the living and the dead, as he did with bodies of thought, both ancient and contemporary? Improbable, one might say; after all, there was no mutuality with Martin, no reciprocity of thinking or feeling of the sort that is often said to attest to friendship. Heidegger is not one of those intimates whom Derrida publicly mourns as friends who were members of "my 'generation.'" "For more than a half century, no rigorous philosopher has been able to avoid an 'explanation' with [*explication avec*] Heidegger" ("HP," 182), Derrida comments, as if to say that there is no saying no to Heidegger, not even saying no. So much then depends upon the explanation of the *avec* of this inescapable being-with. If in 1976 Heidegger could nevertheless be said to have "left" Derrida, he could not be said to have done so in the way that we see deeply regretted in remarks Derrida makes about friends such as Jean-François Lyotard, Gilles Deleuze, and Michel Foucault, each of whom were born and who died but a short time before Derrida, each of whom can more readily be described as belonging to a single generation from which one loss is experienced as the loss of all. With good reason, Derrida is instantly wary of the fraternizing homogeneity of the concept of belonging to a particular "generation," as Pascale-Anne Brault and Michael Naas point out.[27] But by thinking of "generation" otherwise, and thus of what constitutes being-together in its name, perhaps Heidegger and Derrida could be said to be coevals after all.

Still, as he says, and in a halting manner that registers the toll of loss on Derrida, "there comes a time, in the course of a generation, the gravity of which becomes for some, myself among them today, more and more palpable, when you reach an age, if you will, where more and more friends leave you, oftentimes younger than you, sometimes as young as a son or daughter" (*WM*, 188). And if the lost friend is the age of a son or daughter, then why not the age of a father, or a mother? Where does the generational divide lie where the work of mourning is concerned? Derrida is said to have described himself toward the end of his life as the last of his generation; could Heidegger be said in some spectral sense to have been the *first*? After all, when Derrida evokes the "yet to come" in Heidegger, he is affirming his irreducible precedence. With the other thinker who comes before, there could only ever be a friendship of the kind that never punctually takes place, a friendship that is therefore always yet to come. The pledge to Heidegger is a "*salut* without return," a promise or appeal made in a night of faith in which the future, including the future of the relationship between Heidegger and Derrida, is, for essential reasons, unknown.

We have not begun to consider the meanings of philosophical belatedness and precedence until we have explored the philosophemes of legacy, inheritance, and generation that structure the history of the relationship between thinkers. But one of the arguments I have been attempting here is that "friendship" offers a kind of conceptual lever, a *mochlos*, with which to think about that history and those relationships otherwise. Perhaps this explains why *Of Spirit* is so taken with scenes of colloquies of professors, both "real" and "fictional." Recall, for example, the way in which the book ends, with Derrida "imagining a scene between Heidegger and certain Christian theologians." In this *mise-en-abyme*, Derrida restages *Of Spirit*'s scrupulously close reading of Heidegger as an improvised conversation between contemporaries, as if to materialize a fantasy that the book has otherwise harbored—a dream of holding a seminar with Heidegger rather than awaiting the arrival of the "ghost or Geist of Martin." The affability and cordiality with which the philosopher and the theologians speak to one another is worth remarking, as is the peculiar way in which each tells the other that what the one claims is most foreign to the thinking of the other is in fact "what is most essential" (*OS*, 110). Each encounters the other by "going to their encounter" and thus "entering, or trying to approach, the space of the other's relation to alterity."[28] Fraternization happens not because friends share a secret among themselves and not with others, but because friends share an otherness that is a secret from themselves. The suggestion is that the first form of intimacy is in fact a displaced expression of the latter. Among friends, once again, this gathering together of nearness and farness, love and respect, affinity dwelling in the heart of difference. And since, as Derrida says, "I'm doing the questions and answers here" (*OS*, 111), one has to wonder in what ways each of the speakers is an avatar of himself, and how the scene rehearses a meeting with Heidegger that never took place and that has since then always taken place.

This imagined community of scholarly friends resonates with others in the book. In a remarkable endnote, for example, Derrida evokes the "fabulous European colloquium" in which "the greatest European minds met" (*OS*, 124n2). Among these acquaintances there is a familiarity and a certain minimal agreement that is nothing if not friendly: "In this imaginary symposium, in this invisible university, . . . they echo each other, discuss or translate the same admiring anguish: '*So* what is happening to us? *So*, what is happening to Europe?'" Derrida treats this colloquy of like-minded and rather close-minded spirits (Fichte, Valéry, Husserl, and so forth) with considerable irony and even disdain. Yet in all rigor could one say that his own work does not itself memorialize cognate gatherings composed of scholarly friends who were not necessarily present to each other, much less literally calling each other friends, as Derrida fondly recalls happening one day at Yale University, but, instead, "invisible" encounters of an other kind, gatherings that are not face to face (assuming for a moment that we know what that sort of intimacy means) but for all that are no less consequential, meetings in the name of friendship between, for example, those who never met in person but who nevertheless lived together (literally apart, yes, but notionally dwelling together, because in concert asking similar questions, having similar worries. As Derrida elsewhere notes, remembering that he is himself part of that "fabulous European colloquium": "Between 1919 and 1940, everyone was wondering—but are we not still wondering the same thing today?—'What is Europe to become?' And this was always translated as 'How to save the spirit?'" [*PH*, 185–86]). Does Derrida's work not then affirm the colloquia between the living and the dead, not to mention the living, the dead, and the yet to be born, the latter being but one way to think of the unthinkable, the "yet to come"? These are the friendships, one is tempted to say, not of flesh and blood, but, after a fashion, *of spirit*, relationships at once forged and violated in the name of the "difficult friendship" with philosophy (as Blanchot says of his cordiality with Levinas).[29] Do

Derrida's friends include not only those long dead and who never declared themselves to be friends to him? Do they include friendships with the yet to be born? I can hardly be alone in counting on that incalculable possibility, in which, surely, the future of theory after Derrida lies. Can one be a friend to someone one never knew, or with whom none of the sociality that is often associated with friendship happened? Derrida and Heidegger did not know each other, or at least never spoke; but perhaps the unspoken and that which goes without saying, themselves conventionally identified as markers of friendship, are also markers of unconventional friendships, of thinking of friendship otherwise and elsewhere. Perhaps it is more accurate to ask if there is friendship *without* these absences or whether it isn't precisely the suffering and nurturing of them? Certainly before the gathering of his intimates at Yale, and out of the to and fro of their colloquy, Derrida talks *as if* he were speaking of a lost friend, upon whose death, as he has often said, the last word must always be given, that is, if there is to be a future; "for me everything still remains to come and to be understood," he says, for example, in the aftermath of Sarah Kofman's death (*WM*, 170). So too with Heidegger, about whom he writes almost the same words, even if, strictly speaking, the relationship with the two thinkers and their respective bodies of thought could not have been more different. Whoever Heidegger was to Derrida, his text's uncertainties, its fugitive movements and suspended remainders, bind him to an incalculable debt and in this way promise him to a future. Heidegger's, yes, but inasmuch as "Heidegger" is "in" Derrida, insofar as "Heidegger" is "for" him, "for me at least," as he says, Derrida's future too. Together, in friendship, they are "yet to come."

Let us return to the text at hand and bring this seminar hurriedly to a close. The colloquy at Yale is a community of friends who have nothing in common, we could say, recalling a phrase from Alphonso Lingis.[10] In the accompanying endnote, cached amid supplemental commentaries that sometimes constitute essays unto themselves, Derrida graciously offers up the names of his fellow seminarists, then makes a solemn promise: "They were Thomas Keenan, Thomas Levine, Thomas Pepper, Andrzej Warminski . . . as well as Alex Garcia Düttmann," Derrida recalls. "I want to express here my gratitude to them," he writes; "this book is dedicated to them, . . . in memory of 'Schelling'" (*OS*, 117n3).

Gratitude, dedication, remembrance. Such gestures of acknowledgment and commemoration are of course a commonplace of scholarship. But as Derrida argues, the conventionality of our expressions of remembrance and indebtedness forms a kind of recognizable and repeatable placeholder for acts of singular responsibility. The named names remember the absolutely unique nature of each friend, even if the rhetorical setting of that remembrance threatens to carry off that singularity, obscuring it from sight. As Derrida asks: "How do we speak otherwise and without taking this risk? Without . . . generalizing what is most irreplaceable in it?" (*WM*, 58). That which is said with certain familiarity stands in for what is unfamiliar and difficult about the other to whom Derrida turns in gratitude. "*In memory of him*: these words cloud sight and thought," Derrida writes in "Mnemosyne," reminding us that what we call "memory" and what we claim to think and do in its name remains irreducibly obscure, confused, and confusing; this rather ordinary word that names the self's faculty of acquaintance with itself (and its principal means of self-propriation) remains for Derrida not only unthought but also, in some sense, *in the way* of thought, and never more so when the memory of an other is at hand. And when is memory not the memory of an other, which is to say, the memory of something or someone that remains an *alterity*, at once irreducibly obscure and uncertain? In memory we mourn, but the object of our mourning can never be ascertained with confidence. In a private seminar given in remembrance of his then recently dead wife, Caroline, Schelling himself argued that "the concept of memory is far too weak," pointedly reminding his auditors that the infirmity at hand lies not only in the capacity to remember—whose finitude we might imagine to be a given—but also in the philosophical language with which we struggle to understand that capacity.[31] In the spirit of Schelling, then, Derrida asks, "What is said, what is done, what is desired through these words: *in memory of . . . ?*" (*M*, 19).

On the margins of Derrida's text, thanks are given and a commitment to remembrance is made, each complexly performative actions that, among many other things, remind us that whatever else *Of Spirit* is, it is irreducible to neither theory nor critical practice. The dedication, like all dedications, performative utterances, promises, contracts, engagements, and founding or instituting acts, puts to us that the book is something else than (scholarly) work or perhaps that this work is simultaneously and in its entirety both work and something *other* than work. A *Trauerarbeit*, let us call it, since Derrida himself has just rendered his book as such, in memory of another, or in the name of an other. In one sentence, then, we find an expression of appreciation to the living and a promise of loyalty to the dead, even if the name of the dead is subjected to the prophylaxis of

Derrida's quotation marks, in a ghostly reminder of how *Geist* is sometimes treated in the Heideggerian texts that Derrida reads so attentively. It is not clear that one could rigorously distinguish between the two gestures of thanking and memorialization, of naming and the quotation of a name. The deliberate citation of the name of the dead and the just-as-deliberate naming of the names of the living make it seem *as if* such a distinction were possible and even necessary. Yet this dedication *to* others—who are alive—in remembrance *of* an other—who is long dead—raises many more questions than it answers. A felicitous debt is discharged, to be sure, of a kind that is familiarly pleasurable to all those who write and think, which is to say all those who write and think with others and for others. Yet this is hardly a settling of accounts, for no sooner has Derrida offered his thanks than he reopens the account, as it were, this, by promising the fruits of his considerable labor to someone else, mortgaging and committing not only himself *and* his American friends—"Derrida & Co.," let us call them—to a name, but also and more specifically to a fidelity *to* that name: a promise of faithfulness is made to "Schelling" that is of necessity analogous—in its interminability, in its performative pledge *to* the future—to the queer philosopheme that Derrida has just called, thinking of Heidegger, "the *yet to come.*" Once again, we see how "the *salut* without return signs the very breathing of dialogue" (*R*, 140). To dedicate a book to friends "in memory of 'Schelling'": these are words that are said with such solemn surety, yet nothing is less certain.

Why "Schelling"? An interminably complicated question. Roughly at the same time that Derrida was dedicating his book to the German philosopher, de Man was wryly counseling others to "forget about [him]," meaning, of course, that he was a thinker no one could afford to fail to remember. As de Man explained to an audience at Cornell, Schelling was one of those spirits "who messes up the works a great deal."[32] Indeed. But why Schelling, here, in a book on Heidegger, who, admittedly, was a very close reader of Schelling but is hardly the focus of Derrida's discussion? As John H. Smith notes, Schelling's masterwork, *Philosophical Inquiries into the Nature of Human Freedom*, and the *locus classicus* of Heidegger's memory of the German idealist's writing, is "referred to only obliquely by Derrida via Heidegger."[33] But oblique references, and relationships between thinkers and bodies of thought that are aslant and that happen through indirection, deferral, and displacement, are what we are attempting to discern here. There are occasions, as Derrida says several times, in which Heidegger's thinking is "literally Schellingian" (*OS*, 63, 106), so intimately acquainted is the one philosopher with the other. We wonder why Derrida presses the point the way that he does, as if incredulous at the haunting of the one thinker by the thoughts and by the very words of an other. This incorporation of the earlier philosopher's words, this ventriloquism of the dead, is not an instance of philosophical mesmerism, however, but instead marks those points in which Heidegger is both himself and other than himself—the very problem upon which *Of Spirit* is wagered. Peter Fenves smartly argues that Heidegger's difficulty with Schelling, and the reason why, eventually, he abandoned reading him, or abandoned reading him in a certain way, was, finally, that he wasn't Heidegger.[34] But it might also be said that in Schelling, Heidegger grasped that he wasn't altogether "Heidegger" either, and that his absorption of certain Schellingian concepts and phrases into the body of his work, both early and late, was a way of registering that mixed state of dispossession and accommodation. As Jean-Luc Nancy notes, Heidegger's disavowals of his predecessor hint symptomatically at a "secret, imperceptible, ontodicy."[35] In Schelling's presence, Heidegger is not himself, Derrida argues; but then in Heidegger's presence, or Derrida's, neither is Schelling, as anyone reading Heidegger's 1936 lectures on the *Freedom* essay or Derrida's essay on Schelling's *Of University Studies* quickly realizes. Is this chiasmus or intersection, this scene in which each philosopher is read through the other, and through the other's difference from himself, an oblique autobiographical reference to the complexity of Derrida's engagement with Heidegger? In what way is "Schelling" a figure for the "yet to come" in Heidegger, just as "Heidegger"—a certain "Heidegger," certain problems, questions, and openings to thought that "Heidegger's text" obscurely bequeaths to the future—remains a figure for the "yet to come" in Derrida?

The fact that Derrida unexpectedly dedicates *Of Spirit* "to the memory of 'Schelling'" would seem extremely suggestive in this regard, Derrida here locating himself in the still-churning wake of philosophical negotiations with, for example, the problem of "the demonic" and the question of "evil" going back at least as far as German idealism, if not long before. Heidegger mourns Schelling, finds himself caught up in "a movement in which an interiorizing idealization takes in itself or upon itself the body and voice of the other, the other's visage and person, ideally *and* quasi-literally devouring them" (*M*, 34). Heidegger eats his—Schelling's—words; in his vividly realized lectures on the German idealist's 1936 masterwork on the nature of human freedom, he offers, as Nancy remarks, "nothing other than a kind of continuous harmonic composition, where Heidegger's own discourse would create an incessant counterpoint to Schelling's, without making the matter explicit on its own, and without the latter's discourse being given a clear interpretation by that of the former."[36] Does an analogous incorporation and introjection characterize Derrida's encounter with Heidegger? The minuteness and literality of Derrida's attention to the fate of *Geist* would perhaps be the most vivid case in point, but many others could be cited, including the remarkable ventriloquization of the German philosopher that Derrida performs in the last pages of the book. Whatever he is doing with Heidegger, it is passionately invested, an experience of readerly endurance that is at once "unbearable and fascinating" (*PH*, 182). Is Schelling's curious survival in Heidegger's text, then, a figure for self-differences haunting Derrida's text, and indeed ensuring its heterogeneous living-on? For Derrida, Schelling activates possibilities and causes disturbances in Heidegger that might otherwise have lain dormant. It is there, where Derrida appears most intimately acquainted with Heidegger, that he affirms Heidegger's uncertain difference from himself. This move with respect to Heidegger in no way guarantees mastery over the elder philosopher, whose text, Derrida insists, continues to surprise him and with which, therefore, as I have suggested, he finds himself in a condition of continual extemporization. *Of Spirit* remembers Derrida's faithfulness to this complex fidelity and, indeed, calls exemplarily for others to suffer similarly contingent passages, even if, as Spivak remarks, the book has often not been read as such.[37] Derrida's reading of the other thinker is not a settled matter, not even in prospect, as a kind of future possibility; the "yet to come," as Derrida never ceases to explain, is not something that comes; it is not a discrete future that awaits its present materialization. It is *coming*, which is why it is important to hang on to the fact that Derrida's text remains itself *uncertain* about Heidegger's uncertainty. Remembering Heidegger, he is of necessity also recalling Schelling, Heidegger's "Schelling," among others, and it is this plurality, "still in movement," that ensures that the object of mourning is never punctually available to thought. For this reason, Derrida does not have the last word on Heidegger, and to demonstrate that point, he gladly and at every point gives his text over to the voice of the dead philosopher, who, in truth, has never ceased talking and who was never one voice.

Reading the roll call that begins with the names of his American friends and ends with that of a German philosopher we might ask, Why is the name of the long since dead so incongruously yet so effortlessly included with the names of the living, all these souls gathered together in friendship in New Haven and perhaps elsewhere to share in Derrida's hospitality and he in theirs? Derrida thanks the living and dedicates himself as author of the work to them, but in the mode, so to speak, of remembering the dead, thereby collapsing thanking, dedicating, and memorializing into a heterogeneously gracious but also mournful gesture that figures "Schelling" as if he were a kind of intellectual currency or promissory note more or less privately exchanged among these politely named seminarists. "Schelling" is what signs their intimate fraternity, so it functions as a kind of shibboleth. The quotation marks with which his name is cited would in this sense mark a form of winking confidentiality, signally to those in the know, those who were at Yale, that the content of Derrida's more or less public declaration of his indebtedness to "Schelling" is also more or less secretive. Derrida pays tribute to "Schelling," but the quotation marks also act to remind us of what an uncertain legacy this is, as if the marks were there to guard us against too quickly assuming that we knew what we meant when we said, as I have often done and in fact do here, "Schelling," meaning "Schelling, as such." Whoever or whatever Schelling is, he is "in them"; what is left of him, what remains of him, is now "with us," so that the best we can ever hope to say of Schelling, by way of remembering him, is "Schelling," the quotation marks pointing to an interiorized and idealized version of Schelling as that which lives on. "Schelling" is not Schelling, not the man who once answered to that name, the man who incomparably loved others and mourned the loss of others, not the philosopher who famously wrote that a "veil of melancholy" is draped over the nature of things, or the philosopher who himself held a sort of private seminar, this, in Stuttgart, under the dreadful pall of the death of Caroline, his friend, his wife, no, not *that* "Schelling," but *this* "Schelling," Schelling as he is or at least as he appears in Derrida's memory, among many others', including those who attended the seminar held in his memory, or in memory of his name. The quotation marks thus mark a certain transformation of Schelling and bear the trace of the necessary infidelity that Derrida, like all of us, demonstrates uncontrollably toward the other, whether dead or alive. To repeat: "Schelling" is not Schelling but, rather, Schelling in us, for us. But where is "Schelling"? What is this strange interiority, at once somehow shared and singular, a privacy that is to some degree also public? As Derrida has argued, mourning-work can be said to begin with the incorporation of the other, "a movement in which an interiorizing idealization takes in itself or upon itself the body and voice of the other, the other's visage and person, ideally *and* quasi-literally devouring them" (*M*, 34). But as Naas and Brault ask, "what does it mean to say that the dead are 'in' us?"[38] Unless we succumb to narcissistic temptation, the dead cannot be contained, not without assuming that the psyche possesses a stable topography in which the inside is divided from the outside, rather than thinking of it as the scene of multiple partitions and interminable involutions. What's uncanny about dedicating *Of Spirit* to the memory of "Schelling" is that Schelling is precisely the philosopher who dared to put this conventional psychic topography into question and, indeed, attributed maximal importance to its impossibly convoluted features by speaking of it in the context of discussing the Absolute: "Something must be in God that is not *He Himself*," Schelling insists in his Stuttgart private seminars.[39] In other words, even the divine is doomed to the burden of interiorizing what cannot be interiorized, and thus to sharing its space with "something" that violates all available topological concepts. In Schelling's imaginings, God is not a tranquil abstraction but a creature who is beside himself with languor and loss. It was Schelling's great insight to have identified this condition of impossible but irrepressible interiorization not only with the work of mourning but with a mourning work without end.

We have already noticed that *Of Spirit* is not a text included among those memorializations collected in *The Work of Mourning*. De Man, Deleuze, Marin, Foucault, Levinas, Lyotard, Kofman: the names of the dead in whose memory Derrida dedicates and lovingly entrusts his words do not include Schelling, no more than Heidegger. What can it mean, then, to write and to publish a book in memory of "Schelling" and thus to observe and to nurture a rapport with the work, the thought, and the person for whom that name stands as a ghostly reminder? That the name is cited in quotation marks is the first sign that this specter, although powerful enough to oblige Derrida and to *extract* a promise from him, is also curiously indeterminate, a phantom whose very determination as quote-unquote "Schelling" ensures that it is haunted by alterities, that he, it, whatever the name names, is never what he or it seems to be. Had Schelling himself not said that the best that we can expect of each other "in this life" is an "appearing man" [*erscheinend Mench*], thereby rendering provisional and fictional "himself" and those who observed, encountered, and remembered him, including "himself"?[40] It is worth saying right away that the alterities troubling the name are to a certain extent unheard, since of course "Schelling" and "'Schelling'" sound exactly the same: their difference, like the difference that obtains between *différence* and *différance*, is of another order, that of *écriture*. He writes not "Schelling" but "'Schelling'" (assuming for the moment that there is a fundamental difference), as if there were always *a priori* more than one, as if the "Schelling" *Of Spirit* remembers were at best an approximation or a kind of shorthand, "Schelling," *as it were*, or "Schelling" as a metonym for certain works by or about him, a certain "Schelling" or a certain reading of "Schelling." Heidegger's 1936 *Schellings Abhandlung über das Wesen der menschlichen Freiheit* certainly comes to mind, not least because it is a text Derrida remembers in *Of Spirit*, and remembers at the precise point in which Heidegger not only reads Schelling but is also said to adopt his "point of view" (*OS*, 71). Where "Schelling" is, we might say, there is always "a doubling of essence" and a multiplication and othering of "identity"— questions and phenomena about which the German philosopher indeed has—*had*, for this is in memory of "Schelling"— a great many things to say. As Thomas Pfau has argued, "Because pronouncing the identity of the subject means primarily a certain engagement with otherness within a *specifically* controlled and restricted economy of difference, as Schelling well knew, identity involves, prima facie, not the birth of the subject but that of a certain ethical practice."[41]

More strangely still, it is as if Derrida were harboring a secret—an open secret, to be sure, since his "Schelling" and that of his companions make no secret that they are together dedicated to this name, but still a secret— "Schelling," yes, a name with which any number of us are familiar but *he who is (or was) for-us*, encrypted within those quotation marks. "My 'Schelling,'" or rather "Our 'Schelling,'" the work by him and about him, signed in his name, that we once shared—shared once, uniquely, together, once upon a time. "We'll always have 'New Haven,'" Derrida seems to be saying, the quotation marks registering a certain shared intimacy, sealing in memory what is also bequeathed to the future. In this seminar that was "private," or at least "sort of private," one is momentarily reminded of the critique of cults and of the crypto-politics of the cults that Derrida explores with considerable circumspection in Kant. Among certain mourners of Derrida, those triumphalists who wished him dead long before he died, or who wished for the demise of the questions and ideas signed in his name, among those who claimed to know the secret of "deconstruction" (as "nihilist," for example, or "obscurantist"), "Derrida" and "Yale" remain to this day coarse metonyms for the putative clubbishness and threatening privacy of theory. To them, Derrida's classroom memory may well conjure up "the pent-up phantasm of a few experts closeted with their students in a seminar."[42] Yet this "Schelling," whose uniqueness is at once the burden and the possibility of his memorialization, hardly promises anything like narcissistic self-possession, a dream of incorporation shared among acolytes. We are right away reminded that for Derrida names and remembrance are in fact intimately related phenomena—and something more than phenomena—because the condition of the possibility of a name is that it is a memorialization of "itself," that the name is always "itself" *as* another, always "itself" *and* an other: the name "is from the outset 'in memory of,'" he writes in *Memoires*: "We cannot separate the name of 'memory' and 'memory' of the name; we cannot separate name and memory" (*M*, 49). To say that *Of Spirit* is written "in memory of 'Schelling'" is thus in some sense to say that it is written in memory of memory, a folding or doubling of the power of recollection and the force of mourning that, far from offering the phantasmatic consolation of hypermnesia, of a totalizing archive so perfect that it archives itself, promises instead interminable loss and the advent of what Schelling so evocatively calls "the indivisible remainder"[43]—that is, that which falls out of even the most powerful of interiorizing remembrances.

"What does it mean to fall in love with a writer?"[44]

Your last letter to me (there were only a few) almost didn't make it, having been misdirected to Wales before being sent to me in Canada. Did I in fact ever receive it? Was it for me? I cannot see for the tears. There—where?— you spoke of not having "the time or strength" to begin certain new projects. "*Ce sujet est magnifique, j'aurais tant aimé prendre part au numéro spécial que vous y consacrez,*" you wrote; "*Malheureusement, le temps et les forces me manquent trop pour que je puisse même y songer. Avec ma reconnaissance et mes voeux les plus cordiaux. . . .*" Your defencelessness made and makes me tremble. Why? In your absence, this without-force of "time and strength [*les forces*]" feels irrepressible. You were the one who taught me, as if in a private seminar, that the time and strength of *Trauerarbeit* cannot be fathomed and cannot not be fathomed. For the work of mourning is a matter of the without-force of time and strength, the refusal, at once tender and vigorous, simply to harness death and the dead to a question of time and strength. To the extent that the work of mourning is in defiance of arithmetic, it is not only work. The work of mourning is a matter of work and of something other than work. That is what makes the phrase terrible and confusing, as you often said. That is why, when I mourn you, I am at a loss for loss, unsure of when or how to mourn. For you who went before me, always before me. And I come to understand, fitfully, that this incompetence will be the death of me. "What is this 'without force,' this state of being drained, without any force, where death, where the death of a friend, leaves us, when we also have to work at mourning force? Is the 'without force,' the mourning of force, possible?" It is with this question that you left us, "like rich and powerful heirs, that is, both provided for and at a loss, given over to being forlorn and distraught, full of and fortified by him, responsible and voiceless" (*WM*, 144).

Adieu, mon ami, you whom I never dared to call "friend."

Notes

I am grateful to the Department of English at the University of Wisconsin–Madison, where, under the good graces of Theresa Kelly, and as Halls-Bascom Visiting Scholar, I was given the opportunity to share a much earlier version of this essay. I am thankful as well to Ian Balfour, Stephen Barber, Suzanne Crosta, Grant Farred, Rebecca Gagan, Sean Gaston, Jacques Khalip, Marc Redfield, Patricia Simmons, Orrin N. C. Wang, and Tracy Wynne for their suggestions and for their friendships, and to the members of my 2005 graduate seminar ("Derrida's Wake: On the Futures of Deconstruction") for their attentive readings of Derrida's texts.

1   Jacques Derrida, *Of Spirit: Heidegger and the Question*, trans. Geoffrey Bennington and Rachel Bowlby (Chicago: University of Chicago Press, 1989), 8. Subsequent citations from *Of Spirit* (identified as *OS*) are given parenthetically by page number in the text.

2   I cite David Farrell Krell's turn on Derrida's term *destinerrance*. See Krell, *The Purest of Bastards: Works of Mourning, Art, and Affirmation in the Thought of Jacques Derrida* (University Park: Pennsylvania State University Press, 2000), 206. Derrida uses the term in many places, including "Eating Well, or the Calculation of the Subject," trans. Peter Connor and Avital Ronnell, in *Points . . . Interviews, 1974*, ed. Elisabeth Weber (Stanford, CA: Stanford University Press, 1995), 260.

3   Jacques Derrida, "Heidegger, the Philosopher's Hell," trans. Peggy Kamuf, in *Points . . . Interviews, 1974*, ed. Elisabeth Weber (Stanford, CA: Stanford University Press, 1995), 183. Subsequent citations from this interview (identified as "HP") are given parenthetically by page number in the text.

4   Jacques Derrida, *Rogues: Two Essays on Reason*, trans. Pascale-Anne Brault and Michael Naas (Stanford, CA: Stanford University Press, 2005), 4.

5   Jacques Derrida, *Politics of Friendship*, trans. George Collins (London: Verso, 1997), 299. Subsequent citations from this text (identified as *PF*) are given parenthetically by page number in the text.

6   In the wake of Derrida's work, Gil Anijdar carefully considers the complex relationship joining the "friend" and the "enemy." See especially *The Jew, the Arab: A History of the Enemy* (Stanford, CA: Stanford University Press, 2003). In David Simpson's elegant phrasing, the "Western ethical inheritance" is quickened by "the double imperative . . . to at once punish the enemy and love him as oneself, to be and not to be one's own enemy." See *9/11: The Culture of Commemoration* (Chicago: University of Chicago Press, 2006), 140.

7   Deborah P. Britzman, "Theory Kindergarten," in *Regarding Sedgwick: Essays on Queer Culture and Critical Theory*, ed. Stephen M. Barber and David L. Clark (New York: Routledge, 2002).

8   Thomas Dutoit, review of *Jacques Derrida and the Humanities: A Critical Reader*, ed. Tom Cohen (Cambridge: Cambridge University Press, 2001), *Cercles: Revue pluridisciplinaire du monde anglophone*, available at www.cercles.com/review/r7/cohen.html (accessed October 4, 2006).

9   The exegetical pressure that I bring to bear on the phrase "for me at least" is supported by a small emphasis missing in the English translation of Derrida's text. In French it reads: "En répondant à leurs questions ou suggestions, j'essayai alors de définir ce qui *me* paraissant suspendu; incertain, encoure en movement et donc, pour moi du moins, à venir dans le texte de Heidegger." So much depends upon the accent given to "*me*." See Jacques Derrida, *Heidegger et la question* (Paris: Flammarion, 1990), 19–20.

10 Jacques Derrida, "Rams: Uninterrupted Dialogue between Two Infinities, the Poem," in *Sovereignties in Question: The Poetics of Paul Celan*, ed. Thomas Dutoit and Outi Psanen, trans. Thomas Dutoit and Philippe Romanski (New York: Fordham University Press, 2005), 140. Subsequent citations from this text (identified as "R") are given parenthetically by page number in the text.

11 Jacques Derrida, *Cinders*, trans. Ned Lukacher (Lincoln: University of Nebraska Press, 1991), 75.

12 Jacques Derrida, "Epoché and Faith: An Interview with Jacques Derrida," in *Derrida and Religion: Other Testaments*, ed. Yvonne Sherwood and Kevin Hart (New York: Routledge, 2005), 31; "Faith and Knowledge: The Two Sources of 'Religion' at the Limits of Reason Alone," in *Religion*, ed. Jacques Derrida and Gianni Vattimo (Stanford, CA: Stanford University Press, 1998), 60. Subsequent citations from these texts (identified, respectively, as "E" and "F") are given parenthetically by page number in the text.

13 Jacques Derrida, *The Other Heading: Reflections on Today's Europe*, trans. Pascale-Anne Brault and Michael B. Naas (Bloomington: Indiana University Press, 1992), 78.

14 Jacques Derrida, *Memoires: For Paul de Man*, rev. ed., trans. Cecile Lindsay, Jonathan Culler, Eduardo Cadava, and Peggy Kamuf (New York: Columbia University Press, 1989), 229. Subsequent citations from this text (identified as *M*) are given parenthetically by page number in the text.

15 Martin Heidegger, *What Is Called Thinking?* trans. Fred Wieck and J. Glenn Gray (New York: Harper and Row, 1968), 77; David Wood, *The Step Back: Ethics and Politics after Deconstruction* (Albany: State University of New York Press, 2005), 54.

16 Jacques Derrida, *The Work of Mourning*, ed. Pascale-Anne Brault and Michael Naas, trans. Pascale-Anne Brault (Chicago: University of Chicago Press, 2001), 41–42. Subsequent

citations from this text (identified as *WM*) are given parenthetically by page number in the text.

17 Jacques Derrida, *Envois*, in *The Post Card: From Socrates to Freud and Beyond*, trans. Alan Bass (Chicago: University of Chicago Press, 1987), 21. Subsequent citations from this text (identified as *E*) are given parenthetically by page number in the text.

18 In a brief but important text that forms the concluding focus of Derrida's *Politics of Friendship*, Maurice Blanchot underlines the importance of never speaking *of* but always *to* the friend. See *L'Amitie* (Paris: Gallimard, 1971), 328.

19 J. Hillis Miller, "Literary Study among the Ruins," *Diacritics* 31.3 (Fall 2001): 58.

20 Jacques Derrida, "The Future of the Profession or the University without Condition (Thanks to the 'Humanities' What *Could Take Place* Tomorrow)," in *Jacques Derrida and the Humanities: A Critical Reader*, ed. Tom Cohen (Cambridge: Cambridge University Press, 2001), 31–34.

21 Simpson, *9/11: The Culture of Commemoration*, 7, 8.

22 Gayatri Chakravorty Spivak et al., "The Politics of Mourning," Slought Foundation Conversation in Theory Series, December 27, 2004, http://slought.org/content/11252/ [online discussion].

23 This refrain about friendship forms, of course, the hypotext for *Politics of Friendship*.

24 Spivak et al., "The Politics of Mourning."

25 Heidegger: "Hearing even constitutes the primary and authentic openness of Da-sein for its ownmost possibility of Being, as in hearing the voice of the friend whom every Da-sein carries with it." *Being and Time*, trans. Joan Stambaugh (Albany: State University of New York Press, 1996), para. 163. Jacques Derrida, *Politiques de l'amitié: Suivi de L'oreille de Heidegger* (Paris: Galilée, 1994).

26 Letter from Martin Heidegger to Lucien Braun, May 16, 1973. A facsimile of the letter is reproduced in Jacques Derrida, Jean-Luc Nancy, Philippe Lacaoue-Labarthe, et al., *Penser à Strasbourg* (Ville de Strasbourg: Galilée, 2004), 30. In another letter to Braun (September 29, 1967), Heidegger writes: "Je vous sais gré de m'avoir rendu attentif aux publications de Jacques Derrida" (29).

27 Pascale-Anne Brault and Michael Naas, "Editor's Introduction: To Reckon with the Dead: Jacques Derrida's Politics of Mourning," in *The Work of Mourning*, 17–19.

28 I recall David Wood's phrase in *The Step Back*, 54.

29 Maurice Blanchot, "Our Clandestine Companion," trans. David B. Allison, *Face to Face with Levinas*, ed. Richard A. Cohen (Albany: State University of New York Press, 1986), 42.

30 Alphonso Lingis, *The Community of Those Who Have Nothing in Common* (Bloomington: Indiana University Press, 1994).

31 Friedrich Schelling, *Stuttgart Seminars*, in *Idealism and the Endgame of Theory: Three Essays by F. W. J. Schelling*, trans. and ed. Thomas Pfau (Albany: State University of New York Press, 1994), 239.

32 Paul de Man, *Aesthetic Ideology*, ed. Andrzej Warminksi (Minneapolis: University of Minnesota Press, 1996), 161.

33 John H. Smith, "Of Spirit(s) and Will(s)," in *Hegel after Derrida*, ed. Stuart Barnett (London: Routledge, 1998), 65.

34 Peter Fenves, "Foreword: From Empiricism to the Experience of Freedom," in *The Experience of Freedom*, trans. Bridget McDonald (Stanford, CA: Stanford University Press, 1993), xxviii.

35 Jean-Luc Nancy, *The Experience of Freedom*, trans. Bridget McDonald (Stanford, CA: Stanford University Press, 1993), 134.

36 Ibid., 36.

37 Jean-Michel Rabaté, Gayatri Chakravorty Spivak, Eduardo Cadava, and Aaron Levy, "The Politics of Mourning," Slought Foundation Conversation in Theory Series, December 27, 2004, http://slought.org/content/11252/.

38 Brault and Naas, "Editor's Introduction," *The Work of Mourning*, 10.

39 Schelling, *Stuttgart Seminars*, 224.

40 Ibid., 237.

41 Pfau, "Critical Introduction," in *Idealism and the Endgame of Theory*, 45.

42 Jacques Derrida, "Privilege: Justificatory Title and Introductory Remarks," in *Who's Afraid of Philosophy: Right to Philosophy 1*, trans. Jan Plug (Stanford, CA: Stanford University Press, 2002), 59.

43 F. W. J. Schelling, *Philosophical Inquiries into the Nature of Human Freedom*, trans. James Gutmann (La Salle, IL: Open Court, 1936), 34.

44 Eve Kosofsky Sedgwick and Adam Frank, "Shame in the Cybernetic Fold: Reading Silvan Tomkins," in *Shame and Its Sisters: A Silvan Tomkins Reader* (Durham, NC: Duke University Press, 1995), 23.

Elisabeth Weber

Suspended from the Other's Heartbeat

Suspendu au battement du coeur de l'autre,"[1] "suspended from the other's heartbeat"—this fragment of a sentence from Derrida's *Politics of Friendship* describes a decisively critical moment, a decisively critical space. "Suspendu au battement du coeur de l'autre"—this is what occurs in the space or lapse of undecidability that necessarily precedes any decision, if that decision is to occur as something else than the predictable application of a calculable program.

Such suspension, the event of being "suspended from the other's heartbeat," cannot happen to a subject if the subject is defined as sovereign self-presence.

"Undoubtedly," Derrida writes, "the subjectivity of a subject, already, never decides anything; its identity in itself and its calculable permanence make every decision an accident which leaves the subject . . . indifferent.[2] *A theory of the subject is incapable of accounting for the slightest decision.* But this must be said *a fortiori* of the event, and of the event with regard to the decision."[3] A theory of the subject is incapable of accounting for what effectuates the latter's interruption: a decision, a call, a gift, forgiveness, hospitality, in short, for what fractures his or her indifference—and it is

South Atlantic Quarterly 106:2, Spring 2007
DOI 10.1215/00382876-2006-026   © 2007 Duke University Press

only what fractures the subject's indifference and capacity of appropriation that deserves the name "event."

"Suspendu au battement du coeur de l'autre"—if that happened, one could not remain "indifferent." It would be a matter of life or death. The English translation, that I have corrected until now, actually reads: "suspended *over* the other's heartbeat." It betrays a defense against the *folie*, the sheer madness of the suspension Derrida names. Being "suspended *over* the other's heartbeat" reinstates the security of domination over an event of radical vulnerability and fragility. In Derrida's French, the one who is suspended does not hover *over* the other's heartbeat, in what could only be an overtowering, if not menacing, movement. Rather, "suspendu à" means hanging "by a support from above"; in Derrida's formulation, then, the other's heartbeat is the support above. The one who is suspended is at the mercy of the other's heartbeat. Such a radical suspension happens in the moment of undecidability in which any decision, in spite of the declared autonomy of the decider, is "founded," and thereby, in fact, forever unfounded.

It is a lack of precision, albeit an unavoidable one, to speak of *"being suspended from the other's heartbeat"*: The event "suspended-from-the-other's-heartbeat" *is* not necessarily; or perhaps, rather, necessarily *is* not: "It perhaps does not *exist* nor ever *present* itself, nevertheless, it happens, there is a chance of it happening.[4] Perhaps . . ."[5]

Such a "perhaps," first introduced into philosophy as an unheard-of dimension by Nietzsche, to whom Derrida's book dedicates a long section,[6] does not, as Derrida specifies, belong "to a regime of opinion. . . . Our unbelievable *perhaps* does not signify haziness and mobility, the confusion preceding knowledge or renouncing all truth. If it is undecidable and without truth in its own moment (but it is, as a matter of fact, difficult to assign a proper moment to it), this is in order that it might be a condition of decision, interruption, revolution, responsibility and truth." Pursuing his comment on Nietzsche's aphorism on the "new friends of 'truth,'" the "philosophers of the future," Derrida writes: "The friends of the *perhaps* are the friends of truth. But the friends of truth are not, by definition, *in* the truth; they are not installed there as in the padlocked security of a dogma and the stable reliability of an opinion. If there is some truth in the *perhaps*, it can only be that of which the friends are the friends. Only friends."[7]

"Perhaps" is the hinge on which friendship and future, the *avenir*, which, in French, reads "the to-come," move. It indicates the fracture of calculability and predictability, and, as such, of a certain "rationality" and the related concepts of politics and justice. "Perhaps" introduces the chance of an event that for once deserves its name: a radical arrival, which Derrida, in the creation of the neologism "arrivance," invites to enter into a resonance with the term that, over four decades ago, provoked a fracture in established philosophy, *différance*, but also into a resonance with another term of invention of the future: *aimance* ("lovence").

The difficulty to think such an event becomes apparent in the words themselves. The French word for "perhaps," "peut-être," is, as Derrida points out, "perhaps, too rich in its two *verbs* (the *pouvoir* [literally: to have the power to do] and the *être* [to be]),"[8] whereas the English *perhaps* and the German *vielleicht* still resonate with the chance of an unforeseeable happening. On the other hand, the English translation reintroduces the power of being, when it renders Derrida's "il y a" as "there is." Where Derrida points out "la différence entre 'il y a' et 'est' ou 'existe,'" the English translation reads "the difference between 'there is' and 'is' or 'exists.'"[9] In these instances, the English translation does not escape the "words of presence" that Derrida tries to avoid, and perhaps it cannot escape those words, unless others are invented. Which is what Derrida urges his readers to do.

This is not just a question of philosophical subtleties. It is precisely the "words of presence" that define the subject, and with it, the political subject. The problems in the English idiom are not limited to this particular language: they betray how difficult it is to move beyond a tradition marked through and through by the "words of presence," and by their corresponding practices and institutions, such as representation, calculation, legislation.[10]

Derrida always insists on the question of the idiom, as, for example, at the beginning of the interview conducted in English on October 22, 2001, with Giovanna Borradori in New York City. He starts his reflection by proposing to decipher the ceaseless invocation of the so-called "major event" of "September 11," in which "a language . . . admits its powerlessness and so is reduced to pronouncing mechanically a date, repeating it endlessly, as a kind of ritual incantation, a conjuring poem, a journalistic litany or rhetorical refrain that admits to not knowing what it's talking about."[11] Derrida underlines the necessity to analyze not only the "content," but, perhaps more importantly, the provenance of this compulsive repetition. We need to "try to understand . . . what is pushing us to repeat endlessly and without knowing what we are talking about, precisely there where language and the concept come up against their limits: 'September 11, September 11, *le 11 septembre*, 9/11.' . . . From where does this menacing injunction itself come to us? . . . *Who* or *what* gives us this threatening order (others would already say this terrorizing if not terrorist imperative): name, repeat, rename 'September 11' . . . even when you do not yet know what you are saying and are not yet thinking what you refer to in this way."[12] It is, according to Derrida, crucial to insist here "on the English" because this injunction "comes first of all from a place where English predominates," not just in the sense that the United States was targeted, "but because the world order that felt itself targeted through this violence is dominated largely by the Anglo-American idiom, an idiom that is indissociably linked to the political discourse that dominates the world stage, to international law, diplomatic institutions, the media, and the greatest technoscientific, capitalist, and military power."[13]

The injunction to repeat compulsively, and that means by implication *not* to "work through," *not* to analyze, occurs in the idiom that ultimately dominates the definition and practice of international law, international economy, and international politics, an idiom in which powerfully effective policies of a resistance against the inventions of a "democracy-to-come," the inventions of a "justice-to-come," including of a just economy, are drafted, as, for example, U.S. foreign policy interventions in Central and South America have made abundantly clear over the last decades. This idiom is also the one in which, as Amnesty International's Secretary General Irene Khan pointed out in Amnesty's Annual Report of April 2005, "the US government has gone to great lengths to restrict the application of the Geneva Conventions and to 're-define' torture."[14]

Derrida's attention to language in all its aspects is not a philosophical luxury, it is a philosophical and political necessity: "Semantic instability, irreducible disturbance of the border between concepts, indecision in the very concept of the border: all this must not only be analyzed as a speculative disorder, a conceptual chaos or zone of passing turbulence in public or political language. We must, on the contrary, recognize here strategies and relations of force. The dominant power is the one that manages to impose and, thus, to legitimate, indeed to legalize (for it is always a question of law) on a national or world stage, the terminology and thus the interpretation that best suits it in a given situation."[15] The "irreducible disturbance" not just "on" (as the English translation reads), but "of the border between concepts" is potentially highly productive: It is not a "zone of passing turbulence," a temporary "disturbance" (*trouble*) that will be followed by stability. *Au contraire*, "on the contrary," it is our responsibility (*"il faut"*: "we must," it is necessary), to recognize here the zone of exploration of irreducible aporias, such as, to quote *Politics of Friendship*,

> the aporia of the *perhaps*, its historical and political aporia. Without the opening of an absolutely undetermined possible, without the radical abeyance and suspense marking a perhaps, there would never be either event or decision. Certainly. But nothing takes place and nothing is ever decided without suspending the *perhaps* while keeping its "living" possibility in living memory. If no decision (ethical, juridical, political) is possible without interrupting determination by engaging oneself in the *perhaps*, on the other hand, the same decision must interrupt the very thing that is its condition of possibility: the *perhaps* itself. In the order of law, politics or morality, what would rules and laws, contracts and institutions indeed be without steadfast determination, without calculability and without violence done to the *perhaps*, to the possible that makes them possible?[16]

Throughout his writings, from the earliest to the latest, Derrida recalls relentlessly the moments of radical unfoundedness that work in our practices without, in most cases, being accounted for, reflected on, remembered, or honored, even though the most complex systems, and institutions, and the most far-reaching decisions, hinge on them, are suspended from them. Derrida's work persists in uncovering the fragility and aporias of this suspension, its risks and its *chance*, the potential of its *arrivance* and *aimance*, by meticulously deconstructing the layers of asserted foundation, origin, or presence that have been heaped onto it.

The exemplary case in *Politics of Friendship* is, as the book's title announces, the friend, because, as Derrida's reading will develop, the "friend" and his definition through an "equality of birth," through the sameness of "blood," proves to be at the core of the Greek notion of "democracy." In his close reading of Plato's *Menexenus*, Derrida shows how "everything called democracy here (or aristo-democracy) founds the social bond, the community, the equality, the friendship of brothers"—and not of sisters—"*identification qua fraternization*," in the link between civic equality and equality of birth,[17] the "bond between the political and autochthonous consanguinity," in the presumably "natural bond between *nomos* and *phusis*," in short, in the unquestioned bond between two "structurally heterogeneous ties."[18] Moreover, the civil equality is bound to the equality of a good or noble birth (*eugéneia*), by the repetition of an act of memory: it implies and performs, by "necessity," the "promise" or "oath" of fidelity to dead ancestors.[19] This "is the place of fraternization as the symbolic bond alleging the repetition of a genetic tie. Responsibility must imperatively answer for itself before what is, at birth and at death. In more modern terms, one might speak of the foundation of citizenship in a nation."[20] To the Greeks of Plato's time, "the memory of their dead—their fathers of noble birth—recalls nothing less than their truth, their truth *qua* political truth. The obligatory necessity of this bond of memory forms the condition of their political freedom. It is the element of their freedom, the sense of their world as the truth of their freedom. It is their freedom—indeed, for them, the only imaginable freedom. Truth, freedom, necessity, and equality come together in this politics of fraternity."[21]

The goal of Derrida's analysis is not to assert a straight line from Plato's reflections on "democracy" to today's notion of "democracy." However, in light of the current debates, in Europe, the United States, and elsewhere, surrounding "immigration" and the legislation of "naturalization," Derrida asks an unsettling question: "Are we certain that throughout all the mutations of European history (of which, of course, the most rigorous account must be taken), any concept of the political and of democracy has ever broken with the heritage of this troubling necessity? Made a radical, thematic break with it? This is the question we are concerned with here."[22]

Derrida's interest in the "origins" of "democracy" is motivated by the fact (which he sees as a chance) that for Plato, "democracy" is an uncertain, divided concept, and by the fact that in today's experience and understanding of "democracy," unacknowledged residues of the "old," Platonic, definition can be detected which are a massive threat to "democracy." The analysis of these residues shows that the very definition of the political is, in the tradition of the West, inseparable from the reference to the founding fathers, and the descent, by birth or by oath, from this genealogy and the fraternity and "friendship" created by it. Western democracies, but also the Western understanding of "friendship," are haunted by their unquestioned, repressed foundation in blood ties. They are haunted by their foundation in a concept of politics rooted de facto in the priority of the sameness of blood, that is, the sameness of a good or noble birth, and in the determination of friend and enemy according to this priority, this "necessity." Even if the public discourse rejects the foundation of the community through the sameness of blood and its corresponding hierarchization of bloodlines as undemocratic, the political practice of Western democracies betrays all too often the perseverance of this phantasm and its devastating influence on the life of subjected communities.

A longer passage from *Politics of Friendship* describes the stakes:

> Considered in itself, beyond the ruses and irony that may mark *Menexenus*, [Plato's] hesitation over the name "democracy" will always provide food for thought. If, between the name on the one hand, the concept and the thing on the other, the play of a gap offers room for rhetorical effects which are also political strategies, what are the lessons that we can draw today? Is it still *in the name of democracy* that one will attempt to criticize such and such a determination of democracy or aristo-democracy? Or, more radically—closer, precisely, to its fundamental *radicality* (where, for example, it is *rooted* in the security of an autochthonous foundation, in the stock or in the genius of filiation)—is it still in the name of democracy, of a democracy to come, that one will attempt to deconstruct a concept, all the predicates associated with the massively dominant concept of democracy, that in whose heritage one inevitably meets again the law of birth, the natural or "national" law, the law . . . of autochthony, civic equality (isonomy) founded on equality of birth (isogony) as the condition of the calculation of approbation and, therefore, the aristocracy of virtue and wisdom, and so forth? What remains or still resists in the deconstructed (or deconstructible) concept of democracy to guide us endlessly? To order us not only to engage a deconstruction but to keep the old name? And to deconstruct further in the name of a *democracy* to come? That is to say, further, to enjoin us still to inherit from what—forgotten, repressed, misunderstood, or unthought in the "old" concept and throughout its history—would still be on the watch, giving off signs or symptoms of a stance of survival coming through all the old and tired features?[23]

What, in the "old name" of "democracy," "resists" its foundation on the "equality of birth" to the extent that it "orders" us to "keep the old name"? The injunction to keep the "old name" stems from the fact that we have already inherited something that was "forgotten, repressed, misunderstood or unthought in the 'old' concept." The necessity to address the phantoms of what has remained "unthought" or "repressed" cannot occur but in the phantoms' language. If, as Derrida asserts, the "old" concept "democracy" implies the chance of the "perhaps," this chance can be opened and seized only at the condition of acknowledging and addressing the specters that continue to haunt "democracy."

One of the disturbing questions Derrida raises is how the definition of "democracy" through blood filiation may be related to what he describes as the intrinsically "suicidal" essence without essence of "democracy." Commenting on the example of Algeria, where a democratic election was canceled in 1992 because of the imminent victory of an Islamic antidemocratic party, Derrida deciphers in this abolishment of democracy in the name of the preservation of democracy the always impending risk of an "aporia" intrinsic to the concept of democracy, rather than a historical contingency. In the post-9/11 United States, where the legitimacy of torture and other abusive practices has been reinstated in the name of the protection of democracy, an analysis of this aporia in the concept of democracy is particularly urgent. Those willing, to quote Alfred McCoy, "to tolerate torture as a necessary excess in defense of democracy"[24] actualize, together with the "suicidal" aporia of democracy, what Derrida calls its "auto-immune processes" and "the perverse effect of the autoimmunitary itself. For we now know that repression in both its psychoanalytical sense and its political sense—whether it be through the police, the military, or the economy—ends up producing, reproducing, and regenerating the very thing it seeks to disarm."[25] Derrida's provocative assertion "La démocratie a toujours été suicidaire," "democracy has always been suicidal," is followed by an equally provocative challenge: "et s'il y a un à-venir pour elle, c'est à la condition de penser autrement la vie, et la force de vie":[26] "If there is a future and a 'to-come' of democracy, it is at the condition of thinking otherwise life, and life's force." The task is enormous: the future of democracy, a democracy-to-come, requires thinking otherwise "life" and "life-force," which means, first and perhaps foremost, "filiation," "genealogy."

It is, therefore, particularly troubling that sexual humiliation is, as Alfred McCoy has shown, one of the "two key techniques" with which the commanders at Guantánamo "perfected the CIA torture paradigm" between 2002 and 2003, and which were exported to Abu Ghraib prison in August 2003, when the commander of Guantánamo, General Geoffrey Miller, was sent to what had been Saddam Hussein's most notorious torture and execution compound. "If you look at the most famous of photographs from

Abu Ghraib, of the Iraqi standing on the box, arms extended with a hood over his head and the fake electrical wires from his arms . . . you can see the entire 50-year history of CIA torture. It's very simple. He's hooded for sensory disorientation, and his arms are extended for self-inflicted pain. And those are the two very simple fundamental CIA techniques, developed at enormous cost."[27] Those "fundamental" techniques, sensory deprivation or sensory assault on the one hand, and self-inflicted pain on the other, were "perfected" by adding to them "an attack on cultural sensitivity, particularly Arab male sensitivity to issues of gender and sexual identity."[28]

If it is certainly not by chance that, as Susan Sontag has noted in her reaction to the publication of the images emerging from the U.S.-run Abu Ghraib torture chambers in spring 2004, "rape and pain inflicted on the genitals are among the most common forms of torture,"[29] it is noteworthy that in its "global war on terror," specifically against suspected terrorists who are Muslim, the CIA has resorted to sexual humiliation as one technique of its "three-fold total assault on the human psyche." As McCoy develops in his detailed history of fifty years of CIA interrogation, "forced nudity and explicit photography" were introduced into the coercive interrogation and systematic torture of Iraqi prisoners in 2003, "on the theory that 'Arabs are particularly vulnerable to sexual humiliation.'"[30] "Guantánamo's integration of psychologists into routine interrogation perfected the CIA's paradigm, moving beyond a broad-spectrum attack on human senses, sight and sound, to a customized assault on individual phobias or cultural norms, sexual and religious."[31]

It was an American general, Brigadier General Janis Karpinski, the military police commander for Iraq in 2003, who spelled out what the treatment documented in the Abu Ghraib photographs means in the Middle East: "Do you know what this does in an Arab culture? Do you know what you are doing? This is the equivalent of castrating them in public."[32] It is, beyond the devastating humiliation tantamount to rape, the symbolical denial of procreation, of future filiation and generations. The specter of *eugéneia* which, in Plato's *Menexenos*, is deemed necessary for "democracy," returns here, exhibiting its intrinsic perversity.

Derrida's analyses allow to connect the unquestioned "foundation" of "democracy" with what is, usually, understood as being fundamentally contrary to "democracy": torture, and specifically, in the historical situation that is ours, sexual assault as form of "customized" torture of suspected terrorists or insurgents, tailored over the last four years in the U.S.-run prisons of Guantánamo and Iraq and, as McCoy shows in chilling detail, tolerated by a large segment of the American public in defense of "democracy."[33]

In this dark light, the questions Derrida addresses to us, as our task or calling, resonate with particular urgency: "How do you deconstruct the essential link of a certain concept of democracy to autochthony and to eugenics, without, for all that, giving up the name of democracy?"[34] He invites us to the necessity of attempting, "still in the name of democracy, of a democracy to come," to deconstruct "the massively dominant concept of democracy" and all the predicates associated with it, "in whose heritage one inevitably encounters the law of birth, the natural or 'national' law, the law of . . . civic equality . . . founded on equality of birth . . . as the condition of the calculation of approbation."[35] As a consequence, Derrida calls for a deconstruction of the genealogical wherever the latter "commands in the name of birth, of a national naturalness which has never been what it *was said to be*."[36] Such a deconstruction would have enormous repercussions: It would

> concern confidence, credit, credence, *doxa* or *eudoxia*, opinion or right opinion, the approbation given to filiation, at birth and at the origin, to generation, to the familiarity of the family, to the proximity of the neighbour—to what axioms too quickly inscribe under these words. Not to wage war on them and to see evil in them, but to think and live a politics, a friendship, a justice which *begin* by breaking with their naturalness or their homogeneity, with their alleged place of origin. Hence, which begin where the beginning divides (itself) and differs, begin by marking an "originary" heterogeneity that has already come and that alone can come, in the future, to open them up.[37]

It is then imperative to deconstruct the presupposed and rarely questioned naturalness, originality, or homogeneity (all these concepts having their common source in their rootedness in blood ties) of "friendship," of "justice," and of "politics." If these concepts are drenched in blood, both because they are rooted in blood ties, and because, as a consequence, their haunting, unavowable legacy cannot be severed from "eugenics," mass murder, and torture, the imperative to invent the language of a democracy-to-come goes hand in hand with the realization that "radical changes" in national and international law are "necessary." These changes cannot be left to the legislators alone. They are our responsibility, in particular as scholars, intellectuals, "philosophers." For Derrida, a "'philosopher' . . . would be someone who analyzes and then draws the practical and effective consequences of the relationship between our philosophical heritage and the structure of the still dominant juridico-political system that is so clearly undergoing mutation." Among those "practical and effective consequences" figures prominently the task to "demand accountability from those in charge of public discourse, those responsible for the language and institutions of international law."[38] It is particularly heartbreaking that two years after the circulation of a fifty-page memorandum written by Assistant Attorney General Bybee, in which he provided "'sweeping legal authority' for harsh interrogation" by "carefully interpreting key words in the UN antitorture convention and its parallel congressional legislation,"[39] and only weeks after the Abu Ghraib scandal broke, the Harvard Law School faculty "circulated a petition signed by 481 prominent professors of law and political science at 110 top universities nationwide," on the one hand condemning "abuses practiced on detainees under American control," but, on the other, calling "for serious consideration of 'a coercive interrogation policy . . . made within the strict confines of a democratic process.'" In effect, McCoy writes, "America's leading academics were asking citizens to set aside two centuries of Enlightenment principles and think seriously about legalizing torture."[40]

To uncover the unacknowledged legacy of the concepts of "friendship," "politics," and "democracy," Derrida's analyses, again, set in "precisely there where language and the concept come up against their limits."[41] His insistence on keeping, exemplarily, the concept of "democracy" in the formulation "democracy to come" is motivated by at least two factors: First, "the inherited concept of democracy is the only one that welcomes the possibility of being contested, of contesting itself, of criticizing and indefinitely improving itself."[42] But more fundamentally, what Derrida calls the "aporia of the *demos*" yields the promise of a different "democracy to come": "the demos is *at once* the incalculable singularity of anyone, before any 'subject,' the possible undoing of the social bond by a secret to be respected, beyond all citizenship, beyond every 'state,' indeed every 'people,' indeed even beyond the current state of the definition of a living being as living 'human' being, *and* the universality of rational calculation, of the equality of citizens before the law, the social bond of being together, with or without contract, and so on."[43] In other words, Derrida recognizes that in spite of the heavy legacy of the Greek understanding of democracy and its foundation in blood ties, the *perhaps*, the event of an uncalculable singularity, the *arrivance*—perhaps—can move the concept and experience of democracy to the promise of a "democracy to come." Which can come, paradoxically, only at the condition of an achievement of the "equality of the citizens before the law."

In *Politics of Friendship*, Derrida gives another formulation to this aporia:

> There is no democracy without respect for irreducible singularity or alterity, but there is no democracy without the "community of friends" . . . , without the calculation of majorities, without identifiable, stabilizable, representable subjects, all equal. These two laws are irreducible one to the other. Tragically irreconcilable and forever wounding. The wound itself opens with the necessity of having to *count* one's friends, to count the others, in the economy of one's own, there where every other is altogether other. But where every other is *equally* altogether other. More serious than a contradiction, political desire is forever borne by the disjunction of these two laws. This disjunction also bears the chance and the future of a democracy whose ruin it constantly threatens but whose life, however, it sustains, like life itself, at the heart of its *divided virtue*, the inadequacy to itself.[44]

The insistence on working in the zones where language and concepts "come up against their limits"[45] yields a "hauntology" that has at least three motivations: The concept "democracy," for example, is deconstructed in order to uncover the specters that have not been laid to rest because their life-blood is, precisely, blood. Derrida's analyses demonstrate how the invocation of the founding fathers cannot not invoke at the same time the specter of eugenics, the determination of belonging via blood and the corresponding bloody exclusion of the other. Simultaneously, the ghost of this other is shown to always already in-sist, and the brutality of the exclusion is deciphered as a reaction to the haunting unavoidability of the other. A third (in order of importance first) motivation for Derrida's "hauntology" is the urgency to open a space in which the absence of the others' smothered voices is given a room of resonance, and in which, therefore, perhaps, other voices may, perhaps, find breath.

Derrida's work in the limit-zone of language explores, then, a logic of the phantom, a "hauntology" that has far-reaching consequences for a political theory, as a text on the "final solution" describes with particular clarity:

> I ask myself whether a community that assembles or gathers itself together in order to think what there is to be thought and gathered of this nameless thing that has been called the "final solution" does not have to show, first of all, its readiness to welcome the law of the phantom, the spectral experience and the memory of the phantom, of that which is neither dead nor living, more than dead and more than living, only surviving, the law of the most commanding memory, even though it is the most effaced and the most effaceable, but for that very reason the most demanding.[46]

The necessity of welcoming the "memory of the phantom" marks Derrida's commitment to justice in its entirety and finds its philosophical counterpart in concepts, introduced already in Derrida's earliest writings, such as the "trace," "différance," and the "supplement." The question is not so much how to "address the phantom," and whether one can question or address it, as whether "one can *address oneself in general* if some phantom does not already return."[47] And, referring to Shakespeare's *Hamlet*, Derrida continues: "If, at least, he loves justice, the 'scholar' of the future, the 'intellectual' of tomorrow would need to learn it [to address himself or herself to the other], and of him or her [the phantom]." In order to address oneself to the other in the search for justice, one has *first of all* "to welcome the law of the phantom," precisely because this "law of the phantom" is the "most effaced and effaceable" and, for that very reason, "the most demanding," the most urgent. This is one example for a thinking that would think life "otherwise."

"Beloved" is, in Toni Morrison's novel of the same name, the name on the tombstone of a dead girl, of whom the reader never learns the living name. The violence of her death and the brutality of slavery that caused it make her haunt the lives of her mother, her siblings, and of all their relations. It is of her, the returned and disappeared ghost, that Morrison writes: "Disremembered and unaccounted for, she cannot be lost because no one is looking for her, and even if they were, how can they call her if they don't know her name?"[48] Beloved's memory is, indeed, "the most effaced and effaceable," and, as Morrison's book powerfully shows, "the most demanding." So unbearably demanding that, in the end, her apparition is chased back into invisibility: "It was not a story to pass on."[49] The challenge that Derrida's thought addresses to his readers is to realize the need to "learn," from the other, from the nameless, from the phantom, how to address ourselves to her; how to learn her name with the keen awareness that looking for that name and learning it bears in itself the risk of "losing," forgetting, betraying it in its singularity.

Commenting on the photographs of prisoner abuse and torture in Abu Ghraib, Sontag makes an observation whose implications lead to the very foundations of American democracy: "If there is something comparable to what these pictures show it would be some of the photographs of black victims of lynching taken between the 1880's and 1930's, which show Americans grinning beneath the naked mutilated body of a black man or woman hanging behind them from a tree. The lynching photographs were souvenirs of a collective action whose participants felt perfectly justified in what they had done. So are the pictures from Abu Ghraib."[50]

These pictures, no less than the photographs of lynchings, unambiguously show that they "were meant to be circulated and seen by many people"—they are, as the poses of the tormenters openly indicate, publicly avowable, "in part designed to be photographed."[51] These pictures, Sontag asserts, are "us," because "the issue is not whether a majority or a minority of Americans performs such acts but whether the nature of the policies prosecuted by this administration and the hierarchies deployed to carry them out makes such acts likely." For the Abu Ghraib pictures just as for the lynching photographs, the answer to this question is beyond doubt.[52] In January 2004, a U.S. Army investigation of a Military Intelligence Battalion stationed in Mosul, Iraq, "found evidence that MI personnel and/or translators engaged in physical torture of detainees. As the ACLU lawyer Amrit Singh explained, these documents show that 'torture and abuse of detainees was routine and was considered acceptable practice by U.S. soldiers.'"[53] These pictures are "us" if we consider that, as McCoy documents with the petition signed by 481 prominent U.S. professors, there is "surprisingly widespread advocacy of state-sanctioned torture among American academics," including in the American Psychological Association, which does not discourage its members from participating in "national security endeavors," a euphemism for the APA's "long involvement in military research and CIA behavioral experiments."[54] Finally, those pictures are "us" because mainstream media entertainment may well have been contributing for years to the public acceptability of torture. As McCoy observes,

> With the horrific reality of the Twin Towers attack still resonating and endless nuclear-bomb-in-Times-Square/ticking-bomb interrogation scenarios ricocheting around the media and pop culture, torture

seems to have gained an eerie emotional traction. Polls taken over the last three years have confirmed this. . . . Through the invisible tendrils that tie a state to its society, the media has often reflected aspects of administration policy on such subjects. Television, in particular, has had a powerful effect in its repeated portrayals of harsh, even abusive interrogations as effective and morally justified acts—when, in fact, they are neither. After years of watching television shows such as *NYPD Blue* and *24* with plots that mimic the ticking-bomb scenario, millions of ordinary Americans seem to believe that we have entered an era when abuse, or even torture, is necessary to save lives. Each week, for instance, up to 20 million Americans have watched the fictional detectives of *NYPD Blue* use harsh methods to "tune up" suspects in the "pokey," or interrogation room, risking their careers to extract information that regularly saved lives and made the city safer. Accepting the need to torture just one criminal in this week's episode, or just one terrorist with a ticking bomb in Fox Television's popular CIA drama *24*, opens ordinary Americans to consider whether the torture of real terrorists is not only justifiable but imperative. It seems likely that these televised scenarios have lent a hand in creating a public climate tolerant of governmental torture.[55]

These pictures are "us"; they are a reflection of democratic Americans; they are a reflection of the dominant power's interpretation of national law, in flagrant violation of the latter and of international treaties.[56] But they are also "us" in yet another, almost unfathomable way. They offer a glimpse into an otherwise "invisible universe" of the so-called "black sites," a CIA-run covert prison system around the world in which dozens of so-called "ghost-detainees" are being held in complete isolation for months and years, without being registered with the International Red Cross, without recognized legal rights, without charges brought against them, completely cut off from their families, their lawyers, and anyone other than CIA personnel.[57]

"Camp Echo" was the name of such a "black site" inside Guantánamo.[58] Democracy's call is reflected back from these sites in horrendous self-repetition, and if the Abu Ghraib pictures are "us," we may not even be able to say for sure that it is deformed. No other voices, not even screams, penetrate the two-way mirrors of this "netherworld," as one former senior intelligence officer called the secret prison system.[59] The fact that the prisoners have been "disappeared,"[60] underground cells that one former victim described as "grave-like,"[61] and the "threat of live burials" that constitutes one method of psychological torture[62] are three indications that the term *ghost-detainee* is not just an eerie metaphor.

Derrida's "hauntology" is demanding in several ways. It requires that the scholars of the future face the "specters" of their philosophical, juridical, political legacies (such as the apparent "necessity" of blood ties). It requires, simultaneously, learning, from the ghost, for example from the ghosts of the victims of these legacies, how to address ourselves to the other, not just to the ghost, but to the other *tout court*. It requires defending justice not only for the known "other," the familiar and related "other," but also for the *other* "other." For example, and especially, for the other who is the suspected or the self-declared enemy of "democracy." "Democracy" is alive only at this condition, suspended from the other's heartbeat. Derrida's insistence on the responsibility of the "scholar of the future" toward the "phantom" or the "ghost" (if "at least" he or she "loves justice") is not to be lessened in the case of the "enemies" of democracy. It is not to be lowered for those "ghosts" caught in the CIA's "global gulag"[63] created in defense of American "democracy."

The "scholar of the future"—that is, the scholar committed to a democracy-to-come: Today.

Notes

1   Jacques Derrida, *Politiques de l'amitié* (Paris: Galilée, 1994), 88, *Politics of Friendship*, translated by George Collins (London: Verso, 1997), 69, translation modified. The French pagination will be indicated followed by the pagination of the English translation.

2   The English translation adds "unchanged and," which don't figure in the French original.

3   Derrida, *Politiques de l'amitié/Politics of Friendship*, 87/68.

4   Ibid., 59/39, translation modified.

5   Ibid., 59/39.

6   Ibid., esp. chaps. 2, 3.

7   Ibid., 63–64/43. The Nietzsche text in question is in *Beyond Good and Evil*, 2, paragraph 44; see also paragraph 43.

8   Ibid., 59/39, translation modified. "Le pouvoir et l'être": Derrida adds the definite article to both verbs, because they can serve, in French, as substantives as well, in which case they are translated as "power" and "being."

9   Ibid., 59/39.

10   Cf. Jacques Derrida, "Force of Law," *Cardozo Law Review* 11.5–6 (July/August 1990): 963.

11   Jacques Derrida, "Autoimmunity: Real and Symbolic Suicides," in *Philosophy in a Time of Terror*, ed. G. Borradori (Chicago: University of Chicago Press, 2003), 86.

12   Ibid., E87–88.

13 Ibid., F137/E88.

14 Amnesty International, Foreword to Annual Report (April 2005), available at www
    .amnesty.org/ailib/aireport/ (accessed September 25, 2006). The U.S. government, Kahn
    continues, "has sought to justify the use of coercive interrogation techniques, the practice
    of holding 'ghost detainees' (people in unacknowledged incommunicado detention) and
    the 'rendering' or handing over of prisoners to third countries known to practice torture.
    The detention facility at Guantánamo Bay has become the gulag of our times, entrench-
    ing the practice of arbitrary and indefinite detention in violation of international law."

15 Derrida, "Autoimmunity," F159/ E105, translation modified.

16 Derrida, *Politiques de l'amitié/Politics of Friendship*, 86/67. See also "Force of Law," where
    Derrida points out that a decision made on the grounds of accepted laws and rules alone
    would "only be the programmable application or unfolding of a calculable process. It
    might be legal; it would not be just" (963). Derrida recalls that "for a decision to be just
    and responsible, it must, in its proper moment if there is one [s'il y en a un: if one occurs,
    if one happens to happen], be both regulated and without regulation: it must conserve
    the law and also destroy it or suspend it enough to have to reinvent it in each case, rejus-
    tify it, at least reinvent it in the reaffirmation and the new and free confirmation of its
    principle. Each case is other, each decision is different and requires an absolutely unique
    interpretation, which no existing, coded rule can or ought to guarantee absolutely. At
    least, if the rule guarantees it in no uncertain terms, so that the judge is a calculating
    machine—which happens—we will not say that he [or she] is just, free and responsible.
    But we also won't say it if he [or she] doesn't refer to any law, to any rule or if, because he
    [or she] doesn't take any rule for granted beyond his [or her] own interpretation, he [or
    she] suspends his [or her] decision, stops short before the undecidable or if he [or she]
    improvises and leaves aside all rules, all principles" ("Force of Law," 961).

17 See *Politiques de l'amitié/Politics of Friendship*, 127/104.

18 All quotes are from ibid., 121–22/99.

19 Ibid., 122/99.

20 Ibid., 122/99.

21 Ibid., 122/100.

22 Ibid., 122/100, translation modified.

23 Ibid., 126f/103f, translation slightly modified.

24 Alfred McCoy, *A Question of Torture* (New York: Metropolitan Books, 2006), 188.

25 "Autoimmunity," 152/99.

26 Jacques Derrida, *Voyous* (Paris: Galilée, 2003), 57.

27 Alfred McCoy, interviewed by Amy Goodman, "Professor McCoy Exposes the History of
    CIA Interrogation, from the Cold War to the War on Terror," *Democracy Now!* February 17,
    2006, www.democracynow.org/article.pl?sid=06/02/17/1522228&mode=thread&tid=25
    (accessed October 3, 2006). In February 2006, the online newsmagazine *Salon* published
    an archive of 279 photos and 19 videos of Abu Ghraib abuse first gathered by the army's
    Criminal Investigation Command, and in-depth analysis by Joan Walsh, Michael Scherer,
    Mark Benjamin, and others. "The Abu Ghraib files," available to subscribers at www
    .salon.com/news/abu_ghraib/ (accessed September 25, 2006).

28 Interview with Amy Goodman, transcript p. 6. The second "key technique" added in
    the "de facto behavioral research laboratory, a kind of torture research laboratory," into

which the Guantánamo Bay camp was transformed under General Geoffrey Miller, was the participation during interrogations of "behavioral science consultation teams" ("'Biscuit' teams") whose psychologists "would identify individual phobias, like fear of dark or attachment to mother, and by the time we're done, by 2003, under General Miller, Guantanamo had perfected the CIA paradigm, and it had a three-fold total assault on the human psyche: sensory receptors, self-inflicted pain, cultural sensitivity, and individual fears and phobia."

29 Susan Sontag, "Regarding the Torture of Others," *New York Times*, May 23, 2004. "Looking at these photographs, you ask yourself, How can someone grin at the sufferings and humiliation of another human being? Set guard dogs at the genitals and legs of cowering naked prisoners? Force shackled, hooded prisoners to masturbate or simulate oral sex with one another? And you feel naive for asking, since the answer is, self-evidently, People do these things to other people. Rape and pain inflicted on the genitals are among the most common forms of torture. Not just in Nazi concentration camps and in Abu Ghraib when it was run by Saddam Hussein. Americans, too, have done and do them when they are told, or made to feel, that those over whom they have absolute power deserve to be humiliated, tormented. They do them when they are led to believe that the people they are torturing belong to an inferior race or religion. For the meaning of these pictures is not just that these acts were performed, but that their perpetrators apparently had no sense that there was anything wrong in what the pictures show."

30 See McCoy, *A Question of Torture*, 132.

31 Ibid., 187.

32 Quoted in ibid., 142.

33 See ibid., 162, 178–79, 190–91. See also Tomdispatch: Alfred McCoy on How Not to Ban Torture in Congress, available at www.tomdispatch.com/index.mhtml?pid=57336 (accessed September 25, 2006).

34 Derrida, *Politics of Friendship*, 126, nn. 11, 25.

35 Derrida, *Politiques de l'amitié/Politics of Friendship*, 126–27/104.

36 Ibid., 128/105.

37 Ibid., 128/105, translation slightly changed.

38 Derrida, "Autoimmunity," 160/106.

39 McCoy, *A Question of Torture*, 121.

40 Ibid., 178. In addition to an absurdly narrow definition of what constitutes "torture," Bybee's memo rejected "any limitation on commander-in-chief powers to order interrogations" as representing "'an unconstitutional infringement of the President's authority to conduct war.'" When, to use McCoy's formulation, Bybee's "linguistic legerdemain" was published two years later, some prominent legal scholars "mocked its transparently tendentious reading of the law. 'If the president has commander-in-chief power to commit torture,' said the Yale law dean, Harold Hongju Koh, 'he has the power to commit genocide, to sanction slavery, to promote apartheid, to license summary execution.'" Bybee's wording became national policy in August 2002 and was officially replaced by a memo dated December 30, 2004. McCoy, *A Question of Torture*, 122, 162–63.

41 Derrida, "Autoimmunity," 136/87.

42 Ibid., 178/121.

43 Ibid., 178/120. See in this context Peggy Kamuf, "Deconstruction Reading Politics:

Democracy's Fiction," in *Book of Addresses* (Stanford, CA: Stanford University Press, 2005), 172–88.

44 Derrida, *Politiques de l'amitié/Politics of Friendship*, 40/22, translation slightly changed.

45 Derrida, "Auto-immunity," 136/87.

46 Derrida, "Force of Law," 973.

47 Jacques Derrida, *Spectres de Marx* (Paris: Galilée, 1993), 279.

48 Toni Morrison, *Beloved* (1987; reprint, New York: Penguin, 1998), 274.

49 Ibid., 274–75.

50 Sontag, "Regarding the Torture of Others."

51 Ibid.

52 Susan Sontag's argument deserves to be quoted extensively: "The issue is not whether the torture was done by individuals (i.e., 'not by everybody')—but whether it was systematic. Authorized. Condoned. All acts are done by individuals. The issue is not whether a majority or a minority of Americans performs such acts but whether the nature of the policies prosecuted by this administration and the hierarchies deployed to carry them out makes such acts likely. Considered in this light, the photographs are us. That is, they are representative of the fundamental corruptions of any foreign occupation together with the Bush administration's distinctive policies. The Belgians in the Congo, the French in Algeria, practiced torture and sexual humiliation on despised recalcitrant natives. Add to this generic corruption the mystifying, near-total unpreparedness of the American rulers of Iraq to deal with the complex realities of the country after its 'liberation.' And add to that the overarching, distinctive doctrines of the Bush administration, namely that the United States has embarked on an endless war and that those detained in this war are, if the president so decides, 'unlawful combatants'—a policy enunciated by Donald Rumsfeld for Taliban and Qaeda prisoners as early as January 2002—and thus, as Rumsfeld said, 'technically' they 'do not have any rights under the Geneva Convention,' and you have a perfect recipe for the cruelties and crimes committed against the thousands incarcerated without charges or access to lawyers in American-run prisons that have been set up since the attacks of Sept. 11, 2001." As McCoy notes, "The Justice Department memos, and the administration consensus they reflected, would lead, in the coming months, to widespread use of more brutal methods by both CIA and military interrogators." Ibid., 124.

53 McCoy, *A Question of Torture*, 177.

54 Ibid., 178, 183. According to McCoy, "the APA's code of ethics has stricter, more specific standards for the treatment of laboratory animals than for human subjects such as the Guantánamo detainees" (183).

55 Tomdispatch: Alfred McCoy on How Not to Ban Torture in Congress, available at www.tomdispatch.com/index.mhtml?pid=57336 (accessed September 25, 2006). The popularity of *NYPD Blue* is reflected in the fact that, according to ABC's Web site, the show, then in its twelfth season on ABC, "is one of the longest-running police dramas in broadcast history. Since its network debut in September 1993, the series earned 27 Emmy nominations in its first season, won the coveted award for Outstanding Drama Series in its sophomore year and received Emmy Awards for writing and directing in its fourth and fifth seasons. *NYPD Blue* has received an astounding 82 Emmy nominations, winning 20" (http://abc.go.com/primetime/nypdblue/show.html, accessed October 3, 2006).

It is noteworthy that Fox television network thought it necessary to air, on February 7, 2005, a disclaimer read by star actor Kiefer Sutherland that stated: "Hi. My name is Kiefer Sutherland. And I play counter-terrorist agent Jack Bauer on Fox's *24*. I would like to take a moment to talk to you about something that I think is very important. Now while terrorism is obviously one of the most critical challenges facing our nation and the world, it is important to recognize that the American Muslim community stands firmly beside their fellow Americans in denouncing and resisting all forms of terrorism. So in watching *24*, please, bear that in mind" (www.cairchicago.org/mediamonitor .php?file=mm_sutherland02082005, accessed October 3, 2006).

It should be also noted that the drama series expresses criticism of the state, especially of the newly installed president. This echoes a disturbing fact in the debate on torture: The approval of torture is by far not limited to members or supporters of the governing party. The latest and most blatant testimony to this fact is the "Military Commissions Act of 2006," which suspends habeas corpus for "illegal enemy combatants," whose definition is, according to the editors of the *New York Times*, "dangerously broad." Concurrently, the Act allows the president "to decide on his own what abusive interrogation methods" he considers "permissible." It was voted into law in both the House and the Senate on September 28 and 29, 2006, with twelve Democrats joining their Republican colleagues in the Senate. The editors of the *New York Times* called this legislation "a tyrannical law that will be ranked with the low points in American democracy" (September 28, 2006, *New York Times*, www.nytimes.com/2006/09/28/opinion/28thu1.html?ex=1160193600 &en=7d5045259caef4d9&ei=5070&emc=eta1, accessed the same day).

56 See, for example, McCoy, *A Question of Torture*, 123, 172.

57 See Dana Priest, "CIA Holds Terror Suspects in Secret Prisons," *Washington Post*, Wednesday, November 2, 2005, available at www.washingtonpost.com/wp-dyn/content/ article/2005/11/01/AR2005110101644.html (accessed September 25, 2006).

58 McCoy, *A Question of Torture*, 116. The CIA closed Camp Echo in 2004 for fear that U.S. courts would demand greater control over the agency's activities. See Priest, "CIA Holds Terror Suspects in Secret Prisons."

59 Priest, "CIA Holds Terror Suspects in Secret Prisons."

60 Amnesty International declared in 2005 that "'ghost detainees'—or the incommunicado detention of unregistered detainees—bring back the practice of 'disappearances' so popular with Latin American dictators in the past." See http://web.amnesty.org/library/ Index/ENGPOL100142005 (accessed September 25, 2006).

61 Amy Goodman interview, transcript p. 8.

62 McCoy, *A Question of Torture*, 163.

63 See Priest, "CIA Holds Terror Suspects in Secret Prisons," and McCoy, *A Question of Torture*, 117.

David Lloyd

Rage against the Divine

In memoriam Jacques Derrida

Anticipation

In memory of Derrida, after Derrida, in his wake, even, in this context, *at* his wake, it is hard to write without the uneasy shadow of anticipation, of having already been anticipated in anything one seeks to write. To acknowledge this is not only to honor the extraordinary range of his writings that have, over and again, touched on what remains essential in "Western thought," such that it seems impossible to enter upon any terrain without discovering the imprint or impression of his trace already there. That imprint is also, of course, a question of voice or, more properly, of style: following in his wake, it is hard not to be drawn into the groove that his work has laid down. This is not merely a matter of a singular force of personal style, or even of the power and authority (*Gewalt*), the sovereignty, perhaps, of a project that returned again and again to the foundations and institutions of our thinking, unmistakable as those qualities are. Derrida would doubtless have been among the first to wish to undo the establishment of his utterance and its signatures in a kind of charismatic return to a Logos persisting beyond his

South Atlantic Quarterly 106:2, Spring 2007
DOI 10.1215/00382876-2006-027   © 2007 Duke University Press

presence, in his name. It is, rather, a matter of the force of deconstruction itself (if it may be spoken of in the singular),[1] of, precisely, its address to and at the foundations to which, in always already investing them, it does such deliberate nonviolent violence (*Gewalt*). Indeed, the proper response to the university administrator who asked, hopefully, whether deconstruction did not die with Derrida, might have been to say that deconstruction is where it always has been, in the crypt itself, where the violence of the founding of institutions continues to inform and deform the spirit of their laws, where "a silence is walled up in the violent structure of the founding act" ("FL," 14).

Making that silence speak its violence may be the outrage of deconstruction, the trait that has brought down upon it, invoked in its anxious opponents, the manifestations of rage. Even so, deconstruction does not escape, or evade, the problematics of foundation, of its own establishment as a procedure or a style. If the specter of deconstruction already speaks from the cellarage of our state, is it possible not to follow its voice? The uncanny sense of anticipation, of being anticipated, that one feels in doing so bespeaks the force of a repetition one is enjoined to perform. The imperative of such a performative, as a rule, is the compulsion to repeat rules that remain unwritten, the form of the rule without regulations. One repeats, each time anew, not a formula but a form, the form of the thinking of what informs the institution of thinking. If dread accompanies anticipation, is it because the compulsion to repeat that attends this coming performance exhumes not only the violence that founds but that which anticipates the violence of foundation: rage itself? It is with this in mind that I hope to begin by following the tracks of Derrida's "Force of Law," knowing that in this reading of Walter Benjamin's "Critique of Violence" he has already unfolded its problematic turns in ways that anticipate much of what I, or perhaps any of its readers, might have to say of it. It will scarcely be necessary, and would be painfully laborious, to mark here every echo of Derrida's exposition of Benjamin's essay; my aim is rather to read in its track to a moment that opens and then almost instantly closes back into silence in both essays, the moment at which rage as sheer manifestation is distinguished from founding violence.

The Violence of the Divine

The final paragraphs of Walter Benjamin's "Critique of Violence," insofar as they seem to endorse a conception of divine violence as the expiatory and sovereign paradigm for a revolutionary "unalloyed violence," must give pause and raise difficulty for any secular intellect. It is, of course, tempting to read the essay as a whole from a purely secular standpoint, for its extraordinary and radical critique of the violent foundations of law, for its brilliant insights into the ways in which even the strictly nonviolent practice of the revolutionary general strike must appear as violent to the state, precisely insofar as it challenges the foundations of the law itself, and even for its trenchant reflections on myth and violence.[2] But to stop short at that point is to bracket out exactly what is problematic about the essay and what may force the secular reader to take Benjamin against his grain, if not to reject his line of thought in the final analysis, with whatever theoretical consequences may follow. It is to pose the question as to what lies beyond the deconstructible foundations of the law and haunts the possibility of justice itself. In the first part of this essay, I want to read in the gap and the analogy between human and divine rage as Benjamin elaborates each in order to engage a secular critique of Benjamin's understanding of divine violence. In the next section, I will read back into Benjamin's Mosaic text by way of Freud's earlier reading of Moses and the law in his "The Moses of Michelangelo," a text that stumbles no less on the problematic relation of rage and violence in the founding of the law.

Let us begin, then, with the parenthetical example of end-less violence that Benjamin adduces in the "Critique of Violence": "It is not a means but a manifestation [*Sie ist nicht Mittel, sondern Manifestation*]."[3] As Derrida glosses it, very precisely: "The explosion of violence, in anger, is not a means that looks toward an end; it has no object other than to show and show itself."[4] The problem, as we will see, is that Benjamin's manifestation as it unfolds is entirely purposive and is a manifestation of *violence*. To quote the passage in full:

> The nonmediate function of violence [*nicht mittelbare Funktion der Gewalt*] at issue here is illustrated by everyday experience. As regards man, he is impelled by anger [*der Zorn*], for example, to the most visible outbursts [*Ausbrüchen*] of a violence that is not related as a means to a preconceived end [*auf einen vorgesetzten Zweck*]. It is not a means but a manifestation. ("CV," 294/"KG," 60)

Anger or rage (*der Zorn*) is indeed for Benjamin a category of violence, or, more precisely, and in a way that we will see to be typical, a category that slips as if inevitably into violence. For this "manifestation" of violence, though it has no "preconceived end," has nonetheless, if by analogy, a precise *function*, one that is crucial to lawmaking or to the *foundation* of law. Rage is, for Benjamin, analogous to the mythical violence that reveals the intimate link between power and law and that, as we will see, he seeks to distinguish absolutely from *divine* violence.

Let us follow Benjamin's steps here. Like human anger or rage, mythical violence (*die mythische Gewalt*) is in the first place mere manifestation (*blosse Manifestation*). It has, unlike the application of the law through force or coercive violence (*die Gewalt*), neither a preconceived end nor a general rule, a code, for its exercise. It is this that will make mythical violence the archetype, the *Urbild*, as much as the *Vorbild* (model), of the founding violence of the law ("CV," 294/"KG," 60). This is not the place to elaborate Benjamin's radical critique of both naturalist and positivist accounts of the relation of law and violence. Suffice it to remind ourselves of his conclusion:

> The function of violence in lawmaking [*Rechtsetzung*] is twofold, in the sense that lawmaking (as opposed to the law-preserving work of regular policing) pursues as its end, with violence as the means, *what* is to be established as law, but at the moment of instatement [*Einsetzung*] does not dismiss violence; rather, at this very moment of lawmaking, it specifically establishes as law not an end unalloyed by violence, but one necessarily bound to it, under the title of power. Lawmaking is power making [*Machtsetzung*], and, to that extent, an immediate manifestation of violence. ("CV," 295/"KG," 61)

What Benjamin has in mind here is the terrible beauty of the constitutive violence of the state, that is, the moment of the revolution, of conquest, or of the "Declaration of Independence," the moment of an arbitrary performative that established a legitimacy that lacks any foundation, even that of the "people" in whose name it might speak but which in fact it summons. As Derrida puts it, it is the revolutionary situation that will "justify the recourse to violence by alleging the founding, in progress or to come, of a new law. As this law to come will in return legitimate, retrospectively, the violence that may offend the sense of justice, its future anterior already justifies it" ("FL," 35).[5] It is a moment of sheer intentionality (*Vorsatz*), we might say, that brings into being through violence a new state of affairs whose foundation is that violence. Its end folds back onto its means in that, "at the moment of instatement [*im Augenblick der Einsetzung*]," it aims only at its own establishment. That instantaneous imbrication of ends and means is, indeed, captured in the untranslatable slippage in the word *Gewalt*, which means at once "violence" and "authority or power," as in "the separation of powers [*Gewalttrennung* or *Gewaltteilung*]."[6] The term itself condenses the critique of violence, insofar as it aims at the violence always secreted in the apparently legitimate authority of "law-preserving" or policing in the broadest sense.

Mythical violence, then, is constitutive violence, violence one is tempted to term "proformative" as well as performative.[7] It is boundary-making (*grenzsetzend*: "CV," 296/"KG," 62) in more senses than one: literally, each new state establishes its frontiers, marking the divide between those to whom its laws will and will not be applied; figuratively, and especially in the case of the revolutionary or newly established state, it establishes the division between states or conditions, between the before and the after and between conflict and peace as well as between the inside and the outside. In either case, it is decisive (*entscheidend*), marking with its cut the difference between inside and outside, before and after. Mythical, lawmaking violence thus not only stakes out a territory, it inaugurates a *narrative* by which the violence of foundation is represented, if with retrospective force, as legitimate. Violence becomes a fundamentally narrative form within which subjects find their lawful place.[8]

In this, already, we may note a subtle distinction between human rage, as mere "manifestation," an outburst that is explicitly without end, and mythical violence, for which it appeared to furnish an analogy. For mythical violence turns out to be, in fact, manifestation *of something*, in this case, in Benjamin's *urbildlichen Vorbild*, "a mere manifestation of the gods [*blosse Manifestation der Götter*]": "Not a means to their ends, scarcely a manifestation of their will, but first of all a manifestation of their existence [*am ersten Manifestation ihres Daseins*]" ("CV," 294/"KG," 60). We will return to the significance of this analogical hiccup momentarily.

But what is Benjamin's example of "mythical violence"? The story he invokes is that of the unfortunate Niobe, who, in consequence of boasting that she had more children (twelve) than Leto, mother of Apollo and Artemis, is obliged to witness the gods' slaying of her children and turns into a stone that weeps. Niobe's end furnishes, in a wrenching conceptual pun, "a boundary stone on the frontier between men and gods [*ein Markstein der Grenze zwischen Menschen und Götter]*" ("CV," 295/"KG," 60). Her fate is not a punishment for the transgression of an existent law that separates the mortal and the divine; rather, with a certain *Nachträglichkeit*, her unwitting transgression of an unwritten frontier leads to the establishment of that very frontier in an act of unmediated violence: "Their violence establishes a law far more than it punishes for the infringement [*Übertretung*] of one already existing" ("CV," 294/"KG," 60). The vicious circle that emerges here is that the "lawmaking violence" of the gods affirms an as yet unwritten law that preexists its own establishment; the founding violence of the law is, accordingly, always a potentiality of its exercise. Following Georges Sorel, Benjamin notes the "not merely cultural-historical" but also "metaphysical truth" that "in the beginning all law [*Recht*] was the prerogative [*"Vor"recht*] of the kings or of the nobles" ("CV," 296/ "KG," 61, translation modified; Benjamin's quotation marks). Law as the manifestation of the violence that founds it preexists *and* coexists with the law in its quotidian exercise. Hence, in passing, Benjamin's all-too-relevant observations on the simultaneity of the lawmaking and law-preserving functions of the police, particularly under the conditions of a declaration of emergency or, perhaps, of an unending war on terror.

Accordingly, the law in its founding does not put an end to violence but, rather, maintains or preserves violence in its very structure. As Derrida remarks:

> Iterability requires the origin to repeat itself originarily, to alter itself so as to have the value of origin, that is, to conserve itself. Right away there are police and the police legislate, not content to enforce a law that would have had no force before the police. This iterability inscribes conservation in the essential structure of foundation.[9]

Benjamin's account of mythical violence amounts, then, to a deconstruction of the law in its groundless foundations and of the state's claim to a "monopoly on violence" and leads to a call for its destruction:

> Far from inaugurating a purer sphere, the mythical manifestation of immediate violence shows itself fundamentally identical with all legal violence [i.e., *Rechtsgewalt*: legal authority], and turns suspicion concerning the latter into certainty of the perniciousness of its historical function, the destruction of which thus becomes obligatory [*deren Vernichtung damit zur Aufgabe wird*]. ("CV," 296–97/"KG," 62)

The problem is to establish the mechanism by which such a destruction could be achieved: "This very task [*Gerade diese Aufgabe*] of destruction poses again, in the last resort [*in letzter Instanz*], the question of a pure immediate violence that might be able to call a halt to mythical violence" ("CV," 297/"KG," 62).

It is in response to this task (*Aufgabe*) or "obligation" that Benjamin finally sets divine violence over against mythical violence in a rigorous set of antithetical oppositions:

> Just as in all spheres God opposes myth, mythical violence is confronted by the divine. And the latter constitutes its antithesis in all respects. If mythical violence is lawmaking, divine violence is law-destroying; if the former sets boundaries, the latter boundlessly destroys them; if mythical violence brings at once guilt and retribution, divine power only expiates; if the former threatens, the latter strikes; if the former is bloody, the latter is lethal without spilling blood. ("CV," 297)

Given this set of oppositions, it is consistent that against the tale of Niobe, Benjamin poses a biblical story, that of the fate of the company of Korah, the Israelites who oppose the authority of Moses and Aaron during the wanderings of the people. Benjamin understands the tale as exemplifying precisely the difference of divine, expiatory violence from retributive mythical violence, and in reading the story one is indeed struck by the bloodless annihilation of the company and, subsequently, of those who dare to protest their fate. The story, in Numbers 16 to 18, is as follows: Korah, a Levite, and 250 others "challenged the authority of Moses" (16:1), demanding to know by what right they claimed authority over the rest:[10] "They confronted Moses and Aaron and said to them: 'You take too much upon yourselves. Every member of the community is holy and the Lord is amongst them all. Why do you set yourselves up above the assembly of the Lord?'" As before the Egyptian sorcerers, Moses' response is to organize a showdown, and the company of Korah are gathered before the Tabernacle, where, despite Moses' and Aaron's Lot-like remonstrations to the Lord, the whole company is duly annihilated according to Moses' design, bloodlessly indeed:

> Hardly had Moses spoken when the ground beneath them split; the earth opened its mouth and swallowed them and their homes—all the followers of Korah and all their property. They went down alive into Sheol with all that they had; the earth closed over them, and they vanished from the assembly. At their cries all the Israelites round them

> fled, shouting, "Look to yourselves! the earth will swallow us up."
> Meanwhile fire had come out from the Lord and burned up the two
> hundred and fifty men who were presenting the incense. (Numbers
> 16:31–35)

Nor is this instance of shock and awe sufficient to quell the murmurings
of the resistance: "Next day all the community of the Israelites raised com-
plaints against Moses and Aaron and taxed them with causing the death
of some of the Lord's people" (16:41). Once again, the Lord in his wisdom
decides to make an end of all complainers and does so once more bloodlessly, by way of a plague that merely destroys a further 14,700 of the Israelites (Numbers 16:42–50). In this moment, in which "wrath has gone forth
already from the presence of the Lord" (16:46), it is not God's violence
that is expiatory but Aaron's "standing between the dead and the living"
(16:48). Expiation appears as the prerogative of the lawful priest, who establishes a boundary between the worthy and the unworthy, the saved and the
doomed, rather than as a quality of divine violence.

Indeed, reading on into the effects of this rebellion and its violent suppression, it becomes clear that this tale regards the institution (*Einsetzung*) of the priesthood, the establishment of Aaron and his descendants as
the legitimate priests of the tabernacle, alone permitted to enter into the
Presence, and of a division of labor that separates them from the surviving
Levites, who perform some of the functions of the priesthood, and those in
turn from the body of the Israelites who henceforth dare not approach the
Tent of the Presence on pain of death. And as the story unfolds, we see not
only the establishment of the priesthood but also its careful institution of
severely policed boundaries, *Grenzsetzung*.[11] In Benjamin's own terms, this
appears far less like an expiatory, law-destroying manifestation of divine
violence than one indistinguishable from the forms of mythical violence in
its function of lawmaking or inauguration. The carefully posed distinction
between mythical and divine violence collapses in the elaboration of the
example, even in the terms that Benjamin himself has articulated. Indeed,
though it may seem almost blasphemous to say so, given Benjamin's life
and all he stands for, there is an uncanny and disturbing resonance between
the "bloodless" annihilation that characterizes divine violence and the no
less bloodless techniques of the camps that were to represent the founding
violence of the Third Reich. "They went down into Sheol with all that they
had; the earth closed over them, and they vanished from the assembly."[12]

In this resonant collapse of divine into mythical violence, the attempt to read Benjamin's account of divine violence in this early essay as messianic in the later sense of the "Theses on the Philosophy of History" (a sense to which we will return), or as a transformation of the idea of revolutionary violence into conformity with what he termed "ethical anarchism," seems to me to founder irrevocably. Divine violence not only shares with mythical violence a foundational function; it is maintained through a highly elaborate code of law- and boundary-preserving measures whose application is attended with the threat of a merely suspended violence.

Given, then, that divine violence fails, after all, to offer us the instance of "pure unmediated violence"—being, in the last instance, an end-directed founding violence scarcely distinguishable from its mythical counterpart— we are obliged, according to Benjamin's logic, to fall back on mortal rage itself and to the sphere of ordinary human experience for an instance of that "non-mediate function of violence." We have already noted the faltering of the analogy between human rage as "manifestation" and the manifestation of the gods that is mythical violence. Rage, as sheer manifestation, has in fact neither subject nor object. It stands *before* the law- and subject-making moment of violence; indeed, its archetype is the infantile protest at the violence that splits one into subject and object, the no to an ineluctable process of differentiation and subordination to the law. Rage is indifferent to what in its frenzy gets destroyed, the self as object or the self's objects. Hence the terror of the one subjected to rage is not identical with the terror the same subject feels in the face of the violence that may or may not follow rage. However infinitesimal the temporal lag between rage and the infliction of violence, a difference is discernible. If violence is agential, destructive of its objects, transitive, and, in its way, subject-forming in its very transformation of the other into its object, rage is a most un-Hegelian moment of suspension or stasis whose vertiginous oscillations are set in motion by a reciprocal annihilation—the annihilation of the subject in the one who rages and the disappearance of the subject in the one who witnesses the obliterating gaze of the enraged. To be enraged is to be beside oneself, out of oneself; it is to be possessed by a force that is indifferent to the subject in oneself and to the subject in another.[13] Hence the one who witnesses rage witnesses the enraged as a lack of subject and knows that in that absence of subjecthood, his or her own subject is no less annihilated. The enraged does not see the other as subject or even as object: in the sheer transport of rage, differentiation is undone. Rage, therefore, can be neither founding nor destructive, though it may give way to either. It neither institutes nor destroys: it is resolutely nonnarrative and gives rise to nothing out of its stasis, and though, indeed, it may give way almost immediately to violence, it remains another moment with another logic. It is sheer manifestation, but of nothing.

Freud's Steps

Is it perhaps because of this effect of paralysis, of suspension of narrative resolution, that we search in vain for any sustained theoretical analysis of rage as distinguished from violence, aggression, anxiety, and so forth? Is it that, in consuming itself in its very instant, rage preempts the concept? Or is it that, precisely being sheer manifestation, rage lacks the end-directedness that would allow it to be subsumed under a concept? Theory, in any case, seems to turn from rage or turn rage too hastily into what seems to issue from it, as if rage were an embarrassment or, more precisely, an exception: the exception whose exclusion—petrified, walled in, encrypted—allows the narrative of/and law to proceed.[14] Rage is reapprehended as if it were identical with the violence that seems to be what issues from it with apparent inevitability. And yet, as Benjamin, if momentarily, reminds us, rage and violence are not the same: of rage, something remains distinct even after the so-rapid passage to violence, to the relation of means to ends, to narrative. There remains something that troubles theory in the scarcely perceptible yet persistent difference of rage from violence. On the other hand, perhaps it is something of that embarrassment, and a sense of something that awkwardly precedes or anticipates the lawmaking function of violence, that accounts for part of the unease one feels in reading the story of the band of Korah. It is not only the fact of their fate, the bloodless slaughter of some 15,000 Israelites, that disturbs, but the association of such punitive, end-directed violence with the unbounded, excessive divine wrath (*Zorn*) that it shares with the "mythical violence" directed by Apollo and Artemis against Niobe. Faced with such a spectacle, we share something of Niobe's petrified, frozen outrage.

Let us say for the moment that rage is what survives, in the mode of a refusal, the instituting force of violence that the law conserves, iterates, forgets. For the story that the law narrates is one that retrospectively legitimates the violence that is its foundation and its constitutive limit and that would haunt it perpetually were it not, in that very narrative, forgotten. This is the conjunction that Derrida denominates, after Montaigne and

Pascal, "the *mystical* foundation of the law": "It is what I here propose to call the mystical. Here a silence is walled up in the violent structure of the founding act. Walled up, walled in because silence is not exterior to language" ("FL," 14). Following Derrida in the track he will himself trace, and which we will follow in another way shortly, from "Force of Law" to *Archive Fever*, from Benjamin to Freud, we might equally call it "the *arcane* foundation of the law." For not only does the ark, *arca*, contain the stone Tablets of the Law, but *arkhe* itself "names at once the *commencement* and the *commandment*."[15] Like violence, the archive both shelters what it contains and forgets, "shelters itself from this memory it shelters" (*AF*, 2). From the outset of *Archive Fever*, Derrida deliberately recalls "Force of Law" to draw the analogy between violence and the archive, both at once "institutive and conservative," and, indeed, to name the violence encrypted in the archive: "the violence of a power [*Gewalt*] which at once posits and conserves the law, as the Benjamin of *Kritik zur Gewalt* would say. What is at issue here, starting with the exergue, is the violence of the archive itself, *as archive, as archival violence*" (*AF*, 7). But if the archive appears as violence, it would be no less the case, as we have been learning, that violence is crucially archival, sheltering its lawmaking performance in a narrative, a history, that seeks to forget what it shelters. Rage as sheer manifestation, as that which is the refuse or refusal of narration, having neither ends nor instituting force, appears as a tear in the archive of violence. Rage survives the narratives that rationalize violence, that seek even to incorporate rage itself as an expression of object-oriented violence. For that reason, it seems crucial to maintain the distinction between rage and violence as we proceed, difficult, even impossible, as that distinction may be to theorize. It is, indeed, a distinction that eludes even the science that would seem most prepared to elaborate it, psychoanalysis, and for reasons that are profoundly embedded in its own archive.

Yet in the very foundations of a culture so informed by a biblical archive, is there not something profoundly familiar, familial, even, in this deep association of lawmaking violence and the rage that is beyond it? It is an association condensed in the ultimate lawmaking patriarch, Moses, the challenge to whose authority leads to the Korachites' annihilation. The Moses of the Bible is indeed a man of godlike anger. In Sigmund Freud's words:

> The Moses of legend and tradition had a hasty temper and was subject to fits of passion. It was in a transport of divine wrath [*Anfalle von*

heiligem Zorne] of this kind that he slew an Egyptian who was maltreating an Israelite, and had to flee out of the land into the wilderness; and it was in a similar passion that he broke the Tables of the Law, inscribed by God himself. Tradition, in recording such a characteristic, is unbiased and preserves the impression of a great personality who once lived.[16]

Freud's description of Moses here, in "The Moses of Michelangelo," is imbued with all the ambivalence that will emerge in full some two decades later in the essays that make up *Moses and Monotheism* and that explicitly align the patriarch of the Old Testament with the despotic Ur-father of *Totem and Taboo*. But it is here, in an essay devoted to a representation of Moses as the lawmaker, rather than in the later essays, that Freud comes closest to an analysis of the relation between rage and violence. It is also an essay that anticipates Benjamin's analysis of Mosaic violence through a different but no less luminous trajectory.

It is worth following Freud's steps in some detail, not least because the motive that impels him to this trespass into the territory of art history and aesthetics is bound up with the repetition of steps. But I anticipate. Freud commences his essay, published anonymously in the psychoanalytic journal *Imago* in 1914, with a not uncharacteristically diffident disclaimer: "I may say at once that I am no connoisseur in art, but simply a layman" ("MM," 211). His attention to the artwork—in this case, Michelangelo's celebrated statue of Moses, made for the never-finished tomb of Pope Julius II in the Church of S. Pietro in the Roman suburb of Vincoli—is directed not at its "formal and technical qualities" but at its "subject-matter" ("MM," 211). He seeks to understand the affect that a great work produces and is frustrated by the paradox "that precisely some of the grandest [*grossartigsten*] and most overwhelming [*überwältigendsten*] creations of art are still riddles to our understanding" ("MM," 211/*GW*, 173). In order to resolve such riddles, which are only exacerbated by the mass of discordant writings about artworks, one must have recourse to "the application of psychoanalysis" as the mode of access to "the intentions and emotional activities of the artist" ("MM," 212). As the exemplary instance of the effectiveness of psychoanalytic interpretation of artworks, Freud adduces his own and others' reading of *Hamlet* in relation to "the Oedipus theme."

The logic of metonymy might then suggest that when Freud begins his account of the artwork that is now the focus of his attention, we have not strayed far from the terrain of the Oedipus theme. We should follow his steps with care, marked as they are by impress of repetition, sublimity, and abject identifications:

> Another of these inscrutable [*rätselvollen*] and wonderful works of art is the marble statue of Moses, by Michelangelo, in the Church of S. Pietro in Vincoli in Rome. As we know, it was only a fragment of the gigantic tomb which the artist was to have erected for the powerful [*gewaltigen*] Pope Julius II. It always delights me to read an appreciatory sentence about this statue, such as that it is "the crown of modern sculpture" (Hermann Grimm). For no piece of statuary has ever made a stronger impression [*Wirkung*, effect] on me than this. How often have I mounted the steep steps of the unlovely Corso Cavour to the lonely place where the deserted church stands, and have (always/each time) essayed to support the angry scorn of the hero's glance [*habe immer versucht, dem verächtlich-zürnenden Blick des Heros standzuhalten*]! Sometimes I have crept cautiously out of the half-gloom of the interior as though I myself belonged to the mob upon whom his eye is turned—the mob which can hold fast no conviction, which has neither faith nor patience and which rejoices when it has regained its illusory idols. ("MM," 213/*GW*, 174–75)

What motivates this so firmly stressed repetition compulsion on Freud's part, a compulsion that that leads him over and again to mount laboriously the steps that lead him to this overwhelming (*überwaltigend*) statue and to subject himself, painfully indeed, yet surely also with some surplus of delight or even rejoicing, to the anger and scorn of its look?

Freud then commences his own description of the statue, interrupting it with what any reader of Freud's work will recognize as a characteristic deferral: "Were I to give a more detailed description of his attitude, I should have to anticipate what I want to say later on [*so musste ich dem vorgreifen, was ich später vorzubringen habe*]" ("MM," 214/*GW*, 175–76). At this point, Freud fears that his own expository haste, his impulse to reveal what he has already grasped, might forestall the necessary process by which we arrive at the truth in following the steps of his own deductions. What must be seen is already there, but not only is he already there before us; our recognition of the justice of his observations will require that we recognize his anticipation of us and that he not anticipate himself. As the narrative of his investigation unfolds, we will come to see that precisely what we think we grasp (*greifen*) at once is in fact no more than the trace of what has gone before and not, as indeed we might think, the sign of what is to come.

As we proceed through Freud's careful collation of other critics' descriptions of the statue, erroneous as they seem to him, we cannot miss the fact that the first citations in the series turn on Moses's grasping (*greifen*) of his beard with his right hand, a gesture on which, as we shall see, not to anticipate Freud, all turns. For the moment, his point is that the critics do not even agree on what they see, on what is before their eyes. The second set of disagreements concerns the emotional tenor of the gestures that are represented. Is his expression—as Freud's own initial reactions would seem to suggest—"a mixture of wrath [*Zorn*], pain and contempt" or is it indicative of serener emotions, for example, "a proud simplicity, an inspired dignity, a living faith" ("MM," 214/*GW*, 176)? To this apparent ambiguity is added another that concerns the moment that is represented: "Did Michelangelo intend to create a 'timeless study of character and mood' [Freud here cites an unnamed critic] in this Moses, or did he portray [*dargestellt*] him at a particular and, if so, at a highly significant moment of his life?" ("MM," 215/ *GW*, 177). Unsurprisingly, the majority of critics recognize this moment as that of Moses' descent from Mount Sinai, bearing the Tablets of the Law, and the moment of his realization that the Israelites have made themselves a golden calf and are worshipping it. Following Freud's citations, the critics are agreed that this is a dramatic instant, full of anticipation: we wait in this moment of pause for Moses "to start up in wrath [*Zorn*]," "for the explosion of his wrath to burst out with more annihilation the next." The statue would be the representation, then, of the instant at which rage issues in object-directed violence, *und zur Tat überzugehen*, as Freud puts it ("MM," 216–17/*GW*, 178–79).

Yet for reasons that have to do in the first place with observations on the design of the whole monument of which this statue was to have composed part, Michelangelo cannot have meant, following Freud, to have intended this. Freud's first response draws him to agree rather with those critics who see in the statue not the representation of a moment of wrath but that of a "character-type," that of the *vir activus* known to have been the topic of one set of the statues designated for the foot of the sepulcher. Such a character-type would embody "perpetual conflicts," both inner conflict and the conflict between the great man and the "rest of mankind," giving rise to the statue's representation of a contrast between "the inward fire and the outer calm of his bearing" ("MM," 221/*GW*, 184). Much as such accounts explain, Freud finds something lacking in them: *"aber ich vermisse irgend etwas"* ("MM," 221/GW, 184). The excess of the statue's power over their explanations lies, it seems, "perhaps" in "the need to discover a closer parallel" between its attitude and its conflicted emotions, or, properly, a more intimate or *internal relation* between them [*Vielleicht, dass sich ein Bedürfnis äussert nach einer innigeren Beziehung*]" ("MM," 221/GW, 184). To trace such an "inner relation" will involve Freud in the first place in what we might call a "close reading" of the statue, following what he thinks of as a revolutionary method of art historical scholarship that "laid stress on the significance of minor details." This practice of art history, it seems, converges with the practice of psychoanalysis itself: "It too is accustomed to divine secret and concealed things from unconsidered or unnoticed details, from the rubbish-heap (*dem Abhub—dem* "refuse" [in English]), as it were, of our observations" ("MM," 222/GW, 185). From such "unconsidered trifles," from the "refuse" that observation has refused to see, Freud commences his reconstruction of the steps that anticipate the moment in which Moses is represented. On the basis of those details, the moment of rage that appears to first view is resolved into a narrative that tells another tale.

At the heart of this narration lies the secret of the right hand that grasps a strand of Moses' beard, fixing it to the right of the body as the head turns sharply to the left. What resolves the riddle of this "most unusual treatment [*das auffälligste Schicksal*]" ("MM," 223/GW, 186)? Freud's answer proposes that the attitude of the statue represents the last moment in a series that anticipates it:

> If the *left* side of Moses' beard lies under the pressure of his *right* finger, we may perhaps take this pose as the last stage of some connection between his right hand and the left half of his beard, a connection which was a much more intimate one at some moment before that chosen for representation [*so lässt sich dies vielleicht als der Rest einer Beziehung zwischen der rechten Hand und der linken Barthälfte verstehen, welche in einem früheren Momente als dem dargestellten eine weit innigere war*]. ("MM," 224/GW, 188)

This remainder (*Rest*) of a more inward relation (*einer innerigen Beziehung*) is the trace (*Spur*) of a prior action rather than the sign of one to follow, the mark, as it turns out, of a willed inhibition of action rather than of a loss of control that will lead from rage to violence. In a series of cartoons, Freud represents the series of steps that precede the actual statue's posture. Moses is at first seated, holding the Tablets under his right arm, in calm contemplation, a contemplation interrupted by the noises of jubilation from the Israelite camp below. This interruption at first throws Moses into a rage, and as he turns violently to the left to see what is happening, his right hand seizes his beard, risking releasing the Tablets to fall to the ground. The existent posture is thus the trace of his arm's movement back to prevent their fall, leaving a strand of the beard accidentally caught in his finger. It is the image of regained control rather than of eruption into anger:

> What we see before us is not the inception of a violent action [*die Einleitung zu einer gewaltsamen Aktion*] but the remains [*Rest*] of a movement that has already taken place. In his first transport of fury [*in einem Anfall von Zorn*], Moses desired to act, to spring up and take vengeance and forget the Tables; but he has overcome the temptation, and he will now remain seated and still in his frozen wrath [*in gebändigter Wut*] and in his pain mingled with contempt. Nor will he throw away the Tables so that they will break on the stones, for it is on their especial account that he has controlled his anger [*Zorn*]; it was to preserve them that he kept his passion in check. In giving way to his rage and indignation [*leidenschaftlichen Empörung*], he had to neglect the Tables, and the hand which upheld them was withdrawn. They began to slide down and were in danger of being broken. This brought him to himself. He remembered his mission and renounced for its sake an indulgence of his feelings [*Affekts*]. ("MM," 229–30/*GW*, 194)

Freud readily admits that if his theory is correct, it is not the Moses of the Bible that Michelangelo has portrayed, neither in his actions nor in his passionate character:

> Michelangelo has placed a different Moses on the tomb of the Pope, one superior to the historical and traditional Moses. . . . In this way he has added something new and more than human [*Übermenschliches*] to the figure of Moses; so that the giant frame with its tremendous physical power [*gewaltige Körpermasse*] becomes only a concrete expression of the highest mental [*psychische*] achievement that is possible in a man, that of struggling successfully against an inward passion [*der eigenen Leidenschaft*] for the sake of a cause to which he has devoted himself. ("MM," 233/*GW*, 198)

The Moses of Michelangelo is thus the very image of civilization's capacity to overcome and sublimate baser instincts in the name of, or for the protection of, the Law. It translates an external physical force into an inner psychic power, the power, we might say, of *Rechtsetzung*, the institution or establishment of law. Law is established as physical violence (*Gewalt*), undergoes inhibition (*Hemmung*), and is transformed into authority (*Gewalt*). In such an image, the force of the Law is saved from its own emergence in violence. Violence is represented as contained by and contained in the law. It is an image of the foundation of the law in the instant where violence, turned inward as restraint, becomes identical with the law it institutes and preserves. In this instant, both violence and the figure of the punishing father are internalized, subjecting the subject to the law in a movement and a moment that will be repeated incessantly. It is also the instant in which rage will be barred, petrified, bounded—*gehemmt*—as if the manifestation of rage might threaten to undo the narrative of law.

Anarchival Rage

And with this, Freud says, "we have now completed our interpretation" ("MM," 233). And yet. And yet the essay continues with a consideration of the motives that might have led Michelangelo to place such a statue in Pope Julius's tomb, motives that are an intricate mixture of identification and reproach. On the one hand, it is clear that Moses is a model for Julius himself, one who "attempted to realize great and mighty [*gewaltiges*] ends" and did so impatiently, employing violent means (*mit gewalttätigen Mitteln*). In this also, Michelangelo would have seen a resemblance to himself:

> He could appreciate Michelangelo as a man of his own kind, but he often made him smart under his sudden anger [*Jähzorn*] and his utter lack of consideration for others. The artist felt the same violent force of will [*Heftigkeit des Strebens*] in himself, and, as the more introspective thinker, may have had a premonition of the failure to which they were both doomed. And so he carved his Moses on the Pope's tomb, not without reproach [*Vorwurf*] against the dead pontiff [*gegen den Verstorbenen*], as a warning to himself, thus rising in self-criticism superior to his own nature. ("MM," 233–34/*GW*, 198–99)

In this identification of Michelangelo with his own Moses, a triangle of identifications is completed, though not without throwing open another trajectory, that of *Vorwurf*, accusation or reproach, that travels vertiginously around that triangle: Michelangelo's reproach to Julius, which is also a self-reproach that embraces the possibility of mutual failure, yet is at the same time resentment at reproaches from the dead pontiff. Yet the English translation reduces the ambiguity of the German phrase, *gegen den Verstorbenen*, against the dead one, which might logically refer, in this context, as much to the long-dead Moses, whose death famously prevented his entering the promised land and stood as the mark of his failure to master the Israelites and himself—a point Freud explores at great length in *Moses and Monotheism* many years later.[17] Moses is Michelangelo, is Julius, is the ambivalent focus of resentment and rage, perhaps, as much as he is the model of self-mastery.

And so Freud's conclusion returns us to the riddle of the statue of Moses and the affects it provokes just where we thought it resolved. And there we find Freud again, climbing the steps—how often, *wie oft*—to the Church of San Pietro in order to attempt, again and again (*immer*), to sustain the wrathful and contemptuous (*verächtlich-zürnenden*) gaze of the patriarch. One is struck, as so often, by Freud's painstaking subversion of his own archival procedure, a tendency that is part and parcel of the procedure itself. Yielding to us the archeology of his own process of interpretation, insisting on our following his steps back to the first impressions that are the archaic traces of his own motives and motifs, it is as if he demands, even in presenting us with a certain flourish of triumph the completed archive of his findings, that we return to undo that archive, confront and decrypt what it shelters and forgets. As Derrida remarks, "No one has illuminated better than Freud what we have called the archontic principle of the archive, which in itself presupposes not the originary *arkhe* but the nomological *arkhe* of the law, of institution, of domiciliation, of filiation. No one has analyzed, that is to say, deconstructed, the authority of the archontic principle better than he" (*AF*, 95). In the insistent *fort-da* of Freud's returns to and partings from this statue, prefaced as they are by his remarks on *Hamlet*, is it possible not to observe the unresolved rhythms of pleasure and fear in facing and perhaps facing down the rage of the patriarch, that rage before which the subject is annihilated, and in which, moreover, can be discerned no less the failure, the foundering, of the subject and the law in the enraged?

It is precisely from such a reproach that Freud wants to save Moses throughout an essay that is devoted to showing that Michelangelo depicts him not in his rage, but in a moment of regained self-control. But what is being saved here? On the one hand, it may be that Freud seeks to save himself from the possibility of the violence that might be unleashed upon him as Moses' rage issues in deed. On the other, it may be that Freud, more generously, like a boy at once deeply identified with his father and yet ashamed of his father's failings, seeks to save Moses' "character" from the reproach of being subject to transports of rage that lead him to excess and even murder. The motive that Freud attributes to Michelangelo is then his own, the attempt to depict Moses as a reproachless adult, a higher being, an *Übermensch*, rather than as a flawed and even petty human being. Both these motives can be discerned in the strange fantasy that follows in the gloom of the church, that Freud himself "belonged to the mob [*Gesindel*] upon whom his eye is turned—the mob which can hold fast no conviction, which has neither faith nor patience and which rejoices when it has regained [*wieder bekommen hat*] its illusory idols" ("MM," 213/GW, 174–75). Freud places himself here as the potential object of Moses' punishing violence, among the mob, the riffraff, because he identifies with their failure to adhere to "serious causes [*grosse Sache*]." At the same time, he shares their joy in the restoration of their lost idols, precisely what the commandment on the Tablet forbids and what is the object of Moses' reproach and wrath. For what does Freud seek but the restoration of Moses, his transformation in art, in a graven image, from the angry and inconsistent figure of scripture and tradition to a "character-type" more worthy of the boy's idolization? In that transfiguration, Moses becomes not the real and flawed patriarch but the idealized inner image of the Law, an *Übermensch* that is the *Über-Ich*, the internalized image of what the boy wants to be when he is bigger. His *gewaltige Gestalt* must become the outer sign of an inner *Gewalt*, authority rather than violence, the *Darstellung*, presentation, give way to a *Vorstellung*, imaginary representation, in which we can finally say what such works "represent to us" ("MM," 211/GW, 173).

But the narrative transformation of *Gewalt* as violence into *Gewalt* as law remains unachieved, the analysis unterminated. Attentive as Freud is to detail, we may overlook the detail from which, gradually through the essay, his attention turns, that is, Moses' face or look. While in the first instance what impresses itself on Freud is Moses' gaze (*Blick*) or the eye he turns toward the mob, later Freud fixes almost exclusively on the positioning of the right arm which holds the Tables of the Law—and with which, perhaps, the patriarch might strike the idolater. The very details that might communicate his rage—the eye, the brow, and the mouth, the aversion of the glance—are those that Freud forgets. It is as if the narrative course of his analysis releases him, or distracts him, from the anxiety inspired by the prospect of rage, only to impress on him another anxiety, a singularly narrative one at that, the dread of anticipation.

Dread of anticipation is the fear of inadequacy before the law, fear that another will perform the law better, be preferred before one, be first in the eye of the father. It is the dread of failing at the law, of failing to be singular. As such, it is a deeply temporal dread, the fear of faltering as a subject only possible for a subject already formed by the law. It is a dread that maintains the subject in relation to the law as the subject of an iterative performance of what the law has already laid down.[18] The dread of anticipation is thus intimately bound up with the method of reading itself, with the path that is to lead us through the track (*Spur*) of the work's details, that litter of refuse, of *Abhub*, scum, thrown up in the wake of the work, the remainder that survives the passing of the artist's intent (*Absicht*). That intent is lost sight of in the obscure origins of the work, though we continue to be subjected to its "powerful impression [*einem so gewaltigen Eindruck*]" (*GW*, 174, translation modified), the imprint or track of its passage through us, over us. Or, to deploy Freud's other metaphor, our apprehension of the work is the repetition of the affective state of the artist: "Es soll die Affektlage, die psychische Konstellation, welche beim Künstler die Triebkraft zur Schöpfung abgab, bei uns wieder hervorgerufen werden" ("MM," 212/*GW*, 173). Two metaphors for the origin of the work of art and for the sources of its overwhelming (*überwaltigend*) impact upon us: The one suggests its movement through us and our iteration of that movement, in turn, the path by which we return to the steps that led to the representation. Narrative in form, it leads us through the steps that the work itself has already anticipated and imprinted in us, though its overwhelming power may blind us to what we have already seen. The other, that of the constellation, the one that Freud departs from as the essay gets under way, and to which he will not return, instead suggests stasis, the tense, gravitational suspension of relations that remain the same, before which we stand motionless because, being outside worldly time, they are not repeatable. The constellation abolishes time. It can only be summoned up—*hervorgerufen*—again and again, as a specter that erupts into the law.

We may see these metaphors as metaphors for law and rage, respectively. Through his method of narrating the steps that anticipated the form of the statue as we see it, as we fail to see it, in delineating the occult movements that account for these details that are the remainders of past acts, Freud's analysis seeks to redeem the violence of origins and transform it into the authority of a law that can be regularized, subject to rule and *ratio*, grasped in such a way that its power over us can be apprehended and assented to in terms of its genesis. The power of the work, both its *Wirkung* and its *Gewalt*, is subject to a rationality in which every detail is accounted for insofar as it contributes to the *Gesamteindruck* (total effect) of the whole, disposed in "a clear and connected sequence of events [*einen ohne Lücke verständlichen Vorgang*, a comprehensible sequence *without gaps*]" ("MM," 225/*GW*, 189). What threatens the sequence of the law, its coherence as a consequence of the origin with which it is continuous, is the gap still constituted by the occurrence of a rage without issue, rage as "sheer manifestation." It is this rage that survives the narration of Michelangelo's Moses as a break in the sequence, a break, indeed, whose trace informs the details, the refuse, that remain to be read. What remains, after the account of the genesis of the statue's attitude, after the inquiry into Michelangelo's intent and into his identifications, is the specter of a failure—a failure to communicate or transmit those intentions, a failure to make clear, a failure to complete (*vollenden*)—and the reproach that it summons back.[19] In the gap that failure represents, a gap that repeats itself over and over in Freud's own failure satisfactorily to complete his analysis, lurks that which will not be subjected to narrative: the manifestation of rage.

While law sets a limit to violence, both monopolizing and, in principle, regularizing it, an as-yet-unlimited violence remains the foundation of law. And if violence is the threshold at which the law and its iterative temporality are founded, the never-admitted, ever-represented foundation of power, rage is what is encrypted just beyond that threshold, within the law within which it still finds no place. Rage is the atemporal survival of mortality in the subject, the irreducible fact of death entwined in life that negates the subject even as it strives to subject life to the regularity of law, to the realization of ends. In rage, the subject as such is annihilated, confronted with the specter of a mortality that cannot be redeemed. The terror of the subject in the face of rage, and the fascination that summons him or her back time and again to see if he can support it, is not one with the terror at violence. For violence, as lawmaking and law-preserving, makes the subject as much as it undoes him, and, as Kant might say along with Freud, the terror of law's violence is tempered by his accord with the law. The terror in rage is terror at that which persists at the heart of subjectifying violence, the suspension of the subject in its own irredeemable mortality that no power survives. The rhythm of the law, in its iterative enactment or application, is punctuated by rage, which at once exceeds law and is contained within if not by it. Rage haunts the law as a manifestation of the failure of its violence to subject the world of the living, as a remainder and a reminder of its foundering, of the atemporal abyss on which one stands.[20] Rage is the face of life before its own death.

It would be wrong, then, to see rage as simply destructive, merely a modality of the death drive, of *ananke*, manifesting itself in the subject. Unlike violence or aggression, rage is not directed at the conservation of a subject nor at the destruction of its objects, though psychoanalytic work has tended to conflate it with such tendencies.[21] Rage maintains its ambivalent, ambiguous relation to the drives in which the subject is suspended. We might, however, still understand rage as a peculiar form of what Derrida calls the *anarchive*, notwithstanding his association of it with the death drive: "the death drive, the violence of forgetting, *superrepression* (suppression and repression), the anarchive, in short, the possibility of putting to death the very thing, whatever its name, which *carries the law in its tradition*: the archon of the archive, the table, *what* carries the table and *who* carries the table, the subjectile, the substrate, the subject of law" (*AF*, 79). But it cannot be the death drive that undoes the subject, or the archive, so bound up is it with the very formation, in violence, of the subject and its archives: the death drive, we recall from "Beyond the Pleasure Principle" and *Civilization and Its Discontents*, seeks to conserve the ego in homeostasis, not to destroy it. It is, rather, rage, the unnarrativizable, unincorporated surplus over violence, that haunts foundation and casts into relief the violence it shelters and forgets. The remainder of rage as the reminder of what cannot be narrativized, accounted for, in Freud's interpretation of Michelangelo's Moses serves equally as reminder of the fact and the cost of Benjamin's—and Derrida's—passing over of the moment of rage in the passage from mythical to divine violence. Only in the discounting of mortal rage in the face of an immortal, ineluctable violence can the profound injustice of divine violence and its inaugural force be overlooked.

If there is, as we have suspected and as Derrida worries in the postscript to "The Force of Law," a deep affinity between Benjamin's divine violence and the technology of the Holocaust—bloodless and annihilatory as it is—then it may not reside merely in the momentary affinities between Benjamin and Heidegger's thinking of "destruction" or between Benjamin's and Carl

Schmitt's critiques of parliamentarianism. Nor, I think, can it be ascribed to the notion, attractive as it might be in saving Benjamin's terms, that "what Nazism, as the final achievement of the logic of mythical violence, would have attempted to do is to exclude the other witness, to destroy the witness of the other order, of a divine violence whose justice is irreducible to right, of a violence heterogeneous to the order both of right (be it that of human rights or of the order of representation) and of myth" ("FL," 60). On the contrary, not only is the distinction between mythical and divine violence deconstructed in the convergence of their instituting functions, as we have seen, but there is also a terrible convergence between divine and Nazi violence in that both—and not least in Benjamin's desire for a pure expiatory violence—seek to forget through violence the violence that they perform. This desire for annihilation, for the abolition of all record of the destroyed, is the deep injustice immanent in both, the injustice that rage refuses.[22]

Only through a long detour, and one impossible to pursue in detail here, does Benjamin emerge with a philosophy of history commensurate with the significance of the brief moment that rage appears in its own right in the *Critique of Violence*. If, as Benjamin asserts, "the critique of violence is the philosophy of its history" ("CV," 299), it is a philosophy of the history of repetitions, of what appears from "close at hand" merely "a dialectical rising and falling in the lawmaking and law-preserving formations of violence." The "law governing their oscillation" and the possibility of "the breaking of this cycle," which is in its oscillation finally unhistorical, are conceived from the perspective of a thinking of the divine or revolutionary violence that might found "a new historical epoch" ("CV," 300). It is not hard to see how far this conception of history is from the conception of historical materialism that Benjamin would elaborate in the face of what must have seemed the triumph of the "new historical epoch" of the Third Reich. In the terms of the "Theses on the Philosophy of History," divine violence, in its annihilatory force as in its culminative historicism, is absolutely not "messianic," nor indeed does that term attach to it in the critique, tempting as the association may seem. But then, for Benjamin, the messianic has become rigorously secular in the fullest sense of that term—not only as worldly, but as something that occurs in time, through time, punctually but across time—and absolutely not of the future.[23] The horizon of the messianic in Benjamin's late writing is not that of a future yet to come but that of an incandescent interface between present and past. As opposed to the archival procedures of historicism, whose "method is additive (and) musters a mass of data to fill out the homogeneous, empty time," historical materialism "cannot do without the notion of a present which is not a transition, but in which time stands still and has come to a stop."[24] Historical materialism is at once radically antinarrative and deliberately anarchival, devoted to constellation or "configuration" of past and present rather than the methodical steps of causal deduction and interpretation. It is history conceived as outburst, shock, or explosion rather than as progression and relation. It is directed, above all, at the historicism whose function is precisely to forget, to defuse, the violence of the history that it records and archives, in order to ground the legitimacy of the order it serves in the self-evidence of the progress of events. All this is well known. I want only to draw attention to the way in which Benjamin's materialist "image of the past" resumes with such structural correspondence the moment of "rage as sheer manifestation" with which I have been hoping to constellate it. If rage recurs beyond the thinking of the violence that it haunts, it does so surely in the incandescent "time of the now" with which historical materialism refuses the self-evidence of progress and institution.

It is this that places rage not only before violence and distinct from it, but outside the social as constituted in violence. Rage is the site of the disintegration, not of the constitution or maintenance of the subject, and as such cannot be accounted for. Generated in the social, it is not outside the social space but functions nonetheless as a tear in its fabric. Lacking a before and an after, it does not, therefore, mark a border or a point of transition but, rather, delineates a subsidence in the social terrain, the point of the dissolution of subjects damaged, reduced to bare life (which is also death), by the violence of the institution of law. An effect or residue of the violation of formation, rage may be an ineradicable and asocial product of the social. Rage is not the sign of anything to come nor the threshold of the new order, though perhaps it is the manifest of the unredeemed cost of socialization. Not that there is anything self-evident in the hope that rage might be redeemable: falling outside the circuit of means and ends, rage knows no means to be redeemed. Fundamentally, founding nothing, rage is the issueless protest of the mortal against mortality itself—"rage, rage against the dying of the light"—and the inverse of the "blessed rage for order" that seeks to redeem mortality through the subsumption of the subject in the greater life of an institution. But maybe our task is to assume the burden of that mortality, to honor the justness of the protest of rage against the violation of life that the social entails, and to recognize that what is at stake in the long quest for emancipation is not redemption, nor the afterlife, nor the messiah that is always to come. At stake is the desire to shape, without consolation, conditions that, released from the contingent violence of domination, might accommodate the unredeemable charge of life in common.

Rage, then, is that which flashes up before the violence of institution as both witness to and refusal of the drive to domination. That it cannot be incorporated into the forms of the law makes of it at once the trace of the damage domination does to life and a form of life's living on unreduced beyond domination. If it manifests itself in purely negative ways, as that which lacks story, subjectivity, law, we should perhaps not forget that the utopian horizon is always projected from the place of ruin and that the emancipated world, if such there be, is thought ahead in forms supplied by the very texture of damaged life and constellated with the refuse of the past. Might we not then trace in its annihilation of the subject the counterpart of another such annihilation whose name is love? For "how can we love except in this finitude? Where else would the right to love, indeed the love of right, come from?" ("FL," 44). Let us for now leave the last word with Derrida.

Notes

1 "If there is one, and only one, deconstruction . . .": Jacques Derrida, "Force of Law: The 'Mystical Foundation of Authority,'" in *Deconstruction and the Possibility of Justice*, ed. Drucilla Cornell, Michael Rosenfeld, and David Grey Carlson (New York: Routledge, 1992), 56. Subsequent citations from this text (identified as "FL") are given parenthetically by page number.

2 I have explored some of these aspects of the essay in "Ruination: Partition and the Expectation of Violence (on Allan deSouza's Irish Photography)," *Social Identities* 9.4 (December 2003): 475–509.

3 Walter Benjamin, "Critique of Violence," in *Reflections: Essays, Aphorisms, Autobiographical Writings*, ed. Peter Demetz, trans. Edmund Jephcott (New York: Harcourt Brace Jovanovich, 1978), 294. Subsequent citations from this text (identified as "CV") are given parenthetically by page number in the text. The German text is "Zur Kritik der Gewalt," in Walter Benjamin, *Angelus Novus: Ausgewählte Schriften 2* (Frankfurt am Main: Suhrkamp, 1966), 60. Subsequent citations from this text (identified as "KG") are given parenthetically by page number in the text.

4 Derrida, "Force of Law," 51. Derrida passes all too quickly over this moment, but not without leaving it hedged around with the trace of a tantalizing question to which the rest of this essay in some sense seeks to respond: "Is it by chance and unrelated to such a figure of God that he speaks then of the experience of anger, an example of an immediate manifestation that has nothing to do with any means/end structure? The explosion of violence, in anger, is not a means that looks toward an end; it has no object other than to

show and show itself. Let us leave the responsibility for this concept to Benjamin: the in some way disinterested, immediate and uncalculated manifestation of anger" ("FL," 51).

5 See also a text that foreshadows the concerns of "Force of Law," Jacques Derrida, "Déclarations d'indépendance," in *Otobiographies: L'enseignement de Nietzsche et la politique du nom propre* (Paris: Editions Galilée, 1984), 20–21.

6 For a further elaboration of this terminological ambiguity, see Derrida, "Force of Law," 6.

7 This is a somewhat different play than Derrida invokes between permission and promise, *permettre* and *promettre*, that lies in every moment of positing, founding (*Setzung*). See "Force of Law," 38.

8 Allen Feldman, *Formations of Violence: The Narrative of the Body and Political Terror in Northern Ireland* (Chicago: University of Chicago Press, 1991), 13–14, emphasizes this fundamental narrativity of violence, remarking, "Political violence is a genre of 'emplotted' action."

9 Derrida, "Force of Law," 43. It is harder to understand why Derrida considers Benjamin unaware of the self-deconstructing nature of the relation between lawmaking and law preserving, which seems to me the very thrust of his argument in the "Critique of Violence." See "Force of Law," 38, 43–44.

10 It seems that two layers of biblical source material have been woven together here, transforming what was initially a rebellion by a group of Reubenites against Moses' authority "into a protest by another levitical family against the exclusive right of Aaron's family to the Israelite priesthood." See *The Anchor Bible: Numbers 1–20: A New Translation with Introduction and Commentary*, ed. Baruch A. Levine (New York: Doubleday, 1993), 405. The implications of this priestly feud and its resolution for Benjamin's example will be discussed further in this essay.

11 See Levine, *Numbers*, 424, where he suggests that the "immediate purpose" of the priestly writers of these passages "was to lock in the exclusive sanction of the Amramite family, the family of Moses and Aaron, within the larger Kohathite clan of Levites, as the sole legitimate priests." For more detailed commentary see 428–32, and, on the institution of tithing to support the priesthood, 450–52. Jewish legend suggests that precisely what was at stake for Moses and Aaron in this episode was the setting of "definite bounds," in human society as in nature. See Louis Ginzberg, *Legends of the Jews, Volume 1: Bible Times and Characters from the Creation to Moses in the Wilderness*, trans. Henrietta Szold and Paul Radin (Philadelphia: Jewish Publication Society, 2003), 722.

12 See Derrida, "Force of Law," 62: "When one thinks of the gas chambers and the cremation ovens, this allusion to an extermination that would be expiatory because bloodless must cause one to shudder. One is terrified at the idea of an interpretation that would make of the holocaust an expiation and an indecipherable signature of the just and violent anger of God." Such considerations on the convergence of Benjamin's Judaic thought and that of Nazism, in a text "still too Heideggerian, too messianico-marxist or archeo-eschatological," lead Derrida to take his distance from this Benjamin in the name not of "destruction" but of an "affirmative deconstruction" (62–63). Giorgio Agamben, deciphering the troubling convergence at this period between Benjamin's and Carl Schmitt's thought, traces what he sees as an ongoing critique of Schmitt through

Benjamin's evolving considerations of violence. See Giorgio Agamben, *State of Exception*, trans. Kevin Attell (Chicago: University of Chicago Press, 2005), 52–64.

13 Freud links such moments precisely to the splitting of the subject between conscious and unconscious aspects in *Totem and Taboo*: "This original 'duality' (of the primitive distinction of soul and self) . . . is identical with the dualism proclaimed by our current distinction between soul and body and by such ineradicable linguistic expressions of it as the use of phrases like 'beside himself' or 'coming to himself' in relation to fits of rage or fainting." See Sigmund Freud, *Totem and Taboo: Some Points of Agreement between the Mental Lives of Savages and Neurotics*, trans. James Strachey, *Standard Edition of the Complete Psychological Works*, vol. 13 (London: Hogarth Press, 1958), 93. Hereafter cited as Freud, *SE* 13. The peculiarity of rage (and perhaps of fainting) is that they represent states that are neither conscious nor, properly speaking, unconscious: they have no content and no subject.

14 I borrow this formulation from Agamben, *State of Exception*, 35: "*Being-outside and yet belonging*: this is the topological structure of the state of exception"—a structure which he renames immediately with "the oxymoron *ecstasy-belonging*," a formulation suggestive in relation to rage. But while the state of exception is that which Benjamin so cogently analyzes in terms of the iteration of lawmaking violence, as a kind of inside-outside that is the threshold of the law, rage lies rather in a topological cusp, included, like the crypt of melancholia in Abraham and Torok, as an enclosure. See Nicolas Abraham and Maria Torok, "'The Lost Object—Me': Notes on Endocryptic Identification," in *The Shell and the Kernel: Renewals of Psychoanalysis, vol. 1*, ed. and trans. Nicholas T. Rand (Chicago: University of Chicago Press, 1994), 140–41.

15 Jacques Derrida, *Archive Fever: A Freudian Impression*, trans. Eric Prenowitz (Chicago: University of Chicago Press, 1995), 7, 1. Subsequent citations from this text (identified as *AF*) are given parenthetically by page number in the text.

16 Freud, "The Moses of Michelangelo," *SE* 13, 233. Subsequent citations from this text (identified as "MM") are given parenthetically by page number in the text. German text from "Der Moses des Michelangelo," in Sigmund Freud, *Gesammelte Werke*, vol. 10 (London: Imago, 1946), 197–98. Subsequent citations from this text (identified as *GW*) are given parenthetically by page number in the text.

17 See Sigmund Freud, *Moses and Monotheism*, in *The Standard Edition of the Complete Psychological Works*, vol. 23, trans. James Strachey (London: Hogarth Press, 1964), 37, 48, 88–90.

18 If "to be capable of anticipation" is also "to have a future" (*AF*, 74), it is no less the case that to have either is to be capable of dread. A full analysis of this ambiguity would require a lengthy detour through Kierkegaard's *Concept of Dread*, impossible in the present space.

19 Philippe Lacoue-Labarthe has traced this perception of Freud's as to the "inadequation" of Michelangelo's Moses rather to the difficulty presented by the fact that Michelangelo depicts, in the moment of the bearing down of the Commandments, the one who presented "the prohibition against representation." See Philippe Lacoue-Labarthe, "Sublime Truth," trans. David Kuchta, in *Cultural Critique* 18 (Spring 1991): 26. His reference to Freud's Schillerian sources (23–25) is a reminder that for Schiller, the sublime entailed the free submission of the will to force—that the whole drive of Schiller's essay is to show

the way in which free will can be reconciled to a superior violence that is in the first place natural, but implicitly social: "To destroy the very concept of a force means simply to submit to it voluntarily." See Friedrich Schiller, "On the Sublime," in *Naive and Sentimental Poetry and On the Sublime: Two Essays*, trans. Julius A. Elias (New York: Ungar, 1966), 195.

20 I borrow this conceptual pun from Zita Nunes, *Resisting Remainders: Race and Democracy in the Literature of the Americas* (Minneapolis: University of Minnesota Press, forthcoming).

21 See, for example, Melanie Klein's *The Psycho-Analysis of Children*, trans. Alix Strachey (London: Hogarth Press, 1975), where rage appears almost without exception as a mode of aggression.

22 Interestingly, Jewish legend itself does not accord with the notion that the band of Korah were utterly annihilated without trace or memory, though the form of memory is that of their eternal punishment and witness to Moses' and his archive's truth: "They are tortured in hell, and at the end of thirty days, hell casts them up near to the surface of the earth, on the spot where they had been swallowed. Whosoever on that day puts his ear to the ground upon that spot hears the cry: 'Moses is truth, and his Torah is truth, but we are liars.' Not until after the resurrection will their punishment cease, for even in spite of their grave sin, they were not given over to eternal damnation." See Ginzberg, *Legends of the Jews*, 725.

23 As Ian Balfour puts it, in "Reversal, Quotation (Benjamin's History)," *MLN* 106.3 (April 1991): 647: "For all the rhetoric of messianism in Benjamin's corpus, there is scarcely any providential force surveying a prophetic scheme of history unfold in its inexorable course."

24 Walter Benjamin, "Theses on the Philosophy of History," in *Illuminations: Essays and Reflections*, ed. Hannah Arendt, trans. Harry Zohn (New York: Schocken, 1969), 262.

Marc Redfield

Derrida, Europe, Today

In several texts and interventions during the last fifteen years of his life, Jacques Derrida risked "Europe" as a name—a name bound up with others, but not simply one among others—for the possibility of a better world. He was willing to make this claim bluntly when the occasion demanded it, as in a speech that he gave in May 2004 to celebrate the fiftieth anniversary of *Le Monde diplomatique*, and that the journal subsequently published, a month after Derrida's death, in its November issue:

> I am not known as a Eurocentric intellectual. Over the last forty years, people have tended to accuse me of the opposite. But I believe, without Eurocentric illusions or pretensions, without the least European nationalism, without even having much confidence in Europe as it presently is, or seems in the process of becoming, that we must fight for what this name represents today, remembering the Enlightenment, certainly, but also consciously accepting the totalitarian, genocidal and colonialist crimes of the past. We must fight, then, in order that Europe

South Atlantic Quarterly 106:2, Spring 2007
DOI 10.1215/00382876-2006-028   © 2007 Duke University Press

retain that which is irreplaceable within it in the world to come
[*à venir*].[1]

A more conceptually dense and surprisingly hyperbolic version of this
affirmation appears near the end of *The Other Heading* (*L'autre cap*, 1991):
"The *duty* to respond to the call of European memory, to recall what has
been promised under the name of Europe, to reidentify Europe—this *duty*
is without common measure with all that is generally understood by the
name duty, though it could be shown that all other duties perhaps presuppose it in silence."[2]

Why "Europe," "today"? Why should re-calling Europe be a "duty"? And
even if we agree that recalling a heritage and a past can plausibly be thought
of as a duty, how in the world (literally) could this particular act of recollection be thinkable as a duty "without common measure" that "all other
duties perhaps presuppose"? Is yet one more great European philosopher
offering us, in the twilight of his career, a *profession de foi* that, vigorously
boiled, reduces to "Eurocentrism"? Derrida himself, of course, did not
think so. In what follows I shall try to explain why not, both by recalling
Derrida's own explanations and by picking out and thrumming a few of the
longer strands of Derridean writing that lead toward and compose these
claims about Europe. Even if one knows little more about Jacques Derrida
than a few well-circulated biographical facts—his complex relationship to
Algerian and Mediterranean-Jewish culture; his transnational identities
and commitments; his reputation for critiquing "centrisms" of all sorts—
one has grounds for supposing that he was not making these statements
carelessly. He was not altogether properly a "European" philosopher (or
European "philosopher"); and though colonial origins never prevented anyone from identifying with the metropolis, in Derrida's case—as in all other
cases, of course, but surely above all in his—it would be a good idea to
examine the texts and arguments behind this affirmation of Europe before
assuming we know its logic and motivation. The commentary that follows
does not aspire to provide much more than explication; but given the unin-
formed hostility to Derrida still so prevalent, four decades after the land-
mark publications of 1967, in so many journalistic and academic contexts,
explication still seems worth doing.[3]

Derrida suggests in *The Other Heading* that "we no longer know very well what or who goes by this name" of Europe (5); and somewhat later he emphasizes that in his text Europe is "only a *paleonymic* appellation" (30–31). But his strategy of paleonymy—turning an old name like "writing" or "democracy" toward a new meaning—presupposes an analysis of what the old name means, so let me begin by recalling very briefly some of the current political and cultural-ideological meanings of the word "Europe." As a toponym for (parts of) the European landmass, this name goes back some twenty-five hundred years, but it has acquired a political referent only very recently.[4] As a formal political body, Europe is a post–World War II creation. The European Union (EU) emerged out of a series of Cold War–era Western European commercial and political treaties that culminated in the Maastricht Treaty of 1992. The EU remains a work in progress. At present writing it includes Slovenia but not the rest of former Yugoslavia; includes Sweden, Finland, Estonia, Latvia, and Lithuania, but not Norway, Iceland, or Liechtenstein (which, however, unlike Switzerland, belong to the European Economic Area; Switzerland has ratified separate treaties with the EU); incorporates some very far-flung territories and dependencies (French Guyana, the Azores, the Canary Islands, etc.); and has controversial plans to expand eastward, following a political and economic logic that no nineteenth-century analyst could have predicted (Bulgaria and Romania will join the EU in 2007; Turkey may gain entrance in the foreseeable future; Russia probably will not). The "union" has limited sovereign and economic powers (the key member states have retained national sovereignty in the areas of defense and foreign relations, not all member states have accepted the euro, etc.), and remains fractured by internal differences and difficulties (hence the spectacular failure, in 2005, of the European constitutional referendum in France and the Netherlands). To make matters worse, one powerful member state, the United Kingdom, tends to imagine itself separate from "Europe" and often is taken by others to be ambiguously European at best. "There are no English here," Derrida notes of the speakers at the conference at which the original lecture version of *The Other Heading* was given—a colloquium on "European cultural identity" held in Turin in May 1990; and he goes on to suggest the symbolic importance of that absence: "This is one of the essential problems of culture today, of European culture in particular, of which Anglo-American both is and is not a language" (23). (The cover art of the English-language version of *The Other Heading* is ironically unambiguous: it airbrushes Britain and Ireland out of existence.)

Europe's ambivalent political accomplishments are not nugatory, even if, in the quotation with which I began this essay, Derrida expresses understandable skepticism about "Europe as it presently is or seems in the process of becoming." As a political structure, the European Union unashamedly serves market and financial interests. It sits athwart a Europe shadowed—yet again—by genocidal war (Bosnia was of course not the EU, but it was "Europe"): a Europe that, more multiethnic and multicultural than ever, remains more than ever vulnerable to racist, nationalist, and xenophobic movements. Europe as "Union" is a Europe hyperbolically anxious about borders (indeed, Derrida comments in one interview from the 1990s that the task of realizing an ethics of hospitality is difficult "everywhere, but especially in a Europe with the tendency to close up on the outside to the extent that it claims to be open on the inside").[5] Yet if Derrida's affirmation of Europe cannot be reduced to Europe's current or immediately foreseeable political manifestations, it cannot simply be separated from them either. He was certainly not naive about the compromises and limits of the European experiment, yet his philosophical work granted him the ability to read certain politico-cultural events as *promising*. If one were to try to reduce Derridean thought to an epigram, one could do worse than this: deconstruction is the thought that *perhaps promising takes place*. I want to defer for a moment a proper unpacking of that epigram; here let me just note that from *Of Grammatology* on, Derrida presented deconstruction (or what he was then calling "grammatology") as a certain kind of reflection on contemporary events ("the science of writing—*grammatology*—shows signs of liberation all over the world," some of these signs being "the inflation of the sign 'language'"; an impending "death of the civilization of the book"; developments in cybernetics and biology; etc.).[6] When Derrida speaks of "Europe" he is not speaking of the EU, of course, yet he is also not simply *not* speaking of Europe's political articulations. In the EU's abolition of capital punishment, fumbling experiments with shared sovereignty, hospitality toward institutions of international law, and ambivalent openness to transformation, Derrida perceived not just phenomena to be applauded in good liberal-humanist fashion, but signs of something *happening*: a fracturing of sovereignty inseparable from the vast transformations and accelerations set in motion by planetary techno-capitalism (though also inseparable from a fracturing always already at work in the theological notion of sovereignty "itself").[7] Europe, partaking of the measureless violence and the savage inequities of "globalization," at the same time offers the globe a glimmer of hope. A complication awaits us here, however, for the ambivalent civilizing initiatives of the EU are "promising" not in the sense that they mark progress toward an ideal, but in a somewhat more strangely literal sense: they "make promises" (perhaps); they retrace the fragile but stubborn promise of what Derrida famously calls "democracy to come."[8]

But before I say more about the politics of the promise let me loop back again to the idea of Europe. For of course whatever "the name Europe means for us today," it means vastly more than the European Union—more than any formal political entity. *The Other Heading* intervenes in and contributes to a discourse about "Europe" that has deep roots and a particularly rich nineteenth- and twentieth-century history. Derrida's exemplary texts in *The Other Heading* are by Paul Valéry; but since his readings of Edmund Husserl's *Crisis of European Sciences* span the entirety of his career—from *The Problem of Genesis in Husserl's Philosophy* (1953–54) to *Rogues* (2002)— let me offer, as exemplary of this discourse of the European example, a string of remarks from Husserl's "Vienna Lecture" of 1935:

> We pose the question: How is the spiritual shape of Europe to be characterized? Thus we refer to Europe not as it is understood geographically, as on a map, as if thereby the group of people who live together in this territory would define European humanity. In the spiritual sense the English Dominions, the United States, etc., clearly belong to Europe, whereas the Eskimos or Indians presented as curiosities at fairs, or the Gypsies, who constantly wander around Europe, do not. Here the title "Europe" clearly refers to the unity of a spiritual life, activity, creation, with all its ends, interests, cares, and endeavors, with its products of purposeful activity, institutions, organizations. . . . No matter how hostile they may be toward one another, the European nations nevertheless have a particular inner kinship of spirit which runs through them all, transcending national differences. . . . There is something here that is recognized in us by all other human groups, too, something that, quite apart from all considerations of utility, becomes a motive for them to Europeanize themselves even in their unbroken will to spiritual self-preservation; whereas we, if we understand ourselves properly, would never Indianize ourselves, for example. I mean that we feel (and in spite of all obscurity this feeling

is probably legitimate) that an entelechy is inborn in our European civilization which holds sway throughout all the changing shapes of Europe and accords them the sense of a development toward an ideal shape of life and being as an eternal pole.[9]

Europe's is a *spiritual* geography, traversing itself and the world in an economy of inclusion and exclusion that transcends empirical geography (thus the United States—obviously via an essential tautology a "European" United States—partakes of "Europe," whereas Gypsies who "constantly wander around Europe" do not). Husserl's text, written against Nazi barbarism yet so painfully overexposed to the vocabulary of spirit on which modern racism draws, deserves lengthy and scrupulous commentary. Let me simply offer here that this Eurocentrism is not in the first instance a racism; such a "unity of a spiritual life" offers *in principle* a certain limited hospitality to others, so long as these others—Eskimos, Indians, Gypsies, and so on—obliterate themselves *as* other by "Europeanizing" themselves.[10] A missionary-imperialist expansionism or globalization lies at the heart of this idea of Europe precisely because Europe is the idea itself: Europe names the event of the idea as history. Thus, a few sentences later in his lecture, Husserl identifies the "breakthrough of philosophy" in ancient Greece—an event "in which all sciences are contained"—as "the primal phenomenon of spiritual Europe" (276). In essence, Europe, as spirit, records the empirical, historical birth of scientific and philosophical rationality into the world.

Both in his thesis, *The Problem of Genesis in Husserl's Philosophy* (1954), and in his first major publication, *Introduction to Husserl's Origin of Geometry* (1962), Derrida put pressure on this idea of Europe, which precisely *as* idea raises difficulties for a transcendental phenomenology. Europe has to be ideal if it is to be an object of phenomenological analysis:

> Starting from geographical political or economical facticity, the eidetic unity of Europe cannot be defined by anything rigorous. To take in Europe, one must begin from an idea, from a pure and a priori meaning. This idea of Europe is the idea that is born in Europe; it is the idea of philosophy that is, in its absolute originality, Husserl tells us, a European idea. . . . Husserl would not dispute that Europe in its empirical facticity has no privileged relation to the idea of philosophy. And yet, Europe, philosophy's spiritual place of birth, its mysterious and immaterial residence, resists variation. There is a European *eidos* merging itself with the idea of philosophy.[11]

In *The Problem of Genesis* Derrida focuses on "the genetic problem" raised by the emergence of the *eidos* of Europe as philosophy as infinite task: "The passive synthesis ensuring continuity between the worldly and the transcendental, it is no longer possible to distinguish rigorously between empirical constitution and transcendental constitution. There would thus be a genesis of the idea of philosophy out of what is not it" (159). Eight years later, in *Introduction to Husserl's Origin of Geometry*, he draws attention to the problems raised for phenomenology by the Kantian Idea itself: "This idealization, which has for its correlate an infinite Idea, always decisively intervenes in the difficult moments of Husserl's description. The phenomenological status of its evidence remains rather mysterious."[12] For an Idea in the Kantian sense is not accessible to phenomenological presentation as an intuited *eidos*. Because it "never phenomenalizes itself" (137), it registers a danger for phenomenology. "Europe" thus turns out to name a troubled area of the Husserlian project. Not only does this name point to a place where the difference between empirical and transcendental turns uncertain; it also, as the name of an Idea, points to a structure that cannot be made fully present to consciousness.

The paradox of Europe sums up a recurrent Husserlian ambition: to account for the historical or empirical genesis of the transcendental. In his own way Derrida took up this problem; indeed, I think it would be plausible to claim that he found his way toward his own work in large part thanks to Husserl's courageous if problematic attempt to think the historicity of ideality. The audacity of this effort to understand truth as *produced* by an inaugural act of consciousness deserves notice. Unscathed by relativism or empirical contingency, truth, for Husserl, is nonetheless radically historical in the sense that it does not preexist the act constituting it. Hence, as Derrida shows in *Introduction to Husserl's Origin of Geometry*, Husserl's otherwise surprising emphasis on the dependence of ideality on writing. Writing not only permits the originating act to be communicated and handed down; it permits the act—which is an act not of empirical but of transcendental consciousness—to be what it is in the first place: "The possibility or necessity of being incarnated in a graphic sign is no longer simply extrinsic and factual in comparison with ideal Objectivity: it is the *sine qua non* condition of Objectivity's internal completion" (89). The problem of writing then famously makes possible the thought of *différance* and the trace. Following Rodolphe Gasché, these operative terms are often called "quasitranscendental" because they are neither transcendental nor empirical and seek rather to account for such fundamental metaphysical distinctions.[13] For instance: "To think of presence as the universal form of transcendental life," Derrida claims in his culminating study of Husserl, *Speech and Phenomena* (1967), "is to open myself to the knowledge that in my absence, beyond my empirical existence, before my birth and after my death, *the present is.* . . . The relationship with *my death* (my disappearance in general) thus lurks in this determination of being as presence, ideality, the absolute possibility of repetition."[14] And therefore (subsequent, of course, to a good deal of argument I am not reproducing here):

> Only a relation to my-death could make the infinite differing of presence appear. By the same token, compared to the ideality of the positive infinite, this relation to my-death becomes an accident of empirical finitude. The appearing of the infinite *différance* is itself finite. Consequently, *différance*, which does not occur outside this relation, becomes the finitude of life as an essential relation with oneself and one's death. *The infinite* différance *is finite.* It can therefore no longer be conceived within the opposition of finiteness and infinity, absence and presence, negation and affirmation. (102)

The "trace," similarly, is infinitely finite—it is nothing apart from its inscription in history, and it is fundamentally exposed to loss or disappearance—yet it makes ideality (or perhaps one should say quasi-ideality) possible; it is thus "prior" to conceptual pairings such as presence and absence, finitude and infinity, the sensible and the intelligible, or the empirical and the transcendental. Quasitranscendentals provide names—illicitly, through paleonymy—for the fundamental instability of such oppositions.

We may now bring the discussion back to the figure and event of "Europe." Having become the proper name of history itself in Husserl— we shall reemphasize this point in a moment—"Europe" flickers silently in the background in the closing pages of *Introduction to Husserl's Origin of Geometry*, as Derrida first, via Husserl, defines historicity as "the passage of Speech [*Parole*], the pure tradition of a primordial Logos toward a polar Telos," and then, radicalizing the secularizing historicism of genetic phenomenology, submits that "polar Telos" to the uncertain risk of its own movement:

> But since there can be nothing outside the pure historicity of that passage, since there is no Being which has sense outside of this historicity or escapes its infinite horizon . . . this signifies that the *Absolute is*

> *Passage . . .* This movement is also *Danger(ous) as the Absolute* [*l'Absolu d'un Danger*].[15]

Because no external being underwrites or shelters the teleological movement of Europe-as-reason-as history, it becomes exposed to radical loss: the absolute becomes absolute danger.

Derrida's subsequent work might be summarized as a massive development of this insight. Let me leap here from his early work to one of his last texts: the second of the two essays making up *Rogues*, in which Derrida offers a final reading of, and after a fashion homage to, Husserl's *Crisis of European Sciences.* If Europe, according to Husserl, names the historical occurrence of ideality or rational thought, Europe also names the historical unfolding of a malaise or crisis. "The European nations are sick; Europe itself, it is said, is in crisis," Husserl writes.[16] Why? Because reason forgets its origin in subjective acts and falls into specialization and objectivism. Derrida emphasizes that, according to Husserl, "reason itself produces this evil as if by an irresistible internal secretion"; and after quoting a few passages from Husserl's text he ties the knot of the argument with a few rapid gestures, behind which lie forty years of work:

> Husserl knows it and says it: objectivist naïveté is no mere accident. It is produced by the very progress of the sciences and by the production of ideal objects, which, as if by themselves, by their iterability and their necessary technical structure, cover over or consign to forgetting their historical and subjective origin. Scientific reason, in its very progress, spontaneously produces this crisis. It is reason that throws reason into a crisis, in an autonomous and quasi-autoimmune fashion. It could be shown that the ultimate "reason," in the sense of cause or foundation, the *raison d'être* of this transcendental phenomenological autoimmunity, is located in the very structure of the present and of life, in the temporalization of what Husserl called "the Living Present" [*die lebendige Gegenwart*]. The Living Present is produced only by altering and dissimulating itself.[17]

"It could be shown" indeed; *Speech and Phenomena* had shown precisely this, some thirty years previously. In *Rogues* the emphasis falls on the aporetic excess of reason itself: reason, here, is at once rationalizing and prescriptive, calculating and incalculable. Though reason falls prey to itself, reason is also the only cure for itself; thus Husserl calls for a "heroism of reason" (*Heroismus der Vernunft*). The reason of reason is beyond calculation; it is the dignity (*Würde*) of humankind (Kant), the good beyond being (*epekeina tês ousias*) (Plato). Thus, Derrida notes, "a rational and rigorous incalculability presented itself as such in the greatest tradition of rationalist idealism" (133); and in the final pages of *Rogues* he works toward an affirmation of "this *unconditional* rationalism *of the unconditional*" (134) beyond teleology and sovereignty. "Among the figures of unconditionality without sovereignty I have had occasion to privilege in recent years, there would be, for example, that of an *unconditional hospitality*" or "the *gift* or . . . *forgiveness*" (149). Reason itself—the absolute as passage, to recall a much earlier phrasing—drives toward such unconditionals. And "Europe" remains, for Derrida, a name for their impossible possibility: "The invention of these maxims resembles the poetic invention of an idiom whose singularity would not yield to any nationalism, not even a European nationalism— even if, as I would like to believe, within today's geopolitical landscape, a new thinking and a previously unencountered destination of Europe, along with another responsibility for Europe, are being called on to give a new chance to this idiom. Beyond all Eurocentrism" (158).

Europe, in other words, remains *exemplary*. The example and the logic of exemplarity will have to be rethought, but Derrida, after his fashion, remains faithful to this discourse. In the first place Europe, as example, remains inescapable: "avowal, guilt, and self-accusation no more escape this old program than does the celebration of self."[18] Europe has left its mark on history; this old name sums up the tensions, triumphs, and crimes of Western science, culture, and technics. A name, of course, even if in some sense inescapable, can at least be played down (Derrida's surprisingly sharp polemical engagement with Jean-Luc Nancy's *The Experience of Freedom* in *Rogues*, for instance, turns on Derrida's belief that the political figure of "fraternity" should be sidelined as much as possible).[19] As *Specters of Marx* argues powerfully, inheritance paradoxically implies choice: "An inheritance is never gathered together, it is never one with itself. Its presumed unity, if there is one, can consist only in the *injunction* to *reaffirm by choosing*."[20] If for Derrida Europe is inescapable, this is because Europe offers an inheritance worth choosing. The strange imperatives of hospitality, the gift, forgiveness, and democracy haunt and inform this inheritance. *L'Europe, c'est l'autre*, precisely because Europe names the event of reason. Traditionally associated with the head (*caput*) and heading (*cap*), the avant-garde of humanity, Europe is also and therefore the possibility of an other heading:

> And what if Europe were this: the opening onto a history for which the changing of the heading, the relation to the other heading, or to the other of the heading, is experienced as always possible? An opening and a non-exclusion for which Europe would in some way be responsible? For which Europe *would be*, in a constitutive way, this responsibility? As if the very concept of responsibility were responsible [*répondait*], right up to its emancipation, for a European birth certificate [*acte de naissance européen*]?[21]

Derrida proffers his thought as an "if"-clause here, for this Europe, as responsibility—responsibility of and toward the other—is not a fact but a value to be affirmed. Perhaps: perhaps "the very concept of responsibility" countersigns the instituting act, the *acte de naissance*, of the idea of Europe. The very effort (responsibly) to think Europe would in some way be marked or countersigned by this excessive responsibility.

Europe thereby acquires, for Derrida, a peculiar exemplarity, always necessarily and riskily close to the exemplarity it enjoys in Hegel or Husserl or generally in aesthetic humanist discourse.[22] Europe has always been imagined as "a spiritual heading, at once as project, task, or infinite—that is to say universal—idea. . . . The idea of an advanced point of exemplarity is the idea of the European idea, its *eidos*, at once as *arche* . . . and as *telos*" (24). Near the end of his *Introduction to Husserl's Origin of Geometry*, Derrida had paused to reflect on some of the peculiarities of such exemplarity (it is here that we may develop a richer understanding of what Husserl means by Europe's *historicity*):

> The ambiguity of an *example* that is at once an undistinguished *sample* and a teleological *model* is still found here. In the first sense, in fact, we could say with Husserl that every community is in history, that historicity is the essential horizon of humanity, insofar as there is no humanity without sociality and culture. From this perspective, any society at all, European, archaic, or some other, can serve as an example in an eidetic recognition. But on the other hand, Europe has the privilege of being the *good example*, for it incarnates in its purity the Telos of all historicity: universality, omnitemporality, infinite traditionality, and so forth; by investigating the sense of the pure and infinite possibility of historicity, Europe has awakened history to its own proper end. Therefore, in this second sense, pure historicity is reserved for the European *eidos*. The empirical types of non-European

societies, then, are only more or less historical; at the lower limit, they tend toward nonhistoricity.[23]

The Other Heading mines and undermines this logic of (European) exemplarity:

> The value of universality here capitalizes all the antinomies, for it must be linked to the value of *exemplarity* that inscribes the universal in the proper body of a singularity, of an idiom or a culture, whether this singularity be individual, social, national, state, federal, confederal, or not. Whether it takes a national form or not, a refined, hospitable, aggressively xenophobic form or not, the self-affirmation of an identity always claims to be responding to the call or assignation of the universal. There are no exceptions to this law. No cultural identity presents itself as the opaque body of an untranslatable idiom, but always, on the contrary, as the irreplaceable *inscription* of the universal in the singular, the *unique testimony* to the human essence and to what is proper to man. Each time it has to do with the discourse of *responsibility*: I have, the unique "I" has the responsibility of testifying for universality. Each time, the exemplarity of the example is unique. That is why it can be put into a series and formalized into a law.[24]

The value of exemplarity "inscribes the universal in the proper body of a singularity"; cultural identity presents itself as "the irreplaceable *inscription* of the universal in the singular." How should we gloss the meaning of *inscription*? We have already recalled some ways in which Derrida's great texts of the 1960s loom behind this word, for what he describes here is the opening of signification as iterability. The legibility of a mark derives from its ideality: its repeatability as the *same*, elsewhere and elsewhen; yet this transcendental movement fractures the identity it makes possible, composing identity as an exposure to death and alterity. A singularity is always already affected or contaminated by iterability, split and redoubled—yet also always *singular*: never fully mediated by universality into a *particular*. To insist on the *inscription* of the universal in the singular is to remark a primordial violence concealed within the logic of exemplarity, at once driving and ruining this logic. The inscription is "irreplaceable," unique, each time; yet the unique is (also) the formalizable (as example). This aporia names the possibility of Eurocentrism, imperial and aesthetic ideology, and all forms of politico-cultural violence, yet also the possibility of responsibility. Hence the rather dizzyingly rapid move Derrida makes here from the aesthetic humanism he is inheriting ("No cultural identity presents itself as the opaque body of an untranslatable idiom, but always, on the contrary, as the irreplaceable *inscription* of the universal in the singular, the *unique testimony* to the human essence and to what is proper to man") to his own ethical idiom ("Each time it has to do with the discourse of *responsibility*: I have, the unique 'I' has the responsibility of testifying for universality").

The heading must launch itself into the unknown. It calculates its chances only by anticipating the unanticipatable. It inscribes the universal in the singular, yet remains open or exposed to the event, the surprise of singularity. The heading heads toward "an other that the heading can no longer even relate to itself as *its* other, *the other with itself*" (76). Hence, remembering Europe becomes a "duty without common measure with all that is generally understood by duty." Yet all genuine duty—or responsibility, as Derrida usually puts it—is without "common measure"; duty is duty precisely because it is *beyond measure*: beyond mensuration, calculation, exchange. And if remembering Europe involves remembering the excess of responsibility over knowledge, then "it could be shown that all other duties perhaps presuppose" this reidentification of Europe "in silence." Once again we note the *perhaps*. Reidentification is spectral, for Europe, as heading—as the good example—is a specter, and haunted by specters ("The experience of the specter, that is how Marx, along with Engels, will have also thought, described, or diagnosed a certain dramaturgy of modern Europe, notably that of its great unifying projects").[25] Such a Europe, like the democracy it promises, will always remain to-come, *à venir*. As heading, it can never be present. Its "today" is a taking place in excess of any presence-to-self or temporal *punctum*; and this lag or anticipation is what paleonymy seeks to record: "This event takes place as that which comes, as that which seeks or promises itself *today*, in Europe, the today of a Europe whose borders are not given—no more than its name, Europe being here only a *paleonymic* appellation."[26]

And yet the irreducible "perhaps" or "as if" structure of this Europe-to-come does not reduce Derrida's politically oriented work to a "politics of the ineffable," as critics of Derrida have often claimed. It is true that Derrida's thought forbids a programmatic articulation of political *theory*. Much of his later work comes back again and again to the impossibility of subordinating decision or judgment to knowledge. A decision—if there is one—must pass through the ordeal of the undecidable to be a genuine decision or judgment, rather than a program or the unfolding of a potential; it cannot even be taken by *me*, as a sovereign subject: "In order to be a decision, it has to cut off this '[what is] possible [for me],' tear up my history, and thus be first of all, in a particular and strange way, the decision of the other in me: coming from the other with regard to the other in me."[27] This difficult thought of the decision—or of the gift, which to be a true gift must exceed all exchange, even the exchange implied by recognition; or of forgiveness, which to be true forgiveness must forgive the unforgiveable; or of hospitality, which to be true hospitality must be unconditional, a radical openness to the other—does not imply that decisions or gifts or acts of forgiveness or hospitality do not occur. The impossible is in fact *what* occurs. "The 'impossible' I often speak of is not the utopian. Rather, it gives their very movement to desire, action, and decision: it is the very figure of the real. It has its hardness and urgency" (131). None of Derrida's figures of the impossible—Europe, democracy, justice, the gift, forgiveness, hospitality, the invention, and so on—are regulative ideas in Kant's sense; rather, they are "the place from which immediate and concrete matters of urgency are dictated" (ibid.). This is why those who criticize Derridean democracy *à venir* as an "impotent, vague abstraction" are mistaken: a mistake that rhymes with the stubbornly widespread idea that "Derrida is more interested in unmasking hidden oppressions in a totality than in encouraging wholesome collective action."[28] One can always, of course, point to Derrida's record in supporting or participating in "wholesome collective action"; but the point finally to stress is that this (long and distinguished) record is not a contingent or illogical supplement to his "real" philosophical work. The thumbnail definition of deconstruction I offered at the beginning of this essay, that *perhaps promising takes place*, unfolds as a vigilant attentiveness to context and opportunity. A promise is a promise because it is breakable, and it constantly has to be renewed. And thus decisions have constantly to be made (to refuse to make a decision, or to linger too long in indecision, is itself at a certain point to make a decision). Reason itself, as we saw Derrida arguing, forces us to calculate with the incalculable; we must, as it were, have faith in calculation, and calculate with faith.[29]

Derrida's proposals unquestionably maintain or suffer a certain proximity to or contamination by Eurocentrism. Contamination gives deconstruction its chance. One starts within the historical and metaphysical text within which one finds oneself and exploits its fissures and cathexes: such is the import of the much-misunderstood phrase *il n'y a pas de hors-texte*—that we are radically historical beings, unable to extricate ourselves from the processes that have made us. On the one hand, this claim makes genuinely critical thought difficult to achieve. Derrida's chapter on Claude Lévi-Strauss in *Of Grammatology* examines, among other things, the Eurocentric cast of Lévi-Strauss's Rousseauist anti-Eurocentrism (and *Of Grammatology* as a whole nominates "logocentrism" as "the most original and powerful ethnocentrism," as the book's opening paragraph puts it).[30] But if one cannot and should not simply *reject* these "centrisms," on the other hand one can find in them resources for deconstructive thought precisely because the centers do not hold. Europe is an exemplary object of deconstructive thought because it exemplifies exemplarity itself: it thus serves as short-hand for the ruses and promises of "Western" culture, technology, science, metaphysics, and so on, yet always from the singular location of a specific history and field of significance and possibility. As a privileged figure for the "inscription of the universal in the singular," Europe provides a name and an occasion for the loyal disloyalty of deconstruction. The Europe for which Derrida calls—a Europe that does not and cannot simply *exist*—is Husserl's "good example" opened to "the experience and experiment of the impossible."[31] The thought of this Europe thereby becomes a figure for responsibility itself (and such responsibility obviously demands "accepting the totalitarian, genocidal, and colonialist crimes of the past," as Derrida underscores in the extract from the speech with which I began).

My summary therefore cannot pretend even to have begun to cover the wider ramifications of the figure of "Europe" in Derrida's writing. A fuller study would want to read this figure in conjunction with other geo-historico-politico-conceptual figures in Derrida—Algeria, America, Jerusalem, the desert, the island; the figure of placing itself, *khôra*, to which he dedicated numerous pages in the last decade of his life; "spacing" as a figure of *différance*; the signature and the trace in their relation to spaces and places—and thus, ultimately, the entire text of the Derridean archive, every element of which—all those books, essays, conferences, confessions, lectures, and interventions—marks and remarks its occasion, the date and place of its signature. "Europe" haunts those marks, a specter haunted in turn by innumerable others. Perhaps above all, one would want to examine the shadow Europe casts on Derrida's writing on religion ("Difficult to say 'Europe' without connoting: Athens—Jersualem—Rome—Byzantium— wars of religion, open war over the appropriation of Jerusalem and of Mount

Moriah, over the 'here I am' of Abraham or of Ibrahim before the extreme 'sacrifice' demanded of him").[32] Yet the question of religion, for Derrida, leads instantly to questions of media and mediatization, teletechnology, globalization, gender, community and the *ethnos*, autoimmunity, and on and on; and in all of these minitexts one rediscovers that of "Europe," fractured, uncertain, and insistent: "Hence the paradox: globalization is Europeanization. And yet, Europe is withdrawing; it is being fissured and transformed. . . . Europe is in my opinion the most beautiful example, and also the allegory, of autoimmunity."[33]

Wherever Europe haunts itself and its others, there flickers the immense question of language—questions of writing and speech, and of an arche-writing beyond what one ordinarily understands as "language"; yet always also more politically localized questions of idiom: *this* language, "here."[34] Though Derrida never quite said so directly, I believe the figure of "Europe" appealed to him in good part because of the complex politics of language that plays itself out in this word. We saw him noting the ambivalently European status of "Anglo-American," which "both is and is not a language" properly belonging to this strange, exemplary, symbolic, and literal promontory called Europe. This double relation of inclusion and exclusion makes Anglo-American into "one of the essential problems of culture today, of European culture in particular." The fracturing and redoubling of Europe, then, is not simply an "internal" fissuring; Europe both is and is not globalization as global (American) English, is and is not "America" (or even, as we saw earlier, "Great Britain," or even—even more strangely—in some contexts "Ireland"). And the logic of exemplarity that Europe exemplifies repeats itself "internally" as an economy of exemplarity, violence, and opportunity, in which political and linguistic issues constantly intertwine. For the grand "idea of Europe" means certain parts, languages, traditions of Europe—a Europe mediated by the dialects that became "national languages" in a few powerful states: French, German, Italian, Spanish. And yet Europe always also names a(n unequal) plurality of languages and states, and of nation-states and more archaic formations (e.g., Liechtenstein, Andorra, the Vatican); a nonhomology between linguistic and political identity (e.g., Belgium, Switzerland); a proliferation of dialects; convergences between dialectal and "official" languages (e.g., luxembourgeois); language communities few outsiders bother to broach, many place-centered (Dutch, Finnish, the Scandinavian languages, Swiss-German dialects, Slovak, Basque), some mobile or displaced (Romany, Yiddish); to this list must now be added the many languages spoken by immigrant communities (e.g., Arabic, Hindi).

Europe is thus, for Derrida, the very figure of inheritance and decision and of the decision to inherit. We have begun to register the difficulty of the notion of decision here: a decision in excess of knowledge, taken not by me but by "the other in me," can never be known as such (hence Derrida's oft-reiterated locution "if it exists"). Yet precisely for that reason we are constantly driven to decide, and in being driven to decide we are driven to weigh alternatives, calculate chances and probabilities, so as to make *the best* decisions (in the name of what?—once again, in the name of reason itself: reason beyond reason, justice beyond law). Derrida decided to risk strong and cagy affirmations of Europe, all the while insisting on the dangerous and irreducible proximity between "hope, fear, and trembling" and the possibility of "the worst violences": "We come across traps of this sort at every step, and they are not merely traps of language: they are part of the program."[35] I have suggested that within the global scene, Europe as a political event offered a few "promising" signs for him; and he kept faith, through paleonymy, with the old name and idea of Europe for the same reason that he kept faith (in the strong sense: faith-keeping as active inheritance, as a certain breaking-faith in the name of faith) with the great texts of the Western philosophical tradition. Europe meant, among other things, of course, precisely these texts. Always he remained haunted by the *perhaps*; but the *perhaps* is another name for the *promise*. "I hope for it, but I do not see it" was his response, in his October 2001 interview with Giovanna Borradori, to the question of whether or not he sees an important role for Europe in the future:

> I have not seen anything in the facts that would give rise to any certainty or knowledge. Only a few signs to interpret. If there are responsibilities to be taken and decisions to be made, responsibilities and decisions worthy of these names, they belong to a time of risk and of an act of faith.[36]

Notes

1 Jacques Derrida, "L'Europe de l'espoir," *Le Monde diplomatique*, November 2004: www .monde-diplomatique.fr/2004/11/DERRIDA/11677, my translation. A curtailed and inaccurate English version, "Enlightenment Past and to Come," may be accessed at www .mondediplo.com/2004/11/06derrida.

2 Jacques Derrida, *The Other Heading: Reflections on Today's Europe*, trans. Pascale-Anne Brault and Michael B. Naas (Bloomington: Indiana University Press, 1992), 76.

3 That is to say, my essay takes up the peculiar, though in the end I think useful, task of addressing "a paradoxical reader who is supposed not to know anything about Derrida but who is yet imagined able to pick up Derrida's thought in condensed form," as Geoffrey Bennington puts it in *Interrupting Derrida* (London: Routledge, 2000), 2. I cite a few token instances of hostile writing about Derrida in a subsequent note. There is also, of course, an ever-increasing store of very good writing about Derrida; on the specifically political dimension of his thought, see for example (to mention only book-length studies) Richard Beardsworth, *Derrida and the Political* (London: Routledge, 1996); Geoffrey Bennington, *Legislations: The Politics of Deconstruction* (London: Verso, 1994); and Alex Thomson, *Deconstruction and Democracy: Derrida's Politics of Friendship* (London: Continuum, 2005). This is the moment for me to regret that I encountered Michael Naas's fine memorial essay for Derrida, "A Last Call for 'Europe,'" *Theory & Event* 8:1 (2005), only after my own essay was written; luckily the redundancies do not seem crippling.

4 The earliest uses of "Europe" as a toponym refer to mainland Greece, and, subsequently, lands to the north of Greece. Europa is also of course the name of the daughter of the Phoenecian king Agenor, who was raped by Zeus in the form of a bull and carried off to Crete, where she gave birth to Minos. In Homer she is a queen of Crete. The toponym possibly derives from the Akkadian *erebu*, sunset (hence the land to the west, the sunset land). Derrida eschews discussing the etymology of Europe in *The Other Heading* and to my knowledge does not do so anywhere else.

5 Jacques Derrida, *Paper Machine*, trans. Rachel Bowlby (Stanford, CA: Stanford University Press, 2005), 131. This comment comes from an interview with *Die Zeit* in March 1998. Compare a similar point stressed in Derrida's improvised comments in December 1996, during a demonstration in support of the "sans-papiers": this is "a time when everything is being closed everywhere, when every door is being bolted shut, every port, every airport is tightening its nets, when the nation-states of Europe, especially France, are turning their borders into new iron curtains." *Negotiations: Interventions and Interviews, 1971–2001*, trans. Elizabeth Rottenberg (Stanford, CA: Stanford University Press, 2002), 134.

6 Jacques Derrida, *Of Grammatology*, trans. Gayatri Chakravorty Spivak (Baltimore: Johns Hopkins University Press, 1976), 4, 6, 9.

7 On sovereignty, see especially Jacques Derrida, *Rogues: Two Essays on Reason*, trans. Pascale-Anne Brault and Michael Naas (Stanford, CA: Stanford University Press, 2005).

8 For Derrida's most extensive meditation on democracy and the idea of democracy-to-come, see *Politics of Friendship*, trans. George Collins (London: Verso, 1997).

9 Edmund Husserl, "Philosophy and the Crisis of European Humanity," in *The Crisis of European Sciences and Transcendental Phenomenology*, trans. David Carr (Evanston, IL: Northwestern University Press, 1970), 273–75. The "Vienna Lecture" of May 7 and 10, 1935, precedes by six months the lecture series in Prague on which Husserl's *Crisis* was based.

10 I stress *in principle*: in practice (and for reasons that outstrip the difference between principle and practice, and have to do with the deep affinities between modern racism and the language of spirit), the mark of racial identity usually intervenes all the more violently in

the wake of "Europeanization." The literature on racism in relation to European "culture" is vast: two relevant touchstones here would be Frantz Fanon's classic *Black Skin, White Masks*, trans. Charles Lamm Markmann (New York: Grove Weidenfeld, 1968); and (for a helpful meditation specifically on racism and spirit) Philippe Lacoue-Labarthe and Jean-Luc Nancy, "The Nazi Myth," trans. Brian Holmes, *Critical Inquiry* 16 (1990).

11 Jacques Derrida, *The Problem of Genesis in Husserl's Philosophy*, trans. Marian Hobson (Chicago: University of Chicago Press, 2003), 154–55.

12 Jacques Derrida, *Edmund Husserl's "Origin of Geometry": An Introduction*, trans. John P. Leavey Jr. (Lincoln: University of Nebraska Press, 1989), 106. Subsequent citations are given parenthetically by page number in the text.

13 Rodolphe Gasché, *The Tain of the Mirror: Derrida and the Philosophy of Reflection* (Cambridge, MA: Harvard University Press, 1986). Quasitranscendentals have "a structure and a function similar to transcendentals without actually being one" (316); they are "situated at the margin of the distinction between the transcendental and the empirical" (317). Troubling the regime of the what-is, they "seem to be characterized by a certain irreducible erratic contingency" (ibid.).

14 Jacques Derrida, *Speech and Phenomena, and Other Essays on Husserl's Theory of Signs*, trans. David B. Allison (Evanston, IL: Northwestern University Press, 1973), 54. Subsequent citations are given parenthetically by page number in the text.

15 Derrida, *Introduction to Husserl's Origin of Geometry*, 149.

16 Husserl, *Crisis*, 270.

17 Derrida, *Rogues*, 127. Subsequent citations are given parenthetically by page number in the text.

18 Derrida, *The Other Heading*, 27.

19 Derrida, *Rogues*, 49–61. One must ask oneself "at the end of the day whether [a received concept] is receivable, acceptable, and where and why it would be unacceptable" (60).

20 Jacques Derrida, *Specters of Marx: The State of the Debt, The Work of Mourning, and the New International*, trans. Peggy Kamuf (London: Routledge, 1994), 16.

21 Derrida, *The Other Heading*, 17. I give the French for nuance; Naas's translation seems fine to me. The French text is: *L'autre cap, suivi de La démocratie ajournée* (Paris: Minuit, 1991), 22. Subsequent citations are to the English translation and are given parenthetically by page number in the text.

22 On aesthetic humanism and exemplarity, see my *Phantom Formations: Aesthetic Ideology and the Bildungsroman* (Ithaca, NY: Cornell University Press, 1996), esp. 17–27.

23 Derrida, *Edmund Husserl's "Origin of Geometry": An Introduction*, 115.

24 Derrida, *The Other Heading*, 72–73.

25 Derrida, *Specters of Marx*, 4–5.

26 Derrida, *The Other Heading*, 30–31, his emphasis.

27 Derrida, *Paper Machine*, 129. Subsequent citations are given parenthetically by page number in the text.

28 The first citation is from Richard Bernstein, "An Allegory of Modernity/Postmodernity: Habermas and Derrida," in *Working Through Derrida*, ed. Gary B. Madison (Evanston, IL: Northwestern University Press, 1993), 227; the second from Anselm Kyongsuk Min, "The Other without History and Society—A Dialogue with Derrida," in *Philosophy of Religion in the 21st Century*, ed. D. Z. Phillips and Timothy Tessin (New York: Palgrave,

2001), 182. I was led to Bernstein's article by way of Min's. Similar claims are easily found elsewhere: Derrida's writings have been criticized as idealist, ahistorical, apolitical, etc., ever since they first began inspiring debate in the late 1960s. The tone, of course, can vary: Min's, for instance, is a careful essay that only in its final two pages offers what I am arguing are unjustified claims. For an instance of the kind of violent caricature to which Derrida's thought has so often been subjected, see Mark Lilla, "The Politics of Jacques Derrida," *New York Review of Books* 45.11 (June 1998).

29 Derrida's discussions of hospitality offer some clear examples of what he means by calculating with the incalculable, e.g.: "Unconditional hospitality is inseparable from a thinking of justice itself, but as such it remains impracticable. It cannot be written into the rules or in a piece of legislation. If one wanted to translate it immediately into a policy, it would always carry the risk of having perverse effects. But even as we watch out for these risks, we cannot and must not abandon the reference to hospitality without reservations. It is an absolute pole, outside which desire, the concept, the experience, the very thought of hospitality would be meaningless. Once again, this 'pole' is not an 'Idea in the Kantian sense' but the place from which immediate and concrete matters of urgency are dictated." *Paper Machine*, 131.

30 Derrida, *Of Grammatology*, 3. This is actually an extract from the book's second sentence; the very first sentence of the section called "Exergue," commenting on the epigraphs with which *Of Grammatology* begins, draws attention to "the *ethnocentrism* which, everywhere and always, has controlled the concept of writing" (3, italics in the original). "Ethnocentrism" is one of the more persistent words in *Of Grammatology*. At the same time, since the first of the posted epigraphs is drawn from an Ancient Egyptian source, the concept of writing disturbs provincial versions of the *ethnos*.

31 Derrida, *The Other Heading*, 45.

32 Jacques Derrida, "Faith and Knowledge," in *Acts of Religion*, ed. Gil Anidjar (New York: Routledge, 2001), 45. See also Derrida's careful critique of Jan Patocka's philosophical meditations on Christian Europe in Derrida, *The Gift of Death*, trans. David Wills (Chicago: University of Chicago Press, 1995).

33 Jacques Derrida responding to Elisabeth Roudinesco, in Jacques Derrida and Elisabeth Roudinesco, *For What Tomorrow . . . A Dialogue*, trans. Jeff Fort (Stanford, CA: Stanford University Press, 2004), 178.

34 On the ultimate inseparability of questions of language and idiom, see Jacques Derrida, *Monolingualism of the Other, or The Prosthesis of Origin*, trans. Patrick Mensah (Stanford, CA: Stanford University Press, 1998), 8–9, passim.

35 Derrida, *The Other Heading*, 12.

36 Jacques Derrida, "Autoimmunity: Real and Symbolic Suicides—A Dialogue with Jacques Derrida," in Giovanna Borradori, *Philosophy in a Time of Terror: Dialogues with Jürgen Habermas and Jacques Derrida* (Chicago: University of Chicago Press, 2003), 118.

Mary Jacobus

"Distressful Gift": Talking to the Dead

How does one honor, or mourn, the dead, if not by talking to them? This is a question posed by the memorial writings collected in Derrida's *The Work of Mourning* (2001).[1] I want to explore it by means of a little-known elegy by Wordsworth that touches on another subject central to Derrida's work: the relation between the gift and the poem. My subject is the strange afterlife of mourning—as Derrida insists, a non-normative mourning that continues to honor the dead by talking to them. Neither praising nor burying the dead puts an end to this conversation.

In February 1805, Wordsworth lost his sailor brother John when he was drowned off Portland Bill in the wreck of the *Earl of Abergavenny*.[2] Wordsworth was grief-stricken: "The set is now broken," he lamented, calling his brother "a Poet in every thing but words."[3] Writing to a friend, he poured out his overwhelming sense of loss:

> For myself I feel that there is something cut out of my life which cannot be restored, I never thought of him but with hope and delight. . . . I never wrote a line without a thought of its giving him pleasure, my writings printed and manuscript were his

South Atlantic Quarterly 106:2, Spring 2007
DOI 10.1215/00382876-2006-029 © 2007 Duke University Press

delight and one of the chief solaces of his long voyages. But let me stop—I will not be cast down were it only for his sake I will not be dejected. I have much yet to do and pray God to give me strength and power—his part of the agreement between us is brought to an end, mine continues and I hope when I shall be able to think of him with a calmer mind that the remembrance of him dead will even animate me more than the joy which I had in him living.[4]

A strange hope, but a characteristic one: Wordsworth's poetry is animated by the afterlife of memory. In John's words (reported by his brother), this was to have been their agreement: "He encouraged me to persist in the plan of life which I had adopted; I will work for you was his language and you shall attempt to do something for the world."[5] John would have known Michael's covenant with Luke.[6] His side of the bargain had consisted of the potential profit and risk of commanding an East Indiaman that plied the Bengal-to-China trade route during the Napoleonic wars.[7] Preoccupied for months by family grief, Wordsworth was anxious to clear his brother of any imputation of incompetence—and relieved to find that John's sizable financial investment of £20,000 had been fully insured.[8] Any charge of negligence on the part of the East India Company or its employees would have affected the ship's insurance, and an official inquiry followed.[9] John's last recorded words were reported to have been: "O pilot, you have ruined me."[10]

During the months that followed, Wordsworth gradually resumed his own side of the bargain, taking up what his sister called "the Task of his life" in order to "writ[e] a poem upon [John]."[11] But he described himself as overwhelmed by "such a torrent" of verse that he could not hold the pen.[12] Later he wrote a series of intensely personal elegies which he regarded as too melancholy to share with his family or anyone else.[13] One of them—never published in his lifetime—provides my title: "Distressful gift! this Book receives / Upon its melancholy leaves, / This poor ill-fated Book . . ." (ll. 1–3).[14] So begins a poem that apostrophizes both book and brother ("thou, my Friend"), as if the two were equally pitiable, equally ill-fated. The gift-book that is the poem's pretext was apparently a commonplace book, belonging to John. It contained a collection of manuscript copies of Wordsworth's poems: "framed with dear intent / To travel with him night and day, / And in his private hearing say / Refreshing things" (ll. 31–34).[15] The notebook (sealing their bargain) was left behind for Wordsworth as a work in progress, its pages "All fill'd or to be fill'd with store / Of verse for his delight" (ll. 27–28). By the event of his brother's death it became "distressful" instead—at once a reminder of poems written or unwritten, and an unfinished monument to a life cut short: "a Tale / Of Thee thyself; fond heart and frail!" (ll. 8–9). The book's fragile materiality becomes a synecdoche for the vulnerability of the body.[16]

Milton's "Lycidas" is the precursor elegy for a drowned poet, albeit a wordless one ("a Poet in every thing but words"). Subtly invoking the conventions and broken rhythms of lyric elegy—"The sadly-tuneful line, / The written words that seem to throng / The dismal page" (ll. 10–12)—Wordsworth's poem foregrounds the relation between voice and writing, composition and reading: "The sound, the song, / The murmur, all to thee belong; / Too surely they are thine" (ll. 13–14). Sounding, singing, murmuring, his sadly tuneful lines to a dead man stage the most private reading of all: the poet's rereading of his own poetry. This unheard communication is the type of elegiac address: one-sided, intimate, posthumous. The same unheard address to the dead informs Derrida's collected memorials to his dead friends. Derrida shows himself to be a master of the genre—one might almost say, the gesture—of mourning, alert to its self-congratulatory pitfalls and to its opportunities for eloquence. I will be concerned both with the gift of death, as he and Emmanuel Levinas define it, and with what Derrida (in his *hommage* to his friend Louis Marin) calls "the point of view of death." Derrida's memorials to Levinas and Marin are representative of the varied tributes to his dead friends included in *The Work of Mourning*: posthumous replies, unfinished conversations, and personal rereadings. These tributes—often continuing dialogues that had been conducted in print and in person over many decades—are characterized by Derrida's intellectual generosity, by their affective response, and (in some cases) by subtle yet provocative statements of difference. Derrida's memorial stance is to put the *différance* back into reading. He reads not only in the wake of his friends, but beyond them. His elegies are both replies and afterthoughts.

The missing figure in *The Work of Mourning* is Maurice Blanchot, given his pervasive influence on Derrida's thinking and writing since the 1960s. Blanchot's insistence on an impossible outside of writing, or unknown of thought, returns in Derrida's later writings as the "impossible" itself—a concept to which he appeals when he resists the economization of his own thought within political or metaphysical systems. I will close by invoking Blanchot's definition of conversation as interruption, pause, or intermittency. Talking to the dead can be understood as a form of *désoeuvrement*, in Blanchot's sense—a restless un-working that refuses totalization and proceeds not by way of critique, but rather by juxtaposition, divergence, and difference. This is a dialectic without negation, yet capable of responding to disaster, broaching the unknown of one's own thought through repetition, return, and response. In one of the imaginary dialogues included in *The Infinite Conversation* (*L'entretien infini*, 1969), Blanchot writes that "this redoubling of the same affirmation constitute[s] the strongest of dialogues."[17] I will be reading Wordsworth's "Distressful Gift" in just such an attempted dialogue with the questions posed by Derrida, whose own recent death makes the memorials collected in *The Work of Mourning* at once proleptic and strangely posthumous. Finally, I will return to Blanchot's aphorism: "True thoughts question, and to question is to think by interrupting oneself" (*IC*, 340). Talking to the dead, I propose, prolongs this infinitely interrupted conversation. Derrida's insight in *The Work of Mourning* was that his own work might constitute just such a prolongation for those reading in his wake.

Motions of the Life of Love

> Death—as the death of the other [*autrui*] . . . is emotion par excellence.
> —Emmanuel Levinas, *God, Death, and Time*

Among the most eloquent of Derrida's tributes to his dead friends is his 1995 elegy for Levinas, "Adieu" (at once "goodbye" and a benediction, salutation, or prayer: *à-Dieu*).[18] Derrida opens by expressing his wish to find "unadorned, naked words, words as childlike and disarmed as [his] sorrow." The wish—the gesture—resonates with the language of Wordsworth's elegy. Recognizing that the gesture is inherent in the rhetoric of elegy, Derrida goes on to suggest that more than oratorical convention is at stake. He poses a question about the nature of elegiac address itself:

> Whom is one addressing at such a moment? And in whose name would one allow oneself to do so? Often those who come forward to speak, to speak publicly, thereby interrupting the animated whispering, the secret or intimate exchange that always links one, deep inside, to a dead friend or master, those who make themselves heard in a cemetery, end up addressing *directly, straight on*, the one who, as

we say, is no longer, is no longer living, no longer there, who will no longer respond. (*WM*, 200)[19]

The address to another "who will no longer respond" interrupts the secret, intimate exchange that links one to the dead friend. This apostrophe is the supplementary fiction licensed by the public funeral oration in its classical form: the fiction that the elegist is speaking directly to the dead.

Derrida's disarmed and disarming remarks define the elegy as an impossible address to a dead friend who can no longer respond, even if, in reality, his words are addressed to "the dead in me" or to "the others standing around the coffin" (*WM*, 5152). The elegiac mode of "Adieu" announces this urge to speak directly to (rather than of) the dead, drawing attention to a form of address which seeks to avoid—yet always risks—the self-interestedness of language that returns self-reflexively to the self or to the community of mourners when the public elegist comes forward to speak:

> With tears in their voices, they sometimes speak familiarly to the other who keeps silent, calling upon him without detour or mediation, apostrophizing him, even greeting him or confiding in him. This is not necessarily out of respect for convention, not always simply part of the rhetoric of oration. It is rather so as to traverse speech at the very point where words fail us, since all language that would return to the self, to us, would seem indecent, a reflexive discourse that would end up coming back to the stricken community, to its consolation or its mourning, to what is called, in a confused and terrible expression, "the work of mourning." (*WM*, 200)

Derrida's self-proclaimed "law" of "*straightforwardness*" (*droiture*) is "to speak straight on, to address oneself directly *to* the other" (*WM*, 200); to speak for the other before speaking of him (or her). As he insists (allowing his unshed tears to be "heard" in the hesitations of his prose), calling upon the other who keeps silent means addressing someone who does not respond. This "no-response" (*sans-réponse*), Derrida reminds us, is how Levinas himself had defined death (*WM*, 203).[20] Yet to keep on addressing the one who does not respond is also a means of keeping alive *Autrui* (Otherness), perpetuating the secret interior exchange that links the speaker to the dead and keeps him alive within oneself. As Wordsworth insisted, overwrought in the wake of his brother's death: "I shall never forget him, never lose sight of him, there is a bond between us yet, the same as if he were living, nay far more sacred."[21] In his elegy, the unheard link of stanza and rhyme keeps this bond in mind and memory: "Making a kind of secret chain, / If so I may, betwixt us twain / In memory of the past" (ll. 19–21). Elegy is a one-sided agreement that chains the living to the dead.

Derrida suggests that elegiac address perpetually does and undoes the work of mourning, seeing its incompleteness as the type of (the) "work" itself—always unfinished, never brought to a close; an unworking or *désoeuvrement* (in Blanchot's sense). His reference to Freud's "confused and terrible expression, 'the work of mourning'" (*WM*, 200) contests any idea of normative mourning, one that must let the lost object go or else lapse into melancholia.[22] Where Freud emphasizes the slow and painful process by which the ego detaches itself from its objects so that life can go on, Derrida insists that we continue to talk to the dead—hearing their voices, reading their books, and seeing their faces. Freud's account of mourning is complicated, however, by his view that the unconscious knows no tense but the present tense, and therefore takes no account of death. Talking to the dead—apostrophizing the others who do not respond—becomes a way to keep them alive in oneself. Reflecting on the ineradicable impulse to memorialize the dead in his *Essays upon Epitaphs* (1809–10), Wordsworth locates the epitaphic mode in what he calls (quoting Weever's *Ancient Funerall Monuments*) "the presage or fore-feeling of immortality, implanted in all men naturally."[23] Without some counterbalance to the apprehension of death, "a frost would chill the spirit, so penetrating and powerful, that there could be no motions of the life of love." Were it not for this natural belief in immortality, he goes on to say, "neither monuments nor epitaphs . . . could have existed in the world" (*Prose Works*, ii.52). One could read Wordsworth's belief in the religious promise of an afterlife—Derrida's "as if" (*WM*, 52)—not as a denial of death but as a form of realism: when it comes to our love-objects, there is no such thing as memory; our exchanges with them continue as if they were still alive.[24] The work of mourning is always unfinished because we never fully let go of the dead.

Writing within a different theological framework, Levinas defines death as "a departure towards the unknown, a departure without return" (*GDT*, 9). Derrida quotes his definition of our affective relation to death as "a purely emotional rapport" that orients us toward the unknown: "It is an emotion, a movement, a disquietude within the *unknown*" (*GDT*, 16; *WM*, 205); the apprehension of death is "emotion *par excellence*. Affection of being affected *par excellence*" (*GDT*, 9): emotion—apprehension—takes the place of cognition. The elegy is the literary form of affectivity without *telos*—not so much a clinging to life, as an orientation toward the unknown. Wordsworth's sense of the disquietude that underlies his communing with the dead, even in the most peaceful of rural settings, is recorded in a well-known passage from *Essays upon Epitaphs* that silently recalls his brother's drowning five years previously. A country churchyard may look like a smooth sea on a summer's day, yet its depths are stirred with anxieties, perturbations, and rancor:

> The image of an unruffled Sea has still remained; but my fancy has penetrated into the depths of that Sea—with accompanying thoughts of Shipwreck, of the destruction of the Mariner's hopes, the bones of drowned Men heaped together, monsters of the deep, and all the hideous and confused sights which Clarence saw in his Dream! (*Prose Works*, ii.64)

Clarence's dream, in *Richard III*, envisages these hideous and confused sights from the vantage point of the drowning man—"O Lord! Methought what pain it was to drown, / What dreadful noise of waters in my ears, / What sights of ugly death within my eyes. / Methoughts I saw a thousand fearful wrecks" (*R III*, I.iv.21–24). The ocean depths become a place of hideously gnawed and disfigured corpses, scattered treasure, mocking skulls with gems for eyes. As Levinas puts it succinctly, "Death is decomposition" (*DT*, 11), however green the graveyard.

Clarence's murderous dream had formed the discomfiting "motto" or epigraph to the official account of the wreck of the *Earl of Abergavenny* compiled soon afterward from survivor testimonies and reports.[25] It took six weeks for John Wordsworth's body to wash up; by then it must have been almost unrecognizable: "The Body of our dearest John ha[s] been found by dragging and was buried. . . . This is a great comfort to us—his grave is a resting place for our thoughts—the end of all in this world."[26] But "Six weeks beneath the moving Sea / He lay in slumber quietly" (Curtis, 610, ll. 36–37), before being buried in a mass grave. This fiction of the sleeping corpse (in another unpublished elegy, "To the Daisy") makes the period that elapsed between wreck and burial the sleep of a quiet conscience: "All claims of duty satisfied" (l.40). Two years before, however, in a proleptic sonnet based on the story of Simonides ("I find it written of Simonides"), Wordsworth had emphasized the restlessness of the sailor's unburied corpse: "Travelling in strange countries, once he found / A corpse that lay expos'd upon the ground" (ll. 2–3). Piously, Simonides has the body buried and pays for the performance of "due obsequies." In recompense, the dead man appears to him and warns him against an impending voyage; Simonides stays on shore, while the ship is wrecked at sea with all on board: "Thus was the tenderest poet that could be . . . Saved out of many by his piety" (ll. 12–14).[27] In the first of his *Essays upon Epitaphs*, Wordsworth again alludes to this story in support of his thesis that Simonides—because, rather than in spite of, his exaggerated respect for bodily remains—was capable of "communing with the more exalted thoughts that appertain to human nature" (*PW*, 52). Otherwise, he writes, the corpse of a stranger would have meant no more to him than "the dead body of a seal or porpoise which might have been cast up by the waves" (*PW*, 52). Then there would be no need of epitaphs or monuments.

Writing of the relation between lyric poetry and elegy's traditional consolations—its monumentalizing impulse and its promise of immortality— Barbara Johnson notes that despite appearances, "even the most traditional elegy contains the guilty secret that desire is not all for life."[28] The desire for writing and the desire for death are both associated with a particular kind of performance. The ghost of an undead corpse asks Simonides for burial, laying claim to more than mere corporeality. It asks for the gift of death—not forgetfulness, but recognition: burial rites, reverence, restitution. What makes mourning terrible as well as confused is the nature of this demand on the survivor, for whom it may be experienced not just as a claim to a proper burial, but as a persecutory tax levied by the dead on the living. Melanie Klein's autobiographical account of mourning in the wake of her son's death brings to light the uneasy triumph of the survivor and its murderous accompaniment—its residue of hatred, denial, and control.[29] Klein takes a leaf from Wordsworth's book when she appeals to the classical gesture of elegy: "The poet tells us that 'Nature mourns with the mourner.'"[30] For her, the surfacing of a traditional trope of mourning signals not only a freer and more sympathetic relation to inner and outer worlds but also the mobilization of creative process.[31] Calling on the fiction of sympathetic nature, elegy reimagines the inanimate not as *sans-réponse*, but as responsive—giving it a voice. Just as the trope of the voice allows us to hear the tears in Derrida's "Adieu" to Levinas, so we hear "the sound, the song, / The murmur" (ll. 12–13) in Wordsworth's elegy for his brother. The mourning of nature with the mourner (pathetic fallacy) is the figure of elegiac emotion par excellence, a call anterior even to dialogue: the figure that gives affect.[32]

The Survivor's Gift

> The question of the gift will never be separated from
> the gift of mourning.
> —Jacques Derrida, *Given Time*

"It is for the death of the other that I am responsible" (*GDT*, 43). So says
Levinas. But where Levinas sees responsibility, Derrida sees potential
betrayal. His reflections on the economy of the gift in *Given Time* (*Donner le
temps*, 1991) and *The Gift of Death* (*Donner la mort*, 1992) combine a rereading of Marcel Mauss's seminal anthropological work on the gift with a critique of Levinas's ethics of responsibility.[33] Derrida points out in *The Gift of
Death* that the biblical sacrificial scenario (the sacrifice of Isaac) means that
the ethics of responsibility "must be sacrificed in the name of duty."[34] In
this monstrous story, responding to the call of the Other means, paradoxically, sacrificing him: "I offer a gift of death, I betray" (*GD*, 68). There is a
scandal at the heart of the ethics of responsibility. In the culture of death,
the experience of internalization and secrecy associated with the work of
mourning (in psychoanalytic terms, incorporation and repression) involves
more than the apportioning of responsibility. Mourning gives rise to the
need "to interpret death, to give oneself a representation of it, a figure, a
signification or destination for it" (*GD*, 10)—contradicting Freud's view
that there is no representation of death in the unconscious, and putting in
question Levinas's unknown destination without *telos*.

In *Given Time*, Derrida questions whether there is such a thing as a gift
at all, arguing (in a familiar move) for its radical and exorbitant impossibility. Mauss, he writes, "speaks of everything but the gift" (*GT*, 24)—his
subject is economy, exchange, contract, sacrifice, and countergift. As soon
as the gift is recognized as such, it ceases to be a gift. Instead, it becomes
an exchange, a circulation, or a return. A Derridean gift must exceed the
economic category of the gift as Mauss had envisaged it (just as elegy must
exceed the category of address to the self or to others, and its recupera-
tion within an economy of sameness). Derrida's language of hyperbole and
excess is rooted in suspicion of self-interest. The gift that returns to the
giver is like the elegy that refers, self-reflexively, to oneself or the mourners round the coffin. For Derrida the gift must by definition be unrecog-
nized, just as it must neither circulate nor be exchanged. The gift is not
only impossible, "but *the* impossible" (*GT*, 7), a figure of impossibility itself
(just as "the work of mourning" is a figure of the work's necessary incom-

pleteness): "For there to be a gift, there must be no reciprocity, return, exchange, countergift, or debt. If the other *gives* me *back* or *owes* me or has to give me back what I give him or her, there will not have been a gift" (*GT*, 12). On the other hand, a poem written to a dead man who has ended his part of the agreement might be seen as eluding the gift economy.[35] What makes Wordsworth's distress into an impossible gift, in Derrida's sense, is its one-sidedness: there is no one to receive it.[36]

As well as reminding us "that Levinas defines the first phenomenon of death as 'responselessness,'" Derrida invokes "a passage in which he declares that 'intentionality is not the secret of what is human'" (*GD*, 47). The gift lies beyond intentionality. Like that of "Adieu" (whether salutation, benediction, or supplication), the gift's agency comes from what it performs rather than from any ontological necessity—from what it does, not from what it is. For Levinas, death is categorical; it exceeds and obliterates not only intentionality but also the psychoanalytic category of the unconscious. The gift that Wordsworth gives his dead brother prompts some categorical language of his own. This is a poem that involves a prohibition: "And so I write what neither Thou / Must look upon, nor others now, / Their tears would flow too fast" (ll. 15–16). Not just will not, but *must* not; as if by proscription as well as by the tragic accident of John's death. The written words belonging to a dead man—"Too surely they are thine" (l. 14)—are destined not to be read by him or by anyone else. More than a secret solace, this private writing is withheld from those whose "tears would flow too fast." The unread poem secretes its solitary grief in the interests of other readers.

For Levinas, responsibility to others gives meaning to self-identity; singularity is given only by death, or by the apprehension of death: "We encounter death in the face of the other" (*GDT*, 105). But for Derrida the Levinasian concept of singularity is problematic: every other, including God, is every "other"; human alterity is indistinguishable from God's. Yes, Levinasian ethics are already religious.[37] And so it proves when Wordsworth makes a request on his own account, at the end of the poem: "but gracious God, / *Oh grant* that I may never find / Worse matter or a heavier mind . . . / *Grant this*, and let me be resign'd" (ll. 38–42; my emphasis).[38] In this combined "question, prayer" (Levinas's phrase—translated as Derrida's "question-prayer"), Wordsworth utters a call that Derrida defines as "anterior to all dialogue" (*WM*, 209). It is not only anterior but also one-sided. "Prayer," writes Levinas, "never asks anything for oneself; strictly speaking it makes no demands at all, but is an elevation of the soul."[39] Here he is discussing Rabbi Hayyim Volozhiner's *Nefesh ha'Hayyim* (*The Soul of Life*), the posthumously published work of a Lithuanian Kabbalistic and Talmudic scholar of the long eighteenth century.

Levinas is drawn to Volozhiner's concept of prayer as a moment of benediction. According to Levinas, Volozhiner conceives prayer as essentially disinterested: "True prayer . . . is never for oneself, never 'for one's needs.'"[40] In answer to the question "Is it right for us to ask, in our prayers, for human suffering to be eased?" (historical Jewish suffering, for instance), his response is that prayer may be justified in the case of the unhappy "I"—provided its basic concern is not with one's own unhappiness: "The suffering self prays on behalf of God's suffering" (because God suffers with man's affliction).[41] This is not quite how Wordsworth would have viewed it. In Christianity's bargain, Christ does the suffering for humanity, while God makes the unthinkable sacrifice of his only beloved son. Nevertheless, Wordsworth's "For those who yet remain behind, / Grant this" (ll. 41–42) strikes a less orthodox note than some of his subsequent poetry.[42] His prayer on behalf of "those who yet remain behind" (l. 41) includes those whose "tears would flow too fast" (as well as himself). Wordsworth's distressful gift is not only a supplication; it is also a benediction for "those who yet remain behind."

Derrida points out that Christianity's themes of infinite love, sin, repentance, salvation, and sacrifice revolve around "the fathomless gift of a type of death" (*GD*, 49). God's exorbitant gift-giving and incommensurable sacrifice make for a paradigmatic gift. Only God is allowed to make the radical substitution that apparently exceeds the terms of the gift-economy: "the gift of death—and of the death of that which is priceless—has been accomplished without any hope of exchange, reward, circulation, or communication" (*GD*, 96). But as Derrida argues, such a gift "re-appropriates the *an*economy of the gift as a gift of life or, what amounts to the same thing, a gift of death" (*GD*, 97). God hands out his own rewards, whether transcendental or metaphysical. But Wordsworth, we know, had worldly rather than otherworldly ends in view: "I will work for you was his language and you shall attempt to do something for the world."[43] This ethical work for the world was to have been underwritten by John's venture capitalism at sea. Both, for sure, involve willingness to take deferred profits. Derrida's reading of biblical gift-economy paraphrases Matthew 6:19–21, where heaven is called "the place of true riches, a place of treasures, the placement of the greatest *thesaurization* or laying up of treasures. The correct location of the heart is the place that is best placed" (*GD*, 97). In this celestial tax haven, affective capital can never be devalued; it yields infinite profit, immune to accidents such as shipwreck or uninsured capital, but in the future tense: "The heart will thus be, in the future, wherever you save real treasure" (*GD*, 98)—a good savings plan in the face of worldly insecurity.

Derrida's tongue-in-cheek deconstruction of what he calls the "cardio-topology" of the Gospels identifies a hidden accumulation of self-interest. Wordsworth's entire unfinished oeuvre, of which "Distressful Gift" is a synecdoche, might be thought of as a form of poetic accumulation laid up for his future readers: "All fill'd or to be fill'd with store / Of verse for [our] delight" (ll. 27–28). Like *The Prelude* itself, his "Distressful Gift" was to remain unpublished, although not altogether unread. But, as Derrida points out, the writing subject "never gives anything without calculating, consciously or unconsciously, its reappropriation, its exchange, or its circular return" (*GT*, 101); indeed, the subject becomes visible precisely via the operation of such psychic calculation (including, presumably, concern for the living). Hence the truly disinterested Derridean gift is thinkable only on condition of the "death"—not just the anonymity—of the donor/subject. But, as Derrida is careful to say, "only a 'life' can give, but a life in which this economy of death presents itself and lets itself be exceeded. Neither death nor immortal life can ever give anything, only a singular *surviving* can give" (*GT*, 102). Wordsworth's "Distressful Gift" is the survivor's gift par excellence; a gift not without (self-)interest, to be sure, but a gift that presents and exceeds the economy of death, just as it exceeds both intentionality and the unconscious.

Derrida's question remains to be answered: what is the relation between gift and grief? And why is the question of the gift inseparable from that of mourning (*GT*, 36, 129n)? For Derrida at least, the answer turns out to lie in the poem itself, which is at once gift and performance. A poem is already, from its first line, a figure for the melancholy gift of itself. He cites Stéphane Mallarmé's baleful "Don du poème" ("The Gift of the Poem")—a hyperbolically wretched poetic gift, pale, full of suffering, bearing the traces of its solitary conception, and requiring a readerly (i.e., feminine) supplement.[44] Derrida reads Mallarmé's "Don" as the type of all poems, and the poem's gesture as the type of the gift. His definition of the gift is not so much that it is a "free" gift, but rather that it lacks both essence and ontology. It is pure *différance*, trace, or dissemination—a redefinition designed to supersede both Claude Lévi-Strauss's structuralist analysis of the floating signifier (*hau*) and Émile Benveniste's semantically ambiguous "give" and "take" (the *dô* and *dâ* of Indo-European languages).[45] According to this logic, the Derridean gift becomes—perhaps predictably, certainly hyperbolically in its turn—synonymous with the problematic of writing (*différance*), reading (*dissemination*), and the give and take of mourning (unfinished work). Grief and *désoeuvrement* converge on the impossibility (that is, the unthinkability) of both the work and the gift. Exceeding the metaphysics of presence, signs, essence, or value, Derrida's theory of the gift takes the poem as both its question and its *point de depart*. The gift-poem is placed outside all systems of exchange: incalculable, exceptional, neither authentic nor counterfeit. At the end of *Given Time*, in the footnote that gives him his final lines, Derrida signs off with a poem called (what else?) "Donnant": "Que désirer-vous donner / C'est le geste qui compte" (What do you desire to give, / It's the gesture that counts"; *GT*, 172 n).[46] The *geste* (gesture) is at once sign and action.

The Look of the Book

> A la place de quelque chose qui est présent ailleurs, voici *présent* un donnée, *ici*: image? [In place of something that is present elsewhere, there is here a present, a given: image?]
> —Louis Marin, *Des pouvoirs de l'image*

"By Force of Mourning," Derrida's 1993 *hommage* to his friend and colleague Louis Marin, opens with a reminder that "all work is also the work of mourning" (*WM*, 142). Here too he goes out of his way to dismiss any normative conception of "successful" mourning, if what is meant by that is banishing the melancholia of uncompleted mourning. He represents himself as drained, forlorn, and distraught, yet preoccupied by the question posed by Marin's last, posthumously published book, *Des pouvoirs de l'image* (1993):[47] what is the force of the image? Taking as his starting point Marin's concern with portraiture—or, rather, with "a particular class representing the dead or death"—Derrida defines what he calls "the point of view of death" as follows:

> For it would be from death, from what might be called *the point of view of death*, or more precisely, of the dead, the dead man or woman, or more precisely still, from the point of view of the *face* of the dead

in their portraiture, that an image would give seeing, that is, not only would give *itself* to be seen but would give insofar as it sees, as if it were seeing as much as seen. (*WM*, 147–48)

It is worth lingering on what Derrida means here by "*the point of view of death.*" The "*face* of the dead" not so much gives itself to be seen, as "sees" the onlooker ("as if it were seeing as much as seen"); in doing so, it displaces the point of view of the living. This constitutive look disturbs both self-presence and temporality (just as for Levinas, death constitutes an interruption from otherness).

Derrida comments at length on a passage from Marin's introduction to *Des pouvoirs de l'image* which emphasizes the dramatic effects of representation on the present tense: "Something that *was* present and *is* no longer is *now* represented. In place of something that is present *elsewhere*, there is here a present, a *given*" (*WM*, 149).[48] Wordsworth's distressful *donnée* (his "given") consists in representing the book as having been present in the past or as present elsewhere (*présent ailleurs*), and at the same time as a representation; that is, it is both monument to and reminder of what is no longer there—his brother's look, his reading of the book. The look or image of the book that is so insistently "here" (*ici*), with its "melancholy leaves" its "written page and white," stands in for the missing body that is elsewhere (*ailleurs*). The book is "framed" for, and read by, the look of the no-longer-present Friend—"He framed the Book which now I see, / This very Book upon my knee" (ll. 29–30). The temporality of this seeing has been utterly changed by the interruption of the Friend's death: "But now—upon the written leaf / I look indeed with pain and grief" (ll. 36–37). The reading of the book brings pain and grief because its readability re-presents the look of the other, but "from the point of view of death."

Wordsworth's opening stanza contains another interruption—a grammatical incoherence—in the form of an abrupt change of tense: "Distressful gift! this Book receives . . . *I wrote*" (1.4; my emphasis). The point of view of death, which is also the point of view of representation, shifts abruptly from a statement about receiving in the present to a completed act of writing in the past, and then, in the space of a few lines, to the future anterior as the writer prereads ahead of himself: "and when I reach'd the end / Started to think that thou, my Friend"—must what? "Must never, never look" (ll. 4–7). This end-stopped look is the look of the book, the startling ("Started to think") and arresting point of view of death. But there is something extra in representation. Reflecting on the "force" of the image in Marin's work, Derrida refers to "an acute thought of mourning and of the phantom that returns, of haunting and spectrality," an effect of the image that "would stem from the fantastic force of the specter" (*WM*, 153). In "Ejaculation at the Grave of Burns," a poem prompted by a visit to Robert Burns's grave in 1803 (the same year that he wrote the sonnet on Simonides), Wordsworth shrinks with pain beside the grave containing the poet's bones. His address, however, is not to Burns but to his ghost—or rather, to the spirit of his poetry:

> And have I, then, thy bones so near?
> And thou forbidden to appear!
> As if it were Thyself that's here
>   I shrink with pain;
> And both my wishes and my fear
>   Alike are vain. (Curtis, 534, ll. 7–12)[49]

Instead of a ghost appearing ("Thyself that's here") we "see" and "hear" its verbal trace: the spirited stanza that is at once Burns's signature tune and his monument. Quotation as a form of *hommage* brings the fierce spirit of the Scots poet to life.[50]

As Marin observes, the effect of representation, or making the image present, is to create an image that is more forceful, more intense, and yet more spectral, than any original. He calls this spectralizing effect the "primitive" of representation. This doubled image of the body (at once real and fictive) takes a specific form in Derrida's *hommage*, namely, his emphasis on the posthumousness of Marin's book as he revisits it and gives it another look. His rereading has peculiar and painful immediacy ("As if it were Thyself that's here"). Derrida writes: "I would especially like to convey to you, trying not to take advantage of the emotion, how difficult and painful it is for me to speak here of this book" (*WM*, 157). The difficulty and pain of his rereading has to do with the strange time of reading that the time of the writing of this book will have, "as if in advance, imprinted in us, the friends of Louis" (*WM*, 157). Derrida imagines Louis Marin "working on a book he knew he might not, while still living, see." By its own citation of images and photographs of those who have "passed away," Marin's book multiplies what Derrida calls "the survival effect, the effect of living on." Yet even "the grammar of the future anterior" is not adequate to convey the tense of this anticipatory yet posthumous reading.

Derrida suggests that "the strange temporality" of Marin's self-portrayal in advance of his own death gives peculiar force to the affect of mourning. The effect is that of "signing the extraordinary utterance . . . that allows one to say 'I died.'" Derrida sees this "incredible grammar, this impossible time or tense" (*WM*, 157)—about which Marin himself had written—as the time of writing: "It is the strange time of his writing, the strange time of reading that looks at and regards us in advance" (*WM*, 157–58). This is none other than graphological time, "the time or tense, the graphological time, the implicit tempo of all writing" (*WM*, 158). The tense or tempo of writing is the signature of the writer's posthumousness. Testifying to his emotion on rereading Marin's book, Derrida attributes its intensity to something more than "the emotion of mourning that we all know and recognize, . . . an emotion that overwhelms us each time we come across the surviving testimonies of the lost friend" (*WM*, 158). Just as Wordsworth is overwhelmed by the surviving testimonies of his lost Friend (John's manuscript notebook containing his own poems), so Derrida's mourning is overwhelmed by a vertiginous reflexivity that has to do with the time of reading:

> There was another emotion that came to overwhelm this first mourning, this common mourning, coming to make it turn upon itself, I would almost want to say to reflect it to the point of vertigo, another emotion, another quality and intensity of emotion, at once too painful and strangely peaceful, which had to do, I believe, with a certain time of reading. (*WM*, 158)

It is this "strange time of reading," so overwhelming as to be vertiginous, that startles Wordsworth when he comes to the end of his poem, as the pain of loss is caught up in the returns and relays of graphological time-past. Derrida's *hommage* continues to address the question of mourning, alluding (as if to a shared psychoanalytic discourse) to "the image commonly used to characterize mourning [which] is that of an interiorization (an idealizing incorporation, introjection, consumption of the other . . .)" which is ultimately Eucharistic in nature (*WM*, 158–59). Marin writes about the Eucharist as "the great mourning object." Without denying psychoanalytic modes of interiorization and subjectivity, Derrida suggests that if this interiorization "must not—and this is the unbearable paradox of fidelity—be possible and completed," it would be "because of another organization of space and of visibility, of the gazing and the gazed upon" (*WM*, 159). A degree of interiorization is inevitable ("the friend can no longer be but *in us*"); indeed, it is prepared for, both at the moment of death and beforehand, "in the undeniable anticipation of mourning that constitutes friendship." The interiorization of the (dead) friend is reducible to visible scenes and images, their traces in us. Whether memories or monuments, "the other of whom they are the images appears only as the one who has disappeared or passed away, as the one who, having passed away, leaves 'in us' only images" (*WM*, 159). In Wordsworth's poem, the one who has passed away reappears as the visible image of the memorial book. "The written page and white" (l. 24) whose pages he had so often handled, eyed, and turned in anticipation of his brother's reading becomes an image of his look.

It is this image that says so poignantly, in the words of Derrida's threnody: "He is no more, he is no longer here, no longer there" (*WM*, 160). For Derrida, this topology (imago-tropology) of space—neither here nor there—points, not so much to an essential lack, as to a look: "the fact that one is seen there in it. The image sees more than it is seen. The image looks at us" (*WM*, 160). This is the look of the book—not the absence that it reveals (the absence of the reader for whose eyes it had been intended), but the asymmetrical inversion that transforms it into a portrait of the writer-as-reader. The inversion both exceeds and traumatizes the interiority of friendship and of mourning. This a- or dissymmetry of the look is at once anachronous, disquieting, and as much constitutive of the reading subject as any *cogito, ergo sum*: "I know that I am an image for the other and am looked at by the other" (*WM*, 160). Each (necessarily posthumous) reader is looked at "by the one who, with each page, will have providentially deciphered and prescribed, arranged in advance, a reading of what is happening here, of what makes the present scene possible" (*WM*, 160). Just so does Wordsworth write of this prearranged reading: "He framed the Book which now I see, / This very Book upon my knee" (ll. 29–30). Derrida insists of Louis Marin that "we are all looked at" and that the look is interior to the reader: "He looks at us. *In us*. He looks in us" (*WM*, 161). The interiorization of the look (the image or/of seeing) that looks in us, "the experience of this time of reading"—a reading always staged in advance, yet anterior—is caught up in the tempo of a prior writing. Hence not only the sadness of graphological time but also (in Derrida's pregnant phrase) "the torsion of the time of reading" (*WM*, 161)—a torsion that is at once painful, fascinating, and interrupted.

Derrida's tribute to Marin ends with a question that links the gift to death. "Why," he asks, "does one give and what can one give to a dead friend?" (*WM*, 164). Granted that one's relation to the other is also one's relation to oneself—the gaze of Narcissus regards one from the gaze of the other—what can reading do other than repeat, in its echoic way, what comes from the resonance of the other? Derrida's *hommage* tells the story of an interrupted reading ("I wrote," "I . . . started") as well as a prestaged one. He suggests that Marin knew that the work of death begins prior to death; this is why "this book cannot be closed, why it interrupts itself interminably" (*WM*, 164). Derrida's last words narrate a vertiginous speed-reading: "And however prepared I might have been for it, I read it too quickly. In a sort of haste that no mourning will be able to diminish or console. It happened to me too quickly, like Louis's death. I feel as if I were still on the eve of reading it" (*WM*, 164). In this strange torsion of the time of reading, Derrida's words resonate with the dislocated future anterior of Wordsworth's vertiginous opening:

> I wrote, and when I reach'd the end
> Started to think that thou, my Friend,
> Upon the words which I had penn'd
> Must never, never look. (ll. 4–7)

The poem's reading and writing run ahead of themselves, forever unprepared to reach their end, in the sad graphological time that deprives the dead Friend of the reading in which he might see himself interiorized by the look of the book. As Wordsworth's unintended readers, we occupy the same impossible subject-position: the point of view of death, the painful pre-text for his distressful gift.

An Interrupted Line

> . . . an interrupted line that turns about in a coming
> and going.
> —Maurice Blanchot, *The Infinite Conversation*

Blanchot's essay "Interruption (as on a Riemann Surface)," in *The Infinite Conversation* (*L'Entretien infini*, 1969),[51] offers the following definition of conversation: "When two people speak together, they speak not together, but each in turn: one says something, then stops, the other something else (or the same thing), then stops" (*IC*, 75). Conversation, at once a turning movement and a movement that upholds and sustains (*l'entretien*), is not dialogue as we usually understand it. Rather, it consists of interruption and interval, pause and return. Elsewhere in *The Infinite Conversation*, Blanchot locates in the word "turn"—"this turn that turns toward that from which it turns away" (*IC*, 31) what he calls "the original torsion" that speaking tries to disentangle and slacken. The same might be said of the relation between prose and verse: "prose, a continuous line; verse, an interrupted line that turns about in a coming or going" (*IC*, 30). Poetry, then, is a kind of moving conversation, interrupted and undone by the to-and-fro that distinguishes it from prose: "The first turn, the original structure of turning (which later slackens in a back and forth linear movement) is poetry" (*IC*, 30). This poetic form of conversation has its own rhythm, its own detours and deflection: "In this turn that is rhythm, speech is turned toward that which turns aside and itself turns aside" (*IC*, 31). Poetry's *fort/da* movement is a kind of conversation that is constantly turned toward another: an averted apostrophe.

The Infinite Conversation pays tribute to Blanchot's intellectual friendship with Levinas, including his definition of *Autrui* as the mark of a caesura or interruption ("it is this fissure—this relation with the other—that we ventured to characterize as an interruption of being"; *IC*, 69). Prefaced by the staging of an imaginary conversation, and paying tribute to his long dialogue with Levinas, the "infinite conversation" of Blanchot's title refers to "the turn and turn about of plural speech." His metaphor for this alternating plurality is a mathematician's conceptual tool, the Riemann surface: a virtual talking book. Blanchot's footnote to "Interruption (as on a Riemann surface)" explains his title by means of an anecdote told about Paul Valéry:

> Mathematicians use a tool called a Riemann surface: it is an ideal notepad made up of as many pages as necessary, fastened together according to certain rules, and whose total thickness amounts to nearly nothing. Upon this leaved surface numbers are inscribed, some of which occupy the same place upon different sheets. In the course of a conversation, Valéry said . . . "Don't you find that conversations occur on a Riemann surface? I make a remark to you, it is inscribed upon the first sheet; but at the same time I prepare on the second sheet what I will say to you next, and even on a third sheet what will come after. From your side you respond upon the first sheet, while at the same

time putting in reserve on other sheets what you intend to say to me later." (*IC*, 441)[52]

Like Wordsworth, Blanchot uses the metaphor of a book to define both the topographical and temporal turning of the page, in space and time. Turning becomes a metaphor for the temporality of writing, or what Blanchot's note calls "the principle of deferred speech" (*IC*, 441n). Wordsworth, too, computes the material disaster of John's voyage (with all its loss of lives and money) in metrical "numbers" inscribed on "The written page and white."

The turn and turn about of Wordsworth's verse form the "secret chain" that binds him to his drowned brother. Verse is the interruption that links living and dead. The pause permits not just exchange, but an opening for disaster. Some pauses stop the conversation: "and when I reach'd the end / Started. . . ." If poetry's turns and returns, its strange fits and starts of passion, are its mode of conversation—indeed, its mode of thought—each pause or intermittence resembles a small apprehension of death; poet and reader "start" at the end. Blanchot's essay intimates the gravity of the pause, the irreducible distance that already separates two interlocutors. One mode of communicative relation implies an interrelational space, or dialectical relation, whereby the other is regarded as a second self to be brought into harmony and unity with the first. But a second, nondialectical modality relates, more disturbingly, to the ineluctable singularity and separateness of the self: "What is now in play, and demands relation, is everything that separates me from the other" (*IC*, 77)—including time. Here there can be no direct communication, only a hiatus, or unknown mode of being, to which "the interruption in language itself responds, the interruption that introduces waiting" (*IC*, 77). This is the separation that for Blanchot (as for Levinas) constitutes "an *interruption of being*."

Waiting out the turns and pauses of Wordsworth's elegy, the reader "hears" in its syncopated rhythms the writing of intermittence-as-separation. Blanchot's name for the pause where intermittence speaks is "the speech of writing"—something previously unthought or unwritten, "the interruption by which the unknown announces itself" (*IC*, 70). The unknown announces, not just suspension, but (in his phrase) an interruption that "asphyxiate[s] speech," like drowning. Pain or affliction (*Malheur*)—distress—may make it impossible to speak, unless to bring that impossibility to expression: "But now—upon the written leaf / I look indeed with pain and grief, / I do" (ll. 36–37). In the gap or caesura that Blanchot calls "the ultimate, the hyperbolical" interruption, the recognition of death makes itself felt as sheer, meaningless (but not affectless) reduplication: Wordsworth's sad "I do." Blanchot's speculative mode of thought makes self-interruption the prelude to any understanding. Hence his question—whether speech (i.e., writing) "does not always mean attempting to involve the outside of any language in language itself" (*IC*, 78–79). What is excluded from speech is silence. In the pause of waiting, writes Blanchot, "it is not simply the delicate rupture preparing the poetic act that declares itself, but also, and at the same time, other forms of arrest" (*IC*, 79)—death, for instance. This is a Wordsworthian formulation. Pausing in his "mimick hootings to the silent owls" (1805 *Prelude* v. 398), the Winander Boy experiences in their nonresponse the intimation of a longer silence: Blanchot's "impossible interruption" foretells his death.

The turns and returns of Wordsworth's verse in "Distressful Gift" create a reliably returning seven-line stanza (*aabcccb*). But he ends with an eight-line stanza, and an extra rhyme: "find / mind / behind / resign'd" (*aabccccb* instead of *aabcccb*). This extralineal emphasis reinforces Wordsworth's question-prayer: "Oh grant . . . Grant this, and let me be resign'd / Beneath thy chast'ning rod" (ll. 41–42). The distressful gift morphs into resignation and implied obedience, if not punishment. God rhymes unambiguously with "rod." But this shift of address (from book to God) involves another kind of resigning. In "The Absence of the Book," Blanchot writes that whereas the book can be signed, by contrast, "the work . . . requires resignation, requires that whosoever claims to write it renounce himself as a self and cease designating himself" (*IC*, 429).[53] While the book is bound up with completion, the work designates incompletion, *désoeuvrement*, and disaster.[54] For Blanchot, it is the breaking of the tablets ("the set is now broken")—an originary fracture—that renders the writing of the Torah legible. The first law emanating from the disaster, "Thou shalt reject presence in the form of resemblance, sign, and mark" (*IC*, 433–44), thereafter interdicts the sign as a mode of presence. There is no way back, given this radical break, outside the game of indeterminate and inessential chance that Blanchot calls writing, "the game in which everything is each time risked and everything lost" (*IC*, 434). This, you might say, was Wordsworth's side of the agreement with John: the game of risk and loss that underwrites his poetical work for the world, making it not an exchange, but a distressful gift.

Notes

1   Jacques Derrida, *The Work of Mourning*, ed. Pascale-Anne Brault and Michael Naas (Chicago: University of Chicago Press, 2001); subsequently cited parenthetically as *WM*.

2   See Stephen Gill, *William Wordsworth: A Life* (Oxford: Clarendon Press, 1989), 239–41, for a brief account of the wreck and its aftermath, including the succeeding months of Wordsworth family grieving; and see also Richard E. Matlak, *Deep Distresses: William Wordsworth, John Wordsworth, Sir George Beaumont, 1800–1808* (Newark: University of Delaware Press, 2003), for another reading of these entwined relationships.

3   To Richard Wordsworth, February 11, 1805; to Sir George Beaumont, February 11, 1805; *The Letters of William and Dorothy Wordsworth: The Early Years, 1787–1805*, ed. Ernest de Selincourt, rev. Chester L. Shaver (Oxford: Clarendon Press, 1967), 540, 541; subsequently cited parenthetically as *EY*.

4   To James Losh, March 16, 1805 (*EY*, 565).

5   *EY*, 563. For a relevant analysis of the role of exchange as it relates to both Wordsworth's poetry and eighteenth-century accounts of political economy, see Simon Jarvis, "Wordsworth's Gifts of Feeling," *Romanticism* 4.1 (1998): 90–103. Jarvis points to the sustained attempt to separate gifts from exchange, and interest from self-interest, in economic and cultural theory.

6   John's letter of September 12, 1802, to Mary Hutchinson quotes the covenant in Wordsworth's "Michael," ll. 415–17, changing the pronoun: "but, whatever fate / Befall [me] I shall love thee to the last, / And bear thy memory with me to the grave"; see *The Letters of John Wordsworth*, ed. Carl H. Ketchum (Ithaca, NY: Cornell University Press, 1969), 116, 126.

7   For details of John's career, see Ketchum's introduction to *The Letters of John Wordsworth*; in 1801 he succeeded an uncle as captain of the *Earl of Abergavenny* (a thirty-two-gun privateer). The Bengal-China route involved shipping rice, woollens, cotton, tea, opium, and sometimes "bang" (marijuana). Besides their trading cargo, captains transported passengers (as well as troops) on the Bengal leg of the so-called "double voyage." The ship was carrying a combined total of 402 including its crew, of whom only 155 were saved.

8   See Dorothy's letter to Jane Marshall of March 15 and 17, 1805 (*EY*, 561–62).

9   For the main contemporary accounts, see E. L. McAdam Jr., "Wordsworth's Shipwreck," *PMLA* 77 (1962): 240–47. John Wordsworth was exonerated of any responsibility for the wreck at the official inquiry, and the East India Company was acquitted of negligence.

10 Wordsworth reported John's view that "he had indeed a great fear of Pilots and I have often heard him say that no situation could be imagined more distressing than that of being at the mercy of these men" (to James Losh, March 16, 1805; *EY*, 563).

11 "It does [William] good to speak of John as he was, therefore he is now writing a poem upon him. I should not say a *poem* for it is a *part* of the Recluse" (Dorothy Wordsworth to Lady Beaumont, April 11, 1805; *EY*, 576).

12 "At first I had a strong impulse to write a poem that should record my Brother's virtues and be worthy of his memory. . . . I composed much, but it is all lost except a few lines, as it came from me in such a torrent that I was unable to remember it; I could not hold the pen myself, and the subject was such, that I could not employ Mrs Wordsworth or my Sister as my amanuensis" (to Sir George Beaumont, May 1, 1805; *EY*, 586).

13   On July 5, 1805, Wordsworth wrote to Sir George Beaumont: "I have composed lately two small poems in memory of my Brother, but they are too melancholy else I would willingly copy them" (*EY*, 603). On August 7, 1805, Wordsworth copied "To the Daisy" ("written in remembrance of a beautiful Letter of my Brother John"; *EY*, 613).

14   Composed between May 20 and July 5, 1805, and possibly shortly before July 5, 1805, when Wordsworth mentioned having composed "two small poems in memory of my Brother" (*EY*, 603). The text is based on a ms. in Mary Wordsworth's fair copy, with pencil corrections by Wordsworth, in DC MS. 57; see William Wordsworth, *Poems, in Two Volumes, and Other Poems, 1800–1807*, ed. Jared Curtis (Ithaca, NY: Cornell University Press, 1983), 617–18, and, for DC MS. 57, see ibid., xxii. Quotations from "Distressful Gift" are from Curtis's text, cited parenthetically as "Curtis."

15   According to Curtis, "A . . . 'collection,' about which it is possible only to speculate, since the volume does not survive, is mentioned by Wordsworth in his poem 'Distressful gift!' . . . It was apparently left behind before the final voyage. . . . If this commonplace book contained more samples of [Wordsworth's] poems, it seems likely that they were transcribed by John himself from copies sent him from Grasmere" (Curtis, 6).

16   "Why, gifted with such powers to send abroad / Her spirit, must it [the mind] lodge in shrines so frail?" (1805 *Prelude*, vv. 47–48).

17   See Maurice Blanchot, *The Infinite Conversation*, trans. Susan Hanson (Minneapolis: University of Minnesota Press, 1993), 341; subsequently cited parenthetically in the text as *IC*. See also Gerald L. Bruns, *Maurice Blanchot: The Refusal of Philosophy* (Baltimore: Johns Hopkins University Press, 1997), 151–52: "The infinite conversation will be a dialogue without dialectic, a conversation without negation. . . . So we may imagine once more a discourse outside of discourse . . . where the interlocutors neither contest nor supplement one another but have entered into a relation that is structured as an eternal return." Arguably, the same logic structures Derrida's understanding of the gift. See also Leslie Hill, *Maurice Blanchot: Extreme Contemporary* (London: Routledge, 1997), 137–39, where the concept of "impossibility" involved in the Derridean gift (irreducible to any ontology) is shown to replace that of extreme affirmation in *The Infinite Conversation*.

18   First published in *Adieu à Emmanuel Levinas* (1997); see *Adieu to Emmanuel Levinas*, trans. Pascale-Anne Brault and Michael Naas (Stanford, CA: Stanford University Press, 1999); the text referred to here will be that of *The Work of Mourning*. *Adieu to Emmanuel Levinas* also includes Derrida's "A Word of Welcome," a consideration of Levinas's ethics of hospitality, in which Derrida discusses Levinas's understanding of the *à-Dieu* (see ibid., 101–5). Levinas refers to "the pleasure of a contact at the heart of a chiasmus" in "Jacques Derrida: Wholly Otherwise" (1973); see Emmanuel Levinas, *Proper Names*, trans. Michael B. Smith (Stanford, CA: Stanford University Press, 1996), 55–62.

19   Cf. Derrida's remark in "The Deaths of Roland Barthes" apropos of the classical funeral oration: "In its classical form, the funeral oration had a good side, especially when it permitted one to call out directly to the dead, sometimes very informally [*tutoyer*]. This is of course a supplementary fiction, for it is always the dead in me, always the others standing around the coffin whom I call out to." But, he continues, "the interactions of the living must be interrupted" (*WM*, 51–52).

20   See Emmanuel Levinas, *God, Death, and Time*, trans. Bettina Bergo (Stanford, CA: Stanford University Press, 2000), 9; subsequently cited parenthetically in the text as *GDT*.

21 To Sir George Beaumont, February 23, 1805 (*EY*, 547).

22 In a footnote to *Given Time*, Derrida refers to "Fors" (his introduction to Abraham and Torok's *The Wolf Man's Magic Word*), arguing for the blurring of the distinction between introjection and incorporation: "I pretend to keep the dead alive, intact *safe (save) inside me*, but it is only in order to refuse, in a necessarily equivocal way, to love the dead as a living part of me, dead *save in me*, through the process of introjection, as happens in so-called normal mourning"; see Jacques Derrida, *Given Time: I. Counterfeit Money*, trans. Peggy Kamuf (Chicago: University of Chicago Press, 1992), 129n; subsequently cited parenthetically in the text as *GT*.

23. *The Prose Works of William Wordsworth*, ed. W. J. B. Owen and Jane Worthington Smyser, 3 vols. (Oxford: Clarendon Press, 1974), 2.50; subsequently cited parenthetically in the text as *Prose Works*. Weever's 1631 work is a source for Wordsworth's *Essays on Epitaphs*. For the anti-monumentalizing tradition to which *Essays on Epitaphs* belongs, see Samantha Matthews, *Poetical Remains: Poets' Graves, Bodies, and Books in the Nineteenth Century* (Oxford: Oxford University Press, 2004), 159–63.

24 The classic statement is Joan Riviere's, in "The Unconscious Phantasy of an Inner World Reflected in Examples from Literature" (1952); see *The Inner World and Joan Riviere: Collected Papers, 1920–1958*, ed. Athol Hughes (London: Karnac Books, 1991), 317, where she alludes to "countless never-ending influences and exchanges between ourselves and others." Our internal objects, Riviere writes, continue to lead their lives "within us indivisible from ourselves" (ibid., 320).

25 See [William Dalmeida], *An Authentic Narrative of the Loss of the Earl of Abergavenny East Indiaman, Captain John Wordsworth, Off Portland, on the Night of the 5th of Feb. 1805; Drawn from Official Documents, and Communications from Various Respectable Survivors, by a Gentleman in the East-India House* (London: Lane, Newman, and Co., 1805); Wordsworth thought this account the most reliable, mentioning the motto on its title page drawn from *Richard III* (see *EY*, 560–61n, 564–65).

26 Dorothy Wordsworth to Lady Beaumont, March 28, 1805 (*EY*, 574); see also *EY*, 552, for Wordsworth's concern about the burial. John drowned on February 5, but his body was not recovered until March 20, 1805, and it was then buried in an unmarked grave along with other recovered bodies (see Ketchum, *The Letters of John Wordsworth*, 50–51).

27 Wordsworth might well have associated "tender-hearted Simonides" (*PW*, II.52) with his tender-hearted sailor brother—"the tenderest Poet that could be / Who sang in ancient Greece his moving lay" (Curtis, 584, ll. 12–13).

28 Barbara Johnson, "L'Esthétique du Mal," in *Mother Tongues: Sexuality, Trials, Motherhood, Translation* (Cambridge, MA: Harvard University Press, 2003), 26–27.

29 See "Mourning and Its Relation to Manic-Depressive States" (1940), in *The Selected Melanie Klein*, ed. Juliet Mitchell (London: Penguin, 1986), esp. 159–60.

30 Ibid., 162. Cf. Wordsworth in "The Ruined Cottage": "The Poets in their elegies and songs, / Lamenting the departed call the groves, / They call upon the hills and streams to mourn, / And senseless rocks, nor idly" (ll. 73–76).

31 "At this stage in mourning, suffering can become productive. We know that painful experiences of all kinds sometimes stimulate sublimations, or even bring out quite new gifts in some people, who make take to painting, writing, or other productive activities under the stress of frustrations and hardships" (*Selected Melanie Klein*, 163).

32　For the role of affect in writing such as de Man's and Derrida's, see Rei Terada, *Feeling in Theory: Emotions after the "Death of the Subject"* (Cambridge, MA: Harvard University Press, 2001). Terada discusses Derridean emotion, particularly in his *Memoires* for Paul de Man, in relation and response to de Man's figure of prosopopoeia (see ibid., 128–51, esp. 134–40). Terada calls this Derrida's "conversation with the dead de Man" (ibid., 146)—a perceptive reading that bears on *The Work of Mourning*.

33　For a philosopher's discussion of Derrida in relation to Levinas, see Simon Critchley, *The Ethics of Deconstruction: Derrida and Levinas* (Oxford: Blackwell, 1992), esp. chaps. 3 and 4. Critchley's argument relates particularly to the ethical (and political) aspects of deconstruction. See also Colin Davis, *Levinas: An Introduction* (Cambridge: Polity Press, 1996), which addresses the obscurity of Levinas's expression and thought, including his concept of "face."

34.　*The Gift of Death*, trans. David Willis (Chicago: University of Chicago Press, 1995), 67; subsequently cited parenthetically in the text as *GD*.

35　For the status of "impossibility," an influential strand in Blanchot's thought that involves what lies both outside discourse and anterior to being, see Leslie Hill, *Blanchot: Extreme Contemporary* (London: Routledge, 1997), 138, where "the impossible" is defined "as that which escapes affirmation and negation alike and exceeds all such dialectical oppositions or contraries."

36　For a discussion of the gift from a phenomenological perspective, see Jean-Luc Marion, *Being Given: Toward a Phenomenology of Givenness*, trans. Jeffrey L. Kosky (Stanford, CA: Stanford University Press, 2002), 71–118. Marion aligns himself with Derrida only to the extent of finding in his reading the basis for a counterinterpretation, seeing within it the possibility of a problematic return of metaphysics that rests with exposing a contradiction rather than probing its depths (ibid., 79–81). For a penetrating account of Marion's argument about the phenomenology of exchange, see Simon Jarvis, "Problems in the Phenomenology of the Gift," *Angelaki* 6.2 (2001): 67–77; and, for a critique of Derrida for his latent economism, see also Simon Jarvis, "The Gift in Theory," *Dionysius* 17 (1999): 201–22. I am grateful to Simon Jarvis for timely guidance in the area of gift theory; my own emphasis differs in emphasizing the role of both psychoanalysis and Blanchot in Derrida's thought.

37　"Levinas is no longer able to distinguish between the infinite alterity of God and that of every human. His ethics is already a religious one. . . . the border between the ethical and the religious becomes more than problematic" (*GD*, 84).

38　Wordsworth's letters often make use of this turn of phrase, for instance: "God grant me life and strength," "[I] pray God to give me strength" (*EY*, 547, 565).

39　See "Prayer without Demand," in *The Levinas Reader*, ed. Seán Hand (Oxford: Basil Blackwell, 1989), 232. For Volozhiner, according to Levinas, "the act of study constituted in itself the most direct communication with a transcendent, nonobjectifiable God" (ibid., 228).

40　Ibid., 233.

41　Ibid., 234.

42　Cf. the elegy for John written the following year, "Elegiac Stanzas, Suggested by a Picture of Peele Castle" (1806): "Not without hope we suffer and we mourn" (l. 60).

43　See Wordsworth's letter to James Losh, March 16, 1805 (*EY*, 563), quoted above.

44 See *GT*, 58–59. Mallarmé's poem has various titles and versions ("Le Jour," "Le poème nocturne," "Dédicatrice du poème nocturne"). Mallarmé's gender politics are, of course, problematic (conception as masculine, reading as feminine). His miserable neonate is invoked in the course of Derrida's reading of a different transaction, alms-giving ("Aumone")—a stinted giving that leaches the gift of any generosity to the donee (see *GT*, 57–58).

45 See *GT*, 73–78, 78–82. Derrida rereads Claude Lévi-Strauss's tribute to (and critique of) Mauss in his *Introduction to the Work of Marcel Mauss* as "*exchangist, linguisticist and structuralist*" (*GT*, 76). Benveniste's "Gift and Exchange in Indo-European Vocabulary," in *Problèmes de linguistique générale*, is similarly seen as pointing to a semantic ambivalence that belongs more generally to language itself: "Language gives one to think but it also steals, spirits away from us . . . it carries off the property of our own thoughts even before we have appropriated them" (*GT*, 80).

46 The poem is by Michel Deguy, *Donnant Donnant* (Paris: Gallimard, 1981), 57.

47 Louis Marin, *Des pouvoirs de l'image* (Paris: Editions du Seuil, 1993), 11 (*WM*, 149).

48 The passage from Marin's introduction begins: "Le préfixe re-importe dans la terms la valeur de substitution. Quelque chose qui *était* present et ne *l'est* plus est *maintenant* re*presenté*. À la place de quelque chose qui est present ailleurs, voici *présent* un donnée, *ici*; image? Au lieu de la représentation, donc, il est un absent dans le temps ou l'espace ou plutôt un autre, et une substitution s'opère d'un autre de cet autre, à sa place" (*Des pouvoirs de l'image*, 11). Derrida's reading includes the example of the substitution of the body as announced by the angel at the tomb, and relates to the primitive power of this scenario of ontological transfiguration (see *WM*, 149–53).

49 Probably composed in August 1803 and completed in this form between March 1804 and early 1807 (Curtis, 534).

50 For Marin's sense of the voice as inscribed in poetic figures, see the end of his introduction: "Mais si les périodes et les strophes, les phrases et les vers, les mots, les consonnes et les voyelles peignent en montrant et si le langage fait voir, c'est par la force qui le traverse et que ses organizations hierarchisées articulent: c'est part la force qui en déplace, si l'on peut dire, la transparence instituée: c'est par la chair de la voix que signes et letters, mots et phrases informant" (*Des pouvoirs de l'image*, 22).

51 Maurice Blanchot, *The Infinite Conversation*, trans. Susan Hanson (Minneapolis: University of Minnesota Press, 1993), 30; subsequently cited parenthetically in the text as *IC*.

52 The anecdote is cited from Judith Robinson, *L'Analyse de l'esprit dans les Cahiers de Valéry* (Paris: José Corti, 1963). Blanchot comments: " Of course the image remains very unsatisfying since here discourse . . . only calls upon what one might name the principle of deferred speech" (*IC*, 441).

53 "Let us say briefly that if the book can always be signed, it remains indifferent to whoever would do so; the work . . . requires resignation, requires that whosoever claims to write it renounce himself as a self and cease designating himself" (*IC*, 429).

54 See Gerald L. Bruns, *Maurice Blanchot: The Refusal of Philosophy* (Baltimore: Johns Hopkins University Press, 1997), esp. chaps. 6 and 7, for an account of Blanchot's relation to "the work"; cf. also Leslie Hill, *Blanchot: Extreme Contemporary* (London: Routledge, 1997).

Notes on Contributors

IAN BALFOUR teaches in English in the Graduate Programme in Social & Political Thought at York University. He is the author of *The Rhetoric of Romantic Prophecy* (Stanford University Press, 2002). Recently he has edited, with Atom Egoyan, *Subtitles: On the Foreignness of Film* (MIT Press, 2004); and with Eduardo Cadava, a double issue of *SAQ*: "And Justice for All? The Claims of Human Rights" (103.2–3, Spring/Summer 2004). He is currently finishing a book on the sublime.

DAVID L. CLARK is a professor in the Department of English and Cultural Studies and Associate Member of the Health Studies Programme at McMaster University. He is the author of *Bodies and Pleasures in Late Kant* (Stanford University Press, forthcoming) and is working on two other projects: *Mourning Schelling: On the Remains of Idealism* and *Towards a Prehistory of the Postanimal: Kant, Levinas, and the Regard of Brutes*.

MARY JACOBUS is Grace 2 Professor of English at the University of Cambridge, where she is currently director of the Centre for Research in the Arts, Social Sciences and Humanities. She has written books on Wordsworth, romanticism, feminist criticism, and psychoanalysis. Her most recent book is *The Poetics of Psychoanalysis: In the Wake of Klein* (Oxford University Press, 2005). She is currently working on aspects of literary and visual theory.

DAVID E. JOHNSON is an associate professor and the director of graduate studies in the Department of Comparative Literature at the State University of New York at Buffalo. With Scott Michaelsen, he is the coeditor of *Border Theory: The Limits of Cultural Politics* (University of Minnesota Press, 1997) and of the journal *CR: The New Centennial Review*, and the coauthor of *Anthropology's Wake* (Fordham University Press, forthcoming).

DAVID LLOYD, a professor of English at the University of Southern California, is the author of *Nationalism and Minor Literature* (University of California Press, 1987), *Anomalous States* (Duke University Press, 1993), and *Ireland after History* (Cork University Press, 1999) and is currently at work on a further book, *A History of the Irish Orifice: The Irish Body and Modernity*. He is coauthor of several other books, including, with Paul Thomas, *Culture and the State* (Routledge, 1998), and, with Abdul JanMohamed, *The Nature and Context of Minority Discourse* (Oxford University Press, 1990).

J. HILLIS MILLER taught for many years at the Johns Hopkins University and then at Yale University before going to the University of California at Irvine in 1986, where he is now UCI Distinguished Research Professor. He is the author of many books and essays on nineteenth- and twentieth-century English, European, and American literature and on literary theory. His most recent book is *Literature as Conduct: Speech Acts in Henry James* (Fordham University Press, 2005). He is at work on books on Jacques Derrida and on "Communities in Literature."

MARC REDFIELD is a professor of English and John D. and Lillian Maguire Distinguished Chair in the Humanities at Claremont Graduate University. He is the author of *Phantom Formations: Aesthetic Ideology and the Bildungsroman* (Cornell University Press, 1996) and *The Politics of Aesthetics: Nationalism, Gender, Romanticism* (Stanford University Press, 2003). He has co-edited *High Anxieties: Cultural Studies in Addiction* (University of California Press, 2002) and has edited *Legacies of Paul de Man* (Fordham University Press, forthcoming), in addition to special issues of the journals *Diacritics, Romantic Praxis,* and *The Wordsworth Circle.* He is presently writing a book on the late-eighteenth-century origins of the notion of a "war on terror."

REI TERADA is a professor and chair of the Department of Comparative Literature at the University of California at Irvine. She is the author of *Feeling in Theory: Emotion after the "Death of the Subject"* (Harvard University Press, 2001) and is at work on *Phenomenality and Dissatisfaction: Kant to Adorno.*

ELISABETH WEBER is a professor of German and comparative literature at the University of California at Santa Barbara. She is the author of *Verfolgung und Trauma. Zu Emmanuel Lévinas' Autrement qu'être ou au-delà de l'essence* (Vienna, 1990) and the editor of *Questioning Judaism* (Stanford University Press, 2004), a volume of interviews with Jacques Derrida, Emmanuel Levinas, Jean-François Lyotard, and others. She is currently working on a project titled "Torture and the Future."

Cupboards of Curiosity
Women, Recollection, and Film History
AMELIE HASTIE
256 pages, 12 b&w photos, paper, $21.95

Sex in Revolution
Gender, Politics, and Power in Modern Mexico
**JOCELYN OLCOTT, MARY KAY VAUGHAN,
& GABRIELA CANO, EDITORS**
336 pages, 4 b&w photos, paper, $22.95

Mobilizing India
Women, Music, and Migration
between India and Trinidad
TEJASWINI NIRANJANA
288 pages, 46 b&w photos, paper, $21.95

The Academic's Handbook
**A. LEIGH DENEEF &
CRAUFURD D. GOODWIN, EDITORS**
416 pages, paper, $24.95

Public Culture

Invigorated.

There are a number of new things going on at *Public Culture*: new editor Claudio Lomnitz, a new editorial office at the New School for Social Research, and a new design reflecting the journal's commitment to the internationalization of cultural studies.

New features

- Executive editor Dilip Gaonkar's "Doxa at Large" editorial section discussing contemporary cultural questions
- "*Public Culture* Translations," in which notable foreign-language essays are reworked for the English reader
- "Arts in Circulation" initiative, expanding the previous "Artworks" section and featuring both short informative and long reflective pieces

The changes heighten *Public Culture*'s ability to signal new areas of concern and to stimulate new voices in the field.

Subscription Information

Three issues annually
Individuals: $37
Students: $25 (photocopy of valid student ID required)
Single issues: $15

To place your order using a credit card, please call toll-free 888-651-0122 (in the U.S. and Canada) or 919-688-5134, or e-mail subscriptions@dukeupress.edu.

For more information, visit
publicculture.dukejournals.org.